Showing Our Colors

Showing Our Colors

Afro-German Women Speak Out

EDITED BY MAY OPITZ,
KATHARINA OGUNTOYE *&*
DAGMAR SCHULTZ

With a foreword by Audre Lorde

Translated by Anne V. Adams,
    in cooperation with
    Tina Campt,
    May Opitz &
    Dagmar Schultz

The University of
Massachusetts Press
Amherst

Original title:

Farbe bekennen: Afro-deutsche Frauen auf den Spuren ihrer Geschichte

© 1986 by Orlanda Frauenverlag

English translation © 1992 by

The University of Massachusetts Press

All rights reserved

Printed in the United States of America

LC 91–17061

ISBN 0–87023–759–4 (cloth); 760–8 (pbk.)

Set in Linotron Sabon by Keystone Typesetting, Inc.

Printed and bound by Thomson-Shore, Inc.

Library of Congress Cataloging-in-Publication Data

   [Farbe bekennen. English]

Showing our colors : Afro-German women speak out / edited by May
  Opitz, Katharina Oguntoye, and Dagmar Schultz : with a foreword by
  Audre Lorde ; translated by Anne V. Adams, in cooperation with Tina
  Campt, May Opitz, and Dagmar Schultz.

     p. cm.

   Translation of: Farbe bekennen.

   Includes bibliographical references.

   ISBN 0–87023–759–4 (cloth : alk. paper)—ISBN
0–87023–760–8 (pbk. : alk. paper)

    1. Women, Black—Germany—History.   2. Blacks—Germany—History.
3. Race discrimination—Germany.   4. Germany—Race relations.
I. Opitz, May.   II. Oguntoye, Katharina.   III. Schultz, Dagmar.
IV. Title: Showing our colors.

DD78.B55F3713   1991

305.48′896043—dc20
                                            91–17061

                                                 CIP

British Library Cataloging in Publication data are available.

Contents

Foreword to the English Language Edition

In the spring of 1984, I spent three months at the Free University in Berlin teaching a course in Black American women poets and a poetry workshop in English, for German students. One of my goals on this trip was to meet Black German women, for I had been told there were quite a few in Berlin.

Who are they, these German women of the Diaspora? Beyond the details of our particular oppressions—although certainly not outside the reference of those details—where do our paths intersect as women of color? And where do our paths diverge? Most important, what can we learn from our connected differences that will be useful to us both, Afro-German and Afro-American?

Afro-German. The women say they've never heard that term used before.

I asked one of my Black students how she'd thought about herself growing up. "The nicest thing they ever called us was 'warbaby,'" she said. But the existence of most Black Germans has nothing to do with the Second World War, and, in fact, predates it by many decades. I have Black German women in my class who trace their Afro-German heritage back to the 1890s.

For me, Afro-German means the shining faces of May and Katharina in animated conversation about their fathers' homelands, the comparisons, joys, disappointments. It means my pleasure at seeing another Black woman walk into my classroom, her reticence slowly giving way as she explores a new self-awareness, gains a new way of thinking about herself in relation to other Black women.

"I've never thought of Afro-German as a positive concept before," she said, speaking out of the pain of having to live a difference that has no name; speaking out of the growing power self-scrutiny has forged from that difference.

I am excited by these women, by their blossoming sense of identity as they say, "Let us be ourselves now as we define us. We are not a figment of your imagination or an exotic answer to your desires. We are not some button on the pocket of your longings." I see these women as a growing force for international change, in concert with other Afro-Europeans, Afro-Asians, Afro-Americans.

We are the hyphenated people of the Diaspora whose self-defined identities are no longer shameful secrets in the countries of our origin, but rather declarations of strength and solidarity. We are an increasingly united front from which the world has not yet heard.

Despite the terror and isolation some of these Black women have known from childhood, they are freer of the emotional dilemma facing many white feminists in Germany today. Too often, I have met an immobilizing national guilt in white German women which serves to keep them from acting upon what they profess to believe. Their energies, however well intentioned, are not being used, they are unavailable in the battles against racism, antisemitism, hetero-sexism, xenophobia. Because they seem unable to accept who they are, these women too often fail to examine and pursue the powers relative to their identity. They waste that power, or worse, turn it over to their enemies. Four decades after National Socialism, the question still lingers for many white German women: how can I draw strength from my roots when those roots are entwined in such a terrible history? That terror of self-scrutiny is sometimes disguised as an unbearable arrogance, impotent and wasteful.

The words of these Black German women document their rejection of despair, of blindness, of silence. Once an oppression is expressed, it can be successfully fought.

Farbe Bekennen, "Introduction," 1984

It has been six years since I wrote the above. The appearance of this English translation of *Farbe Bekennen* fulfills the dream I had as I wrote these words—of making the stories of our Black German sisters—and Afro-German history as a whole—available to the English-speaking Diaspora.

Farbe Bekennen tellingly presents the particular effects of racism in the lives of thirteen contemporary Black German women. And with the research of May Opitz, it also provides us with the little-known history of white racism in Germany and its influence upon Black German men and women, from the first African arrival to the present. It may come as a surprise to many that this period spans several hundred years.

The first book to be published in Germany dealing with Afro-Germans as a national entity, *Farbe Bekennen* resulted in the formation of the *Initiative Schwarze Deutsche* (ISD), the first national organization of Black Germans. There are now ISD groups in several German cities, both East and West. The material in *Farbe Bekennen* gains new importance now at this juncture in German history, when impending reunification raises critical questions about definitions of German identity.

Those of us who trace our roots back to the continent of Africa are spread across every country on earth. As we proceed upon the specific and difficult tasks of survival in the twenty-first century, we of the African Diaspora need to recognize our differences as well as our similarities. We approach our living influenced by an African mode; life as experiences to be learned from rather than merely problems to be solved. We seek what is most fruitful for all people, and less hunger for our children. But we are not the same. Particular histories have fashioned our particular weapons, our particular insights. To successfully battle the many faces of institutionalized racial oppression, we must share the strengths of each other's vision as well as the weaponries born of particular experience.

First, we must recognize each other.

Some of these women have sustained and nurturing relationships with their African relatives. Others have grown into Blackness in the almost total absence of a Black community. What does it mean to be defined negatively from birth in one's own country because of a father who one may never see or know? How do you come to define a cultural identity when you have seen no other Black person throughout your childhood?*

Yet the presence of Africa in Europe goes back before the Roman Empire. A Neanderthal skull, discovered in Dusseldorf, Germany, dates back to the Old Stone Age and is the earliest African type found in Europe. Julius Caesar brought Black legions to Germany, and many never returned. The historical presence of Black Africans in the courts, universities, monasteries, and bedrooms of seventeenth-, eighteenth-, and nineteenth-century Europe comes as a surprise only to those scholars pseudoeducated in europeanized bastions of institutional ethnocentricity. At the University of Wittenberg in the early 1700s, William Anthony Amo, a Guinean who later became a state counselor in Berlin, obtained his doctoral degree for a philosophical work entitled "The Want of Feeling."**

Two Black German elders who tell their stories here represent the second generation of a four-generation African-German family. One of their granddaughters is also a contributor.

Racism cuts a wide and corrosive swath across each of our lives. The overt climate that racism takes can alter according to society and our national situations. But our connections are real. In addition to shaping our individual national identities within the Diaspora, the question pertains for African Americans and African Europeans and African Asians alike: What is our relationship to Africa as a whole? What should be our input into and expectation from strong and independent African states? What is our role as nationals in the liberation struggles of southern Africa? What is our responsibility?

As members of an international community of people of color, how do we strengthen and support each other in our battles against the rising international tide of racism?

I walk into a shiny tourist sweetshop in the newly accessible East Berlin of 1990. The young white German saleswoman looks at me

*With thanks to Ike Hugel for our conversation of July 10, 1990.
**See May Opitz's discussion; also Ivan Van Sertina, ed., *African Presence in Early Europe* (New Brunswick, N.J.: Transaction, 1985).

with aversion, snaps an outraged answer to my first question, then turns her back upon me and my companion until we leave the shop. Once outside, I look back. She turns also. Through the glass door, our eyes meet. That look of hatred she hurls against the glass in my direction is prolonged, intense, and very familiar. I have survived such looks in Jackson, Mississippi, San Francisco, Staten Island, and countless other North American cities.

I read the pages of *Farbe Bekennen* and there is no question our war is the same.

I write these words at a time when West Berlin, like all of Germany, is becoming a very different place from the insulated, internationally flavored city of six years ago. The grim wall that once enclosed this city kept it at an equal distance from West Germany and the rest of Europe. At the same time, it provided a veil of international glamour. Now the wall is down.

Geographically and politically, Germany stands at the center of Europe. Reunified, it will once again represent a powerful force in European affairs. Historically, this force has not been a peaceful one. A new Germany's potential power, and the relative part they will play in influencing the direction of that power—are part of the destiny of African-Germans, just as the political positions of the United States are a part of the destiny of African Americans.

Without a vision, every social change feels like death. Today, there are passions of violent hatred being loosened in East and West Germany, stoked by furies of bewilderment, displaced aggression at chaotic change, and despair at the collapsing textures of daily living. But these passions are not new in German history. Six million dead Jews and hundreds of thousands of dead, tortured, and castrated homosexuals, so-called gypsies, Poles, and people of color attest to what can happen when such passions are unleashed and directed into an ideology.

In East Germany after World War II, communism suppressed fascism but it did not destroy it. Racism, anti-semitism, and xenophobia were severely legislated against in the East, but never admitted nor examined as a national reality. They remain an unaltered psychic time bomb in the national consciousness. These forces are now finding their physical expression in the sharp increase of attacks upon all people of color, foreign guest workers as well as Black Germans.

Such attacks are also increasing in West Germany, encouraged by the same dormant neo-nazi element and stimulated by the prospect of a unification that will provide an economic and political climate within which to express this element. West Berlin children squirt water guns at a Black woman on the Kurfürstendamm. They use "Jew" as a curse word against any white neighbor their parents dislike, and do not even know what the word means. And this aggressive racism and anti-semitism in Germany have been further nurtured by the spread of a worldwide reactionary conservatism whose chief spokespeople for the past ten years have been Britain's prime minister Margaret Thatcher and the United States' president Ronald Reagan.

Communities of the African Diaspora are national minorities in the countries of their birth, but considered together with the populations of the African continent, the balance changes. Globally, the rising tide of reactionary conservatism can be seen as a case of the white superpowers, East and West, deciding to come together despite their ideological differences, because, with the imminent liberation of southern Africa, even they can see the handwriting on the wall.

In West Germany within the last two months of the summer of 1990, young Turkish boys were stoned to death. A Pakistani student was fatally beaten on the steps of a university in West Berlin. Afro-German women were verbally accosted on the daytime subway in Berlin by skinheads, while the white passengers looked on silently. In Dresden, East Germany, a Turkish woman was beaten and her teeth kicked in by a gang of male sports fans while local police watched.

Two nights after the occurrence, at a poetry reading in Dresden, I speak about the need to organize against such happenings. The audience is mostly white women, and young Afro-German men and women. Black and white women from East and West Berlin guard the door. Through the glass door as I speak, I can see large young white men outside bending down and peering in, laughing and drinking beer. I feel myself assume a fighting stance as I read. For the first time in six years I am afraid as I read my poetry in Germany. I ask our Afro-German brothers to walk with us back to our car as we leave for Berlin. The beer drinkers lining the staircase as we leave do not know one of our Afro-German sisters is a black belt in Tai-kwan-do.

Black Germans are not passively accepting this state of affairs. East and West, Afro-Germans are coming together for support and action, often in coalition with other groups. They are learning to identify and use their power, however relative, for their own survival and toward the redefinition of a national German consciousness.

Members of the African Diaspora are connected by heritage although separated by birth. We can draw strength from that connectedness. African Americans and Afro-Europeans incorporate within our consciousness certain splits and alienations of identity. At the same time we concentrate within our being the possibility of fusing the best of all our heritages. We are the hyphenated people, spread across every continent of the globe, members of that international community of people of color who make up seven-eighths of the world's population.

The essence of a truly global feminism is the recognition of connection. Women in Micronesia bear babies who have no bones because of our history of nuclear testing in the South Pacific. In 1964 the CIA fingered Nelson Mandela for the South African police, resulting in his twenty-seven-year imprisonment. With the connivance of such senators as Jesse Helms, the United States sends millions in aid to the South African–backed UNITA forces in Angola, but less than 2 percent of U.S. aid goes to all the countries of the Caribbean. Women farm workers in Jamaica are some of the lowest paid in the world. Yet at the beginning of 1990, while aid to Eastern Europe ballooned, aid to Jamaica was cut by 80 percent.

American women of whatever color cannot afford to indulge ourselves in the parochial attitudes that often blind us to the rest of the world. The Black German women included in this book offer some insights into the complexities of a future global feminism.

This book serves to remind African-American women that we

are not alone in our world situation. In the face of new international alignments, vital connections and differences exist that need to be examined between African-European, African-Asian, African-American women, as well as between us and our African sisters. The first steps in examining these connections are to identify ourselves, to recognize each other, and to listen carefully to each other's stories.

In the interest of all our survivals and the survival of our children, these Black German women claim their color and their voices.

Audre Lorde
St. Croix, USVI
July 30, 1990

Preface to the English Language Edition

Dear Readers,

Six years have passed since we began work in 1984 on *Showing Our Colors*. In that time, changes—some of which are the result of this book—have taken place in German society. The isolation of Black people in Germany, which is described in the testimonies in *Showing Our Colors,* is still a fact, to be sure, and especially for those who have no contact with other Black Germans.

The question of how many Blacks there are in Germany is a difficult and political one. It is usually asked to silence us and to prove that we are only a marginal problem. But it is obvious that even in countries where there is a greater proportion of Blacks in the population, Blacks are not automatically accorded recognition or equality.

There are no statistics on the number of Black people in the population of the Federal Republic. If there were such data they would be significant only in that they would help us to gauge how many people must cope with the stress that comes with the racism that is subjectively felt and objectively experienced by a Black person living in a majority white—and, most important, self-defined white—society.

It is, however, a given that the number of Afro-Germans is growing. This point can be substantiated on the basis of certain observations: for example, fifteen years ago one could find perhaps one or two Black children in a Berlin school, whereas now there may be between five and ten such children; at least one Black child can be found in most preschool groups. For the individual child and his or her family, this change means that they are able to see their own situation mirrored more widely and that there are greater possibilities for exchange of common concerns and experiences. With regard to the Black Diaspora, a very important and positive development is that Black Germans are coming together and organizing in increasing numbers. The book *Showing Our Colors* was an important stimulus for these initiatives.

The Initiative of Black Germans (ISD) was established in 1986. Its prime movers are Afro- and Asian-Germans, and this book's two black coeditors and several of its writers continue to be active in the organization.

Although this initiative is still very young, it is growing constantly and already provides a variety of cultural, political, and social activities. All of its participants, mostly young people in their twenties and thirties, consider the organization as one that affirms and encourages. To date there are affiliate groups in more than ten cities, from Hamburg to Munich, as well as in the former GDR, which meet together for annual exchanges. Two publications founded in 1988, both quarterly journals, have become important forums for discussion and information. The ISD publishes *Afro Look,* and the nationally based Afro-German Women's Group (ADEFRA) publishes *Afrekete.*

The primary purpose of ISD is to strengthen the self-esteem of its individual members and to assert the rights of Blacks in German society, but it also aims to develop contacts with Black movements in other countries. To this end, Afro-Germans have participated in recent years in events such as the Black Bookfair in London. Several have studied or done professional internships in the United States, Great Britain, and France. Among Black women, there is an enthusiastic and intensive international exchange. Afro-German and Indian-German women have been taking part in international women's meetings; for example, some attended the 1988 Feminist Book Fair in Montreal and the Black Women's Summer Institute, held in New York in 1988 and in Harare, Zimbabwe, in 1989 (the next institute will be held in the FRG in 1991).

In closing, we would like to draw attention to some recent

developments that we find unsettling. Over the last few years, a rising tide of right-wing ideologues and parties has swept across Europe. In 1988, a right-wing extremist party in France, the National Front, received 15 percent of the vote in the National Assembly. In the German election of 1989, "die Republikaner," a new right-wing party, received about 10 percent of the vote. This ominous development in the political landscape has finally set off a long overdue public dialogue about racism (which three years ago was viewed as nonexistent in Germany), and it has made the self-articulation and self-representation of Afro-Germans more urgent today than ever before.

The recent unification of the two German states has not only brought severe economic problems; it has also changed the political and social climate in both the east and the west.

It is significant that with the fall of the wall, white Germans from the GDR were greeted enthusiastically by West Germans, while Black Germans, immigrants, and refugees have been confronted with increasingly open racism. The new immigration law ("Ausländergesetz") of the Federal Republic of Germany, which was drafted long before unification, was passed in 1990 and became valid on January 1, 1991. It contains, among other points, severely intensified restrictions on immigration and residence permits; it also makes civil servants liable for reporting on the living and working conditions and conduct of immigrants. This information can be used as grounds for deportation.

In the GDR, in comparison to the FRG, there had been certain liberal conditions regarding the legal rights of foreigners. For instance, the local voting rights were extended to foreigners in the past years and solidarity actions with certain so-called third world nations had become part of the political program of the GDR. On the other hand, however, the rights of "labor immigrants" were restricted by contracts limited to a certain number of years (usually five). These immigrants generally lived, as did foreign students, in ghettolike conditions and had little contact with the German population. Official ideology held that under socialism there exists neither racism nor antisemitism. For this reason, the East German population never had to confront its own racism (see Raya Lubinetzki's contribution to this book). The reality of daily life in East German society reflected the contradictions of this policy: racism was usually not a subject of discussion and was not demonstrated openly, partially out of fear of conflict with government officials.

With the collapse of the socialist regime in East Germany, racism has erupted into open violence and currently plays a significant role in shaping daily life in East Germany in a more pronounced way than in West Germany. The fact that the new immigration law is valid in West and East Germany significantly undermines the legal rights and status of foreigners in the former East German states and supports the widespread attitude in both the east and the west that "Germany belongs to (white) Germans."

"Skinheads" existed in the GDR long before its political "turning point" in the fall of 1989. Now, however, skinheads and neo-fascists have the opportunity to gather more supporters and to organize, unhindered by internal or external barriers. This is partly the result of connections made with similar groups in West Germany. The effect of these developments is that the physical safety of foreigners, particularly people of color, is in danger, not to mention the fear and threat that is experienced when one lives in a generally hostile environment as an unwanted person.

Until now, the forces against racism and antisemitism in East as well as West Germany have not been able to counter these developments in a decisive way. There are, however, a number of initiatives at both the grass-roots and the institutional levels that are making an effort to promote more communication among people of various ethnic and cultural backgrounds, to mobilize resistance and to work more effectively through more extensive networking activities. Thus the groups of Black Germans who existed in East Germany before unification are now in contact with the ISD (Initiative Schwarze Deutsche) in the west. At the same time, there is more and more contact and cooperation between Black Germans, immigrants, and progressive white Germans on an individual as well as an organizational level. Among women, discussions between Black German women, immigrants, and Jewish women are developing. These beginnings mean more than simply reacting to the threat posed by the political climate: they reflect the need to broaden one's own horizons and to work more intensively at recognizing and defining our differences and commonalities.

Less than a year after German unification we now face the upcoming "European unification" in 1992. Europe is developing into an economic and political bulwark against the rest of the world, above all against the countries and peoples of the so-called Third World. Already today, migratory movements and immigration are being controlled, curtailed, and/or stopped altogether through international agreements (e.g., the Schengen agreement of 1989). As in Germany, there are also countermovements in other European countries. We hope that national and international coalitions that have taken on the goal of eliminating the exclusion of immigrants and people of color and the privileges of white-skinned people in Europe will be able to initiate processes of liberation from which people of color and also white Europeans will profit.

Katharina Oguntoye
May Opitz
1990

Since the first edition of *Farbe Bekennen* was published, some changes have taken place within the white women's movement: at readings and in discussions and private groups, Afro-German women have confronted us directly with our inability or unwillingness to perceive them as Black Germans. At the same time, immigrant and refugee women have challenged white women to deal with the fear, competition, and distance that they sense in white German women's behavior toward them. In similar developments, Jewish women have publicly addressed the antisemitism among non-Jewish women, whose awareness is seriously hampered by their idea that to acknowledge the existence of Jewish women would involve experiencing guilt. Only gradually are white women beginning to realize that accepting responsibility is a viable and necessary alternative to being paralyzed by guilt feelings.

The growing danger from the right in the FRG, the political turnover of 1989 in the German Democratic Republic, and the specter of a Europe united against Africa, Asia, and Latin America have made it more imperative than ever to deal head-on with our entanglement in the racism and antisemitism of this society, instead of treating our (own) concern with racism and antisemitism as merely an intellectual or emotional issue.

In recent years, white women have had numerous opportunities to hear Audre Lorde and to engage in discussions with her and with Black German women. White women have begun to meet among themselves and with women of color over issues of racism. More and more, women's conferences and meetings are focusing on differences among women, although women intellectuals have been particularly slow in changing their perspective. Requests made by women of color and by Jewish women that other women respond when they reveal some of their thoughts, feelings, and experiences are frequently met with silences—silences that indicate that politically meaningful communication is still a long way off. But an increasing number of white women are taking the first steps toward questioning their position in this world and, in Audre Lorde's words, toward moving beyond the first lesson of patriarchy—"divide and conquer"—to "define and empower."

Dagmar Schultz

1990

Editors' Introduction

As Afro-German women almost all of us between the ages of twenty and thirty were accustomed to dealing with our background and our identity in isolation. Few of us had any significant contact with other Afro-Germans and if we attempted to discuss our thoughts and problems with friends, it was always possible that we would alienate someone or be accused of being "too sensitive." Meeting each other as Afro-Germans and becoming involved with each other has been a totally new experience. What several of us did have in common was a socialization unlike that of other Germans; aside from that, we were very different due to the variety inherent in where we came from (Berlin, the GDR, or West Germany), our familial and work situations, our sexual orientations, and our relations with the African or Afro-American part of our ancestry. A spontaneous affinity made it easier for us to move beyond our very diverse life situations and allowed us to enter into a common process: that of sharing our subjective experiences with each other, of considering contacting other Afro-Germans and connecting with them in similar ways, of setting about searching for our history, and, finally—what is occurring with this book—of going public. It was all very exciting, while at the same time it generated so much energy and courage that we overcame many personal and individual anxieties and obstacles. We concluded with a stronger resolve to no longer pass by other Afro-Germans with only a sideways glance.

With this book we want to invoke personal experiences in order to expose the social underpinnings of racism. In the course of our research we met Afro-German women who had lived in Germany under the reign of Kaiser Wilhelm II, in the Weimar Republic, and through National Socialism. Some were immediately willing to meet with us younger ones and recount their lives. Today—several years later—it is difficult to describe how moved and excited we were at these meetings. We suddenly discovered that our history had not begun in 1945. We were brought face to face with our past, and saw it was closely linked with Germany's colonial and National Socialist history. Our unknown background and our invisibility as Afro-Germans are consequences of the suppression of German history.

Our lives will be easier when we no longer continually have to explain our existence. In disentangling the threads of our histories within Africa and Germany and connecting them to our subjective experiences, we are becoming more sure of our identity and are able to assert it more aggressively to the outside world. Perhaps, eventually we will not be simply overlooked by a public steeped in ignorance and prejudice. Possibly our emerging visibility will also clear a path for those who are children today so that they can grow up feeling less isolated, marginal, and exceptional than we did.

With Audre Lorde we created the term "Afro-German," borrowing from Afro-American, as the term of our cultural heritage. "Afro-German" seemed appropriate to us, since many of us have an African father and a German mother. In using this term, our point is not to emphasize that we have a black and a white parent. Our essential commonality is that we are black and have experienced a major part of our socialization and life in confrontation with West German society—a society that is not 99 percent white but that always has behaved as though it were, or should be. By the term "Afro-German" we mean all those who wish to refer to themselves as such, regardless of whether they have one or two black parents. Just as with the similar name "Black Germans," our intent is not to exclude on the basis of origin or skin color. We know what it means to suffer exclusion. More important, we want to propose "Afro-German" in opposition to more commonly used names like "half-breed," "mulatto," or "colored," as an attempt to define ourselves instead of being defined by others.

Katharina Oguntoye
May Opitz

For me [Dagmar Schultz] as a white German woman, working on this book has meant immersing myself in a part of German history that I had known previously only on a very abstract level. I met women of older generations, of whose existence I had known nothing, and once again it became clear to me how much of our "heritage" is kept from us. As children we played with a deck of cards that depicted episodes from the German colonial period—a chapter of German history that was never treated when I was in school, or at least not in the full measure of its brutality. I came together with women of my generation and recalled the Afro-German schoolmate I had and also the girlfriend whose grandfather had been a Native American. But still, I could remember only a few things that gave me any idea about how they—and how we as white schoolchildren—experienced their "difference." Conversations with women interested in writing something for this book made me review the fifties, with its muted consciousness, in a new way.

In the sixties and early seventies, which I spent in the United States, I became familiar with the history of Afro-Americans. My realization that racism was only rarely called by its name in Germany, even in the woman's movement, led me to publish the book *Macht und Sinnlichkeit,* with texts by Audre Lorde and Adrienne Rich. But it was not until I worked on this book that I became aware of the racism that Afro-Germans have experienced and continue to experience. Politically, I have much in common with the younger women whom I came to know—Katharina Oguntoye and May Opitz among them—although our spheres of experience are very different. And from my experience in the United States as well as from here, I knew about racial prejudice, stereotypes, liberalism, and the often inconsiderate or thoughtless political appropriation of "minorities."

In the course of working on this book, these concepts, attitudes, and behaviors took on contours that revealed to me the specifics of the German situation. Much that I had learned from Afro-American women friends and writers and through my political work in the United States now took on a new significance in our working group, in particular the need to identify our differences and to find and build bridges between our worlds. One and a half years of intensive collaboration brought me very close to the other women. Conversations and discussions around the conceptualization of the book, contacts with other Afro-Germans, and preparation of the text were all part of a constant learning process. Through this project and the resulting friendships I have grown personally, and my detachment from Germany, which I had never quite gotten rid of after my life in the United States, has lessened somewhat.

Dagmar Schultz

The initial intention of publishing a book with conversations, texts, and poems of the group of younger women who came together in the summer of 1984 soon expanded to the idea of allowing as many generations as possible the chance to speak. May Opitz's decision to make Afro-Germans and their history the topic of her master's thesis enabled us to provide a framework for the diverse texts and the necessary historical background.

The book is divided into three sections: "Racism, Sexism, and Precolonial Images of Africa in Germany"; "Afro-Germans after 1945: The So-called Occupation Babies"; and "Racism Here and Now." Each section begins with an essay by May Opitz that presents historical, political, and social attitudes with respect to Africa, Africans, and Afro-Germans in Germany or the Federal Republic. This is followed by personal testimonies, interviews, and poems by Afro-German women of the generation corresponding to the chapter's historical context. In the first section we hear from two women who are around seventy and who grew up during the Weimar Republic and lived through National Socialism; in the second section, from women born in the forties and fifties; and in the third section, from the younger generation of the sixties and seventies, including a granddaughter of one of the first women interviewed.

A major portion of our teamwork consisted of encouraging the authors to write and discussing their texts with them. For some it was easier to reveal their experiences in conversations, which we then reworked into a narrative form (at the request of one author, a pseudonym was used). As an editorial team of both Afro-German and white women, we found the collaboration among ourselves and the project editor of the publishing house to be a constructive process, which proved over and over to be a journey of discovery.

Katharina Oguntoye
May Opitz
Dagmar Schultz
1986

Showing Our Colors

Racism, Sexism, and Precolonial Images of Africa in Germany

MAY OPITZ

Portrait of an Ethiopian (an employee in one of the large trading firms of
Augsburg), Albrecht Dürer, 1508

Precolonial Images of Africa, Colonialism, and Fascism

The First Africans in Germany

There is no precise method of determining when the first Africans came to Germany and when the first Afro-Germans were born. The first "half-breed" person in literature appears in *Parsival*.[1] Several paintings have survived from the twelfth century that depict Africans living in Germany. Until well into the nineteenth century, German contacts with Africa were limited to trade relations. The large commercial houses of Fugger, Welser, and Imhoff, in particular, were the first to finance some of the flotillas, which since the Middle Ages have traded under Portuguese and Spanish flags.[2] Initially these commercial ventures brought gold, ivory, spices, and other raw materials to Europe. Later, human beings were also shipped to Europe in increasing numbers as "tokens"—traded or taken as security for contractual agreements. According to historian Joseph Ki-Zerbo, humans were carried away primarily to prove that the Europeans had really been to Africa and to satisfy the curiosity of compatriots who wanted to see what Black people looked like.[3]

There are no figures available as to how many Blacks lived in Germany during the Middle Ages. In the mid-sixteenth century, one-tenth of the population in the Portuguese capital were Black slaves, and, as in France and England, it was probably also true in Germany—albeit less common—that having such an exotic figure in one's livery, parlor, and stable was the thing to do.[4]

The unique story of A. W. Amo has come from the eighteenth century. A Ghanaian, he was brought to Germany in 1703 as a present to Count Anton Ulrich von Wolfenbüttel[5] from the Dutch West India Company, one of the biggest slave trading enterprises of the time.[6] The count and his son assumed sponsorship of Amo and sent him to the University of Halle, whose great fame was enhanced by a faculty that included a number of important figures of the Enlightenment. Given the thinking of the times, it was highly unusual that the count and his son "didn't stick the boy into a servant's outfit and turn him into a rich man's toy."[7]

Amo became one of the most important exponents of Christian von Wolff's philosophy, and, as a follower of John Locke's and Descartes's mechanical philosophy, he was prominent in the fight against the early Lutheran and pietistic clerics. His first scholarly work concerned the rights of the Moors in Europe and was published in 1729 under the Latin title *De juro mauro in Europa*. This work has been lost. Amo later taught as a lecturer at the universities of Halle, Wittenberg, and Jena. Manfred Paeffgen mentions that Amo was appointed by Fredrick William I as a member of the State Council of the Prussian crown at the court in Berlin.[8]

Amo returned to Ghana in 1743, no longer able to withstand the increasing attacks by racial theorists. In Ghana (then known as the "Gold Coast") he once again wound up in the hands of slave traders. He "was surely one of the few Africans in West Africa who knew of the tragic fate of the slaves and was personally affected. For this reason he was moved into Fort San Sebastian, where he was under the complete control of slave hunters. He died shortly thereafter and lies buried in front of the fort."[9]

At the same time, another African had a "career" in Russia as "Peter the Great's Moor," under the name of Ibrahim Petrovich Hannibal. A century later (1847–48), a king's son, Aquasi Boachi, prince of Ashantiland, who was brought to Germany as security for a contract, became the first African to study at the Mining Academy of Freiberg.[10]

The Middle Ages: "Moors" and White Christians

The changes in the use of the terms "Moor" and "Negro" mirror the changes in Germany's and, more generally, Europe's relations with

Africa. "Moor" is the oldest German term for people of different skin color and during the high Middle Ages served to differentiate between Black and white heathens. *Môr,* from Latin *mauri,* was coined in the course of the conflict between Christians and Muslims in North Africa. It was, therefore, physical difference and unfamiliar belief systems that first characterized this concept.[11]

Poliakov et al. point out that in medieval pictures one of the three wise men is depicted as a Black man and conclude that prejudice toward others was not as yet linked to skin color. As further evidence, they point to the medieval preference for fantastic stories set in the Orient.[12] It is hard to know if, in and of itself, this is significant. Henrich Pleticha sees the Blacks in these stories depicted as fabulous creatures neither human nor animal: "They are situated on the level of exotic plants and animals. The essential feature is that the aura of the wild and uncanny is attached to them."[13]

Revealing indications of the low esteem in which Blacks were held are found in the ecclesiastical vocabulary of the time, where "Egyptian" is sometimes used as a synonym for the devil.[14] In addition, there are examples in literature where white people were depicted with the blackness of the Moors, because they deviated in some way from the norm. One example is the version of the "Ywain legend," as written by Hartmann von Aue around 1200 ("Was welt ir daz der tôre tuo?" [What shall the madman do?]).[15] The Tôr turns as black as a "Môr" and frightens people wherever he goes.

In all descriptions of witches, black became the mark of evil, but it was also used in other contexts. For example, an unfeminine woman was often "blackened." Thus the hero in Wirnt von Grafenberg's "Wigalois" is confronted by a female monster: black, ugly, and ill-mannered, a "freak."[16] The same is seen in "Wolfdietrich's Saga," an anonymous poem from the mid-thirteenth century:

> A monstrous woman, born in the wild, came toward him through the trees. There was never a bigger woman. The noble knight thought to himself: "O dear Christ, protect me!" Two monstrous breasts hung from her body. "Whoever gets you," the wise knight spoke, "gets the devil's mother, I do believe." Her body was created blacker than coal. Her nose hung over her chin; long and black was her hair. . . .[17]

The "monstrous woman" who approaches the "noble knight" in the woods ("through the trees") frightens him because of her immeasurable size, projected by her disproportionate ("monstrous") breasts. The knight prays for protection in his hour of need, thinking he recognizes the unmistakable features of the devil's mother in the lips blacker than coal, the nose hanging over her chin, and the long black hair.

In Christian symbolism, "black" embodies the essence of the undesirable, the ugly, the objectionable. Religiously inspired prejudices were thus able to perpetuate the negative image of the Black, by linking it to the particular Christian-patriarchal conceptions of the prototype of the "evil villain," already indicated in the projection of black color on whites (see above). Until the eighteenth century, prejudices toward Blacks were largely unconnected to ideas about the existence of different races. It was only in the age of Enlightenment that a clear change came about as one result of the rapid colonization of African countries south of the Sahara.

From "Moors" to "Negroes"

In the eighteenth century, "Negro" became a German concept. As an expansion and replacement for the term "Moor," it was used to describe people south of the Sahara and served "further as the term for the black race as such."[18] In contrast to "Moor," which did not differentiate between lighter and darker Africans, the new term signified the ideological separation of Africa into white and black regions[19] with the increasing colonization of the continent. Frantz Fanon characterizes the division as follows:

> Africa is divided into black and white, and the names that are substituted—Africa South of the Sahara, Africa North of the Sahara—do not manage to hide this latent racism.[20] Here it is affirmed that White Africa has a thousand-year-old tradition of culture; that she is Mediterranean, that she is a continuation of Europe, and that she shares in Greco-Latin civilization. Black Africa is looked on as a region that is inert, brutal, uncivilized, in a word, savage.[21]

In the course of colonial exploitation, enslavement, and domination "Negro" (from Latin *niger*, i.e., black) became an especially negative epithet. The thinking underlying this label attempted to link physical characteristics with intellectual and cultural ones.

The botanist Carl von Linné, who was the first to illustrate the place of the human within the animal kingdom, in his *Systema naturae* (1735), continued for decades to posit only somatic criteria as distinctive. It was not until the tenth edition of his publication (1758) that he made connections with the psyche.

> In the order now named primate, homo sapiens is identified by varians cultura, loco. The presentation of his varieties refers to skin color, hair, eyes, nose, as well as to posture, character, temperament, and mind, and also to the criteria tegitur and regitur, clothing and customs.[22] Thus, at the same time it takes on a significant valuation, whether it is the acerbic, choleric temperament of the American, the inventive European, . . . ruled by laws, . . . the melancholy, haughty, splendor- and money-loving Asian, or the African, of evil, lazy, and careless disposition, ruled by despotism.[23]

Winckelmann's aesthetic anthropology was oriented in its theory of typology to the classical ideals of beauty of the Greeks. He claimed that the temperate climate of Greece produced the ideal type of human being. "Misformations" increased according to the distance from the climatically favorable center. "The pinched nose of the Kalmucks, the Chinese, and other outlying peoples is . . . a deviation, for it interrupts the unity of form. . . . The protruding, bulging mouth that the moors have in common with the monkeys in their country is a superfluous growth . . . , caused by the heat of their climate."[24]

With the decline of the medieval perception of the world, in which God was accepted as the direct creator of all being, discussions proliferated concerning the genesis and determination of the human race. Central to these discussions was whether all humans shared a common origin. Were the differences among humans the result of genetic difference or mutable environmental influences? George Louis Leclerc, count of Buffon, was the first to draft a theory of evolution based on anatomical knowledge. He started with an assumption of the unity of the human race and linked the various races to climatic zones. In his reflections on the subject,

"Buffon considered very seriously whether Blacks could be transplanted to Denmark and isolated from the rest of the population in order to determine how many generations it would take until they turned white again, thus discovering how long it had taken for them to become black."[25] That the thought did not occur to him to send Europeans to Africa to see whether they would become black over time might be related to the fact that he, too, "esteemed the white European race as the most beautiful and best, above the races of black, red, and yellow people in Africa, America, and Asia."[26]

The concept of an ideal human being, which gained ascendancy in nineteenth-century Europe—that of an emotionless, rational, and efficient person—was developed in accord with the growing needs of industrial capitalism. Other modes of living, cultural forms, and production technologies were similarly devalued, as were physical forms of expression and appearance that did not correspond to the sober aesthetics of classicism.

> With the equating of civilization and work (which, in its limited or modern meaning, was understood as differentiated production of wares for individual profit), evolutionary anthropology of the late nineteenth century identifies civilization with the industrial occident and constructs a typology of society on the basis of its respective technical standards.[27]

The outward appearance of Africans (particularly their color) and their subsistence economy made them the polar opposite of the "beautiful," "modern" man.[28] In general, in the eighteenth century, Africans were seen as the lowest human form, thought to be related to the highest animal form, the monkey.[29] "Europeans appeared . . . , in contrast to the primitives, who were calcifying in a state of backward irrationality, to stand at the head of the cultural and technological evolution of humankind."[30]

Out of this stance, ethnology came to be conceived, in the nineteenth century, as the opposite of historiography—as a science that made "peoples without a history" its subject matter.[31]

The principal objective of ethnological expeditions was not personal contacts with other peoples but rather abstract observation, classification of groups of people, and collection, or appropriation, of artifacts. On this point, an excerpt from the notes of the ethnologic traveler Adolf Bastian:

> There is much talk of the extinction of the primitive peoples. Physical extinction, to the degree that it takes place, is not the crucial issue, for it is dependent on the almighty flow of history, which can be neither stemmed nor averted. But we are concerned here with psychic extinction, the loss of ethnic originalities before they are secured in literature and museums for study. Such a loss threatens our future inductive calculations with all kinds of falsifications and could put the very possibility of a human science in doubt.[32]

Ethnologists used their own group as the standard when defining, valuing, and judging other population groups as "primitive."

Terms for these concepts were invented for the purpose of describing other peoples and cultures, but at the same time they belonged to—or ultimately became—the vocabulary of curse words and invectives of the naming group: "Barbaric," "primitive," "uncivilized" express the ethnocentrically constructed opposite of a world that could at best be associated with remote eras and living conditions overcome long ago (as, for example, in the "deepest dark ages"). The customary differentiation into "primitive" and "civilized" peoples reduces other peoples' forms of expression more to natural reaction than to self-motivated accomplishment. Hidden behind this separation is a conception such as that clearly formulated by Hegel in the nineteenth century:

> As soon as man emerges as a human being, he stands in opposition to nature, and it is this alone which makes him a human being. But if he has merely made a distinction between himself and nature, he is still at the first stage of his development: he is dominated by passion, and is nothing more than a savage.[33]

"Race": The Construction of a Concept

The concept of "race" can be traced to the thirteenth century and the region of the Romance languages. Not until the sixteenth century, however, did it become customary to use it to describe privileged membership and descent.

Two historical events in particular had a decided influence on the early concept of race: The Spanish *Reconquista* and the discussion of nobility in France. With the Spanish mandatory-conversion edict of 1492, Jews entered European consciousness as a "race," their peculiar status being further sealed by the claim for "purity of blood," *limieza de sangre,* designed to exclude them as a powerful group from Spanish society, over and above the conversion.[34]

In France the nobility attempted to use the concept of race to explain its privileges through heredity, thereby securing its position against the rising power of the nonhereditary nobility (the middle class) through the institution of peerage.

Arthur Count de Gobineau (1816–1882) was one of the leading race theorists and the first to propose a biological explanation for *any* inequality in the cultural, social, and political sphere. Enlightenment ideas of equality were necessarily unacceptable to him since as a nobleman he belonged to that group that profited from the static relationships of the aristocratic order. His race theories presented a paradigm diametrically opposed to the ideas of the Enlightenment. Gobineau interpreted every social change as a sign of decay. Using his assumptions about the inequality of human races as a basis, he traced nearly every social hierarchy to racial differences.[35]

From then on the division of humanity into "races" went far beyond the bounds of the classifications suggested in the seventeenth and eighteenth century. Not just whites, blacks, Indians, and yellows were compared. Within the European group there were "historical" races, which were as essentially different from one another as the white and black races could ever be. The white "race" until that time, an example of monolithic integrity, was being broken down into "subraces."[36]

Thus, in the course of the history of its usage "race" became a political catchword that linked social position with kinship. For Michael Traber "race" is "endorsement of a many-sided polarization":

1. spiritual polarization: "chosen–depraved"
2. status polarization: "aristocrats–commoners"
3. class polarization: "bourgeoisie–proletariat"
4. political polarization: "rulers–subjects"[37]

The fact that theories of race were developed and circulated exclusively in continental Europe makes it clear that "race" is a social endorsement that has little to do with biological difference. Consequently, whenever "race" is invoked it is understood as a relational concept that consists of distinctions drawn between one's own group (in group) and another group (out group), whereby ascribed characteristics such as skin color, behavior, religion, and so on are interpreted as "racial characteristics."

Sexism and Racism

I have pointed out that for the classification of other peoples, the qualities taken as the standard were those supposedly characteristic of the ideal type—the modern European. Upon closer examination, a further restriction must be made. "Jews, but also Italians, French, and Slavs counted as female to the Germans."[38] Gustav Klemm (1802–1867), in his ten-volume publication on general cultural history, makes a distinction between "active male" and "passive female" peoples. The former were the peoples of discoveries, inventions, and legal systems; the latter, those "who have always lived their lives, modest in their demands, satisfied with what life afforded them, and without political ambitions."[39]

The racist and sexist oppression and denigration of other peoples and cultures should/must be placed in the context of events following the fifteenth century in central Europe. Early modern times—not the "Dark" Ages—were characterized by religious wars and burnings at the stake. At least nine million women—a number of sources indicate there were as many as thirty-two million—were burned as "witches" during the new, enlightened times, in attempt to purify them of ominous suspicious and alien powers. The triumphal march of science, of alienated industrial labor, and of the new global view was attainable apparently only through the annihilation of everything eccentric or unmanageable, especially women. At the beginning of the eighteenth century, after three hundred years of persecutions and murders of women, the rising bourgeoisie offered a new female ideal, characterized more than ever by passivity:

He [the man] is her natural representative in the State and in the society as a whole. This is her relationship to the society, her public relationship.

A reasonable and virtuous woman can be proud only of her husband and children; not of herself, for she forgets herself in them.[40]

Not until the eighteenth century did "family" become an enclosed entity, which essentially remained limited to a circle of immediate relations (parents and children) and was separate from the remunerated, public sphere of production. The shift developed with the rise of wage labor and the needs of the capitalist economy for a mobile work force that could change its residence. In the preceding centuries, "family" had been a productive economic unit, which, in addition to parents and children, included other relatives and servants and lived largely independent of a market economy.[41] Although in the Middle Ages the family was already patriarchally organized, with legal and social privileges accorded to the husband as head of the household, it was not until conditions of production changed that economic and ideological structures forced unemployed women into economic and emotional dependency on men. With the creation of a private sphere and the relocation of production away from the home, the role developed for the middle-class wife as tender, loving, caring mate, homemaker, and mother—closed off from the world of occupational and political life.[42] This disempowerment was embellished and idealized, although in the eighteenth century the majority of German women did not fit the new feminine ideal because they were doing heavy labor in factories, or in any case, most did not belong to the bourgeoisie.

The concept of marriage as a spiritual and emotional community, of the family as the place for educating a person to a social-cultural being were products of this epoch. On this basis there arose the nineteenth-century model of the middle-class family as a well-situated nuclear family, in which the father determined the social position, the mother created the home atmosphere, both bound in marital love (whatever that might be), bound in the interest of rearing accomplished and well-behaved children, who, in their choice of profession and mate, followed the wishes of their parents.[43]

Thus, the middle-class wife gradually was relegated as "a non-working woman" to the sphere of custodial reproductive *work* (giving birth, rearing children, creating a homey atmosphere); the husband, by contrast, embodied more and more the role of the man operating autonomously, who functioned in the public sphere and, as breadwinner, controlled property and dependent relationships.

The middle-class theoreticians of the Enlightenment did indeed call for substitution of contracts, made by equal partners of their own free will, for tradition and custom, as the basis for human intercourse; but, in truth, the theorists principally represented male interests. Women and children were placed, as a rule, under the "protection" of the man and thus silenced. The thinking of English philosopher John Locke (1632–1704) is an example of Enlightenment theories.

> Rights of women and children to family property occur in Locke only in repudiation of the rights of third parties, particularly the State or other political powers. Within the internal relationship of the family, children and wife had no claims whatsoever against the husband and father.[44]

The subordinate status of women was no longer justified as the will of God and sealed by original sin, but was now seen as derived from the "natural character" of wife and mother. In this manner, social inequality was the result of biology and was still immutable: women were "by nature" passive and emotional, so men were justified in unquestioningly imposing repetitive duties and a housewife existence upon them, which, because these were natural obligations, did not necessitate remuneration.

For Fichte a wife could only exist as a complement to her husband's rational nature provided that she was able to spiritualize her sexual desire and accommodate her husband's needs:

> In the unspoiled wife there is no manifestation of any sexual desire, but rather only love; and this love is the natural desire of the wife to satisfy her husband. . . .
>
> Only in this manner does the desire to give herself take on the character of freedom and duty that it must have, to be able to exist next

to reason. There is probably no man who would not feel the absurdity of the reversal of things, ascribing to the husband a similar desire to satisfy a wife's need; he could neither assume such a need in her nor think of himself as a tool thereof, without being ashamed in the depths of his soul.[45]

Completely contradictory behavior was demanded of the ideal wife. She was supposed to make herself desirable, but not tempting, to be educated, but not self-determining. Indeed, suppression of desire was required of the husband, too, by the constructed contradiction of reason and sensuality, but his socialization led much more easily to a self-conscious, self-responsible, and independent life. Thus the philosopher J.-J. Rousseau demanded an education for his male novice Emile that would make him independent of the opinions of others, but he had entirely different ideas for Sophie:

Nature herself has decreed that woman, both for herself and her children, should be at the mercy of man's judgment. Worth alone will not suffice, a woman must be thought worthy; nor beauty, she must be admired; nor virtue, she must be respected. A woman's honour does not depend on her conduct alone, but on her reputation, and no woman who permits herself to be considered vile is really virtuous. A man has no one but himself to consider, and so long as he does right he may defy public opinion; but when a woman does right her task is only half finished, and what people think of her matters as much as what she really is. Hence her education must, in this respect, be different from man's education. "What will people think" is the grave of a man's virtue and the throne of a woman's.[46]

In that sense women were socialized into a gender-specific role, and the "product" of this training was explained as the true essence of woman.

Thus Scheler claims that

Woman is more guided by closeness to the earth, and to plant life, more unified in all experience and led more strongly by instincts, feeling, and love than Man—she is guardian of tradition, of custom, of all older forms of thought and will, and the eternal braking power of a wagon of civilization and culture racing headlong toward the destination of naked rationality and "progress."[47]

The projections that justify the relationship of men as masters to women as disposable fit the stereotypical image of naturally ascribed characteristics, which is projected onto creatures considered to be "primitive." Hence, the alleged emphasis of "affectivity over rationality, instinct over intellect, immediate perception over abstraction; and mental and cultural immobility over the dynamics of history."[48]

Notes

1. Jörg Becker, *Alltäglicher Rassismus* (Frankfurt, 1977), p. 206. See also Wolfram v. Eschenbach, *Parzival*, ed. Albert von Leitzmann, 7th ed. (Tübingen, 1961), vols. 1–6, no. 1.

2. Manfred Paeffgen, *Das Bild Schwarz-Afrikas in der Öffentlichen Meinung der BRD 1949–1972* (München, 1976), p. 18.

3. Joseph Ki-Zerbo, *Histoire de l'Afrique noire d'hier à demain* (Paris, 1978), p. 208.

4. Ibid., p. 209.

5. My information for this section is drawn primarily from Burkhard Brentjes's essay "Der erste afrikanische Student in Halle," in *Der Beitrag der Völker Afrikas zur Weltkultur*, ed. Burkhard Brentjes (Halle, 1977).

6. In the eighteenth century, Germany was still splintered into many small principalities and did not yet possess a navy.

7. Brentjes, "Der erste afrikanische Student," p. 4.

8. Paeffgen, *Das Bild Schwarz-Afrikas*, p. 9. Paeffgen gives no date.

9. Brentjes, "Der erste afrikanische Student," p. 5. Brentjes gives no geographical specifics about the location of the fort.

10. Ibid., gives some information about their lives.

11. See Sander Gilman, *On Blackness without Blacks: Essays on the Image of the Black in Germany* (Boston, 1982), p. xii.

12. See Léon Poliakov, Christian Delacampagne, and Patrick Girard, *Über den Rassismus: 16 Kapitel zur Anatomie, Geschichte und Deutung des Rassenwahns* (Frankfurt, 1984), pp. 64, 63.

13. Heinrich Pleticha, "Das Bild des Farbigen in der Jugendliteratur," in *Bücher spiegeln die Welt: Das Bild der Rassen und Völker in der Jugendliteratur*, ed. Horst von Schaller (Insel Mainau, 1969), p. 45.

14. See Becker, *Alltäglicher Rassismus*, p. 64.

15. See Gilman, *On Blackness without Blacks*, p. 12.

16. Ibid.

17. "Orneit und Wolfdietrich" from the Wiener Piaristenhandschrift (1906), cited in ibid., p. 12.

18. Uta Sadji, *Der Negermythos am Ende des 18: Jahrhunderts in Deutschland—Eine Analyse der Rezeption von Reiseliteratur über Schwarzafrika* (Frankfurt, 1979), p. 1.

19. Paeffgen points out that black Africa "is a European invention, referring to the area of the African continent with black-skinned people" (*Das Bild Schwarz-Afrikas*, p. 16).

20. At this point I want to refer to the following definition of racism, which, however, does not take into consideration its connection with sexism (gender-specific prejudice and discrimination): "Racism is the belief in the inequality of human races, in whose name certain races, certain cultures, are subjected to economic exploitation, social separation, and even physical extermination. Any person or policy is racist, whose dealings, conscious or not, are influenced by this belief." (Stefanie and Gabriele von Hohenwart, eds., *Taschenwörterbuch der Ethnologie*, 2d ed. [Berlin, 1982], p. 259.)

21. Frantz Fanon, *The Wretched of the Earth*, trans. Constance Farrington (New York, 1965), p. 161.

22. C. v. Linné, *Systema naturae sive regna systematice proposita per clases, ordines, genera et species* (Leiden, 1735).

23. O. Brunner, W. Conze, and R. Kosselek, eds., *Historisches Lexikon zur politisch-sozialen Sprache in Deutschland* (Stuttgart, 1984), p. 145.

24. J. J. Winckelmann, *Zur Geschichte der Kunst des Altertums*, quoted in Fritz Kramer, *Verkehrte Welten: Zur imaginären Ethnologie des 19. Jahrhunderts* (Frankfurt, 1984), p. 145.

25. Poliakov, Delacampagne, and Girard, *Über den Rassismus*, p. 81.

26. Brunner, Conze, and Kosselek, *Historisches Lexikon*, p. 147.

27. Girard Léclerc, *Anthropologie und Kolonialismus* (München, 1973), p. 12.

28. A subsistence economy is based on the family's own need and not geared toward profit.

29. George L. Mosse, *Rassismus—Ein Krankheitssymptom der europäischen Geschichte des 19. und 20. Jahrhunderts* (Königstein/Ts, 1978), p. 11.

30. Poliakov, Delacampagne, and Girard, *Über den Rassismus*, p. 83.

31. Kramer, *Verkehrte Welten*, p. 76.

32. Adolph Bastian, *Der Völkergedanke im Aufbau einer Wissenschaft vom Menschen und seine Begründung in ethnologischen Sammlungen*, cited in ibid., p. 76.

33. Georg W. F. Hegel, *Lectures on the Philosophy of World History* (Introduction: "Reason in History") (Cambridge, 1975), p. 177.

34. Brunner, Conze, and Kosselek, *Historisches Lexikon*, p. 140.
35. Patrick v. Zur Mühlen, *Rassenideologien—Geschichte und Hinter-gründe* (Berlin-Bonn, 1977), p. 62. See also J. A. de Gobineau, *Essai sur l'inégalité des races humaines*, 4 vols., 2d ed. (1883; Paris, 1953–55).
36. Poliakov, Delacampagne, and Girard, *Über den Rassismus*, p. 93.
37. Michael Traber, *Rassismus und weiße Vorherrschaft* (Freiburg, 1971), p. 42.
38. Marielouise Janssen-Jurreit, *Sexismus—Über die Abtreibung der Frauenfrage* (München-Wien, 1976), p. 702.
39. Zur Mühlen, *Rassenideologien*, p. 50.
40. Johann G. Fichte, *Werke* Bd. 3, cited in Annegret Stopczyk, *Was Philosophen über Frauen denken* (München, 1980), p. 143.
41. "Not only was the female labor force thereby devalued to the degree that its critical work functions were eliminated in the course of indus-trialization and the shift to a money economy—the latter having taken place relatively early in the era of the bourgeoisie. In addition, as the result of the burgeoning propagation of a cult of femininity, woman also experienced a redefinition of value, by which, as the representative of home and hearth, she had imposed upon her a new kind of duty and expected behavior that contrasted with the competi-tive, harsh, and hostile outside world." Gertraude Kittler, *Hausarbeit: Zur Geschichte einer "Naturressource"* (München, 1980), p. 49.
42. Heinrich Ebel, Rolf Eickelpasch, Eckehard Kühne, *Familie in der Gesellschaft: Gestalt-Standort-Funktion*, Schriftenreihe der Bundes-zentrale für pol. Bildung, ed. Vorstand der Arbeitsgemeinschaft kath-soz. Bildungswerke in der BR (AKsB), (Darmstadt, 1983), pp. 49 ff.
43. Ibid., pp. 66–67.
44. Barbara Schaeffer-Hegel, "Feministische Wissenschaftskritik: An-griffe auf das Selbstverständliche in den Geisteswissenschaften," in *Mythos Frau, Projektionen und Inszenierungen in Patriarchat*, ed. B. Schaeffer-Hegel and B. Wartmann, 2d ed. (Berlin, 1984), pp. 51–52.
45. Johann G. Fichte, *Fichtes Werke: Erster Anhang des Naturrechts: Grundriß des Familienrechts* (Berlin, 1845-46; Fotomechanischer Nachdruck, 1971), p. 311.
46. From the bildungsroman *Emile* by J.-J. Rousseau (London, 1974), p. 328.
47. Max Scheler, *Vom Umsturz der Werte*, cited in Stopczyk, *War Phi-losophen*, p. 282.
48. Léclerc, *Anthropologie und Kolonialismus*, p. 12.

VI. Jahrg. — Nr. 38, Ausgabe A

Preis **10** *Pf*

Kolonie und Heimat

Unabhängige koloniale Wochenschrift

Organ des Frauenbundes der Deutschen Kolonialgesellschaft

Dem Kaiser!

Dein Tag wird nicht nur in Berlin
Und nur im Reich begangen!
Wo immer Deine Schiffe zieh'n,
Soll heut Dein Name prangen!

Der soll heut stolz und überall
Klingen vor allen Nationen!
Dein Name ist wie ein fester Wall;
Darunter läßt's gut sich wohnen!

Von vielen Stämmen in mancherlei Tracht,
In vielen Farben und Zungen
Wird heute Dir ein Hoch gebracht
Und Dein Kaiserlied gesungen! M. M.

Kolonie und Heimat [Colony and homeland], an independent weekly
published by the Women's Colonial Society

The Germans in the Colonies

The history and present situation of Afro-Germans are closely tied to Germany's colonial history: the first Africans in Germany came here from the colonies to people who considered themselves to belong to the white "master race."

Just as the imperial past has yet to be resolved in the minds of Germans—for it did not end by consensus but by defeat—so too the associated ideologies about "black" and "white" have yet to be surmounted. For an understanding of today's manifestations of racism, it is essential to recall Germany's much repressed colonial history and colonial consciousness.

From the time of the so-called voyages of discovery in the fifteenth century, European powers had colonized Africa's territories. In the thirty years preceding World War I, when more territories were incorporated than in all the previous centuries, Germany was an active participant. Imperial Chancellor Otto von Bismarck was at first restrained in his colonial ambitions, because he had not anticipated any economic gain from colonization. His position changed when he recognized that colonial possessions could be used strategically as an instrument of economic policy to distract attention from Germany's internal social, political, and economic problems.

> The middle class should see in imperialism an objective by means of which the present danger to our economic existence might be overcome. The working class should see in the acquisition of colonies an objective to pursue for the whole nation, equally useful for all sectors of the population. In turning toward this objective they would be diverted

from asserting their legitimate interests here in the country itself. The interests of the individual states whose agricultural or industrial concerns could have torn them asunder—thus casting doubt upon the inherited state and social order forged in the preindustrial era—would be cemented by the objective of imperialism, attractive for both domestic and foreign policy purposes.[1]

In conservative circles, calls were soon heard for the establishment of colonies to which troublesome leftist workers and unionists could be deported. Friedrich Fabri, inspector of the Barmer Mission Society, commented on this idea, as did the colonial propagandist von Weber. In 1897 von Weber wrote to the prince of Hohenlohe-Langenburg:

> The socialist ferment in the heads of our unpropertied, uneducated masses, becomes all the more dangerous, the more it continues to be swelled by intelligent elements from the educated classes, who as a result of the generally bad economic situation will augment their ranks in ever greater numbers. In order to bring the German state back to health and allow emigration to function as a safety valve for all the bad gasses and vapors threatening the mechanism of our state with explosion, at least 200,000 or, better, 300,000 people ought to emigrate annually.[2]

Colonial seizure of power diverted attention from the urgent need for changes in domestic policy and economic restructuring. A similar function was performed by waves of immigration to America and Australia from the mid-eighteenth century onward—as exit restrictions were increasingly liberalized and developments in transportation lowered travel costs. These movements served to relieve Germany's economy of that portion of the population that could no longer be employed.[3] Simultaneously the slave trade came into full boom, for rich Europeans in the New World were seeking the cheapest labor for plantations and industry. Thus the ascent and enrichment of one-half of the world engendered the crippling and enslavement of the other half. "We can assume that Africa, at least as of the fifteenth century, probably lost around 100 million people."[4] According to history professor Heinrich Loth, German authorities directly promoted or indirectly aided and abetted the slave trade and slavery. "In Togo and Cameroon slavery was sanctioned, . . . stabilized by the colonial system; and a consequence of the exploitation of the institution of slavery was also the promotion of the slave trade."[5] Togo, Cameroon, German East Africa (present-day Tanzania), and German Southwest Africa (present-day Namibia) made up the colonial possessions, to which the German Empire had held internationally (European) acknowledged claim since the Congo Conference convened by Bismarck (November 15, 1884–February 26, 1885). The boundaries drawn during that conference, which were determined on the basis of the economic and military interests of European statesmen, remain valid to today.

"Cultural Mission" and "Heathen Mission": The Emigrants' Sense of Mission

The social Darwinist ideology of the right of the strong ("the survival of the fittest") to the assertion of power in nature and society gave a form of legitimacy to placing African peoples and territories under the "protection of the Mother Country" by means of shrewd diplomacy and militarily enforced contractual agreements.

The emigrants' zeal for conquest manifested itself in a corresponding German national sense of mission, which looked upon the task of educating the "natives" to become proper German subjects as an obligation. They saw their educational mission as one of raising the "lower race" to a "higher level of culture." This in spite of the fact that Vasco de Gama and his people had already concluded in 1497 that the inhabitants of the region in present-day Tanzania "were traveling the eastern seas and had better navigational knowledge than they themselves, and they encountered there city-states and governments that were just as flourishing and differentiated as anything similar in Europe."[6]

The conquerors' superiority in weapon technology resulted in defeated populations, forced labor, alienation, destruction of socially evolved structures, and the imposition of foreign structures of consciousness and education.

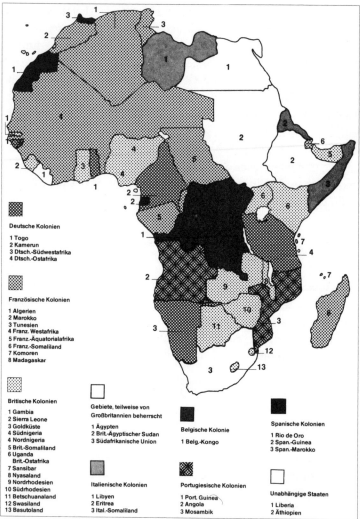

Deutsche Kolonien

1 Togo
2 Kamerun
3 Dtsch.-Südwestafrika
4 Dtsch.-Ostafrika

Französische Kolonien

1 Algerien
2 Marokko
3 Tunesien
4 Franz. Westafrika
5 Franz.-Äquatorialafrika
6 Franz.-Somaliland
7 Komoren
8 Madagaskar

Britische Kolonien

1 Gambia
2 Sierra Leone
3 Goldküste
4 Südnigeria
5 Brit.-Somaliland
6 Uganda
   Brit.-Ostafrika
7 Sansibar
8 Nyasaland
9 Nordrhodesien
10 Südrhodesien
11 Betschuanaland
12 Swasiland
13 Basutoland

Gebiete, teilweise von Großbritannien beherrscht

1 Ägypten
2 Brit.-Ägyptischer Sudan
3 Südafrikanische Union

Italienische Kolonien

1 Libyen
2 Eritrea
3 Ital.-Somaliland

Belgische Kolonie

1 Belg.-Kongo

Portugiesische Kolonien

1 Port. Guinea
2 Angola
3 Mosambik

Spanische Kolonien

1 Rio de Oro
2 Span.-Guinea
3 Span.-Marokko

Unabhängige Staaten

1 Liberia
2 Äthiopien

Colonial Africa, 1914

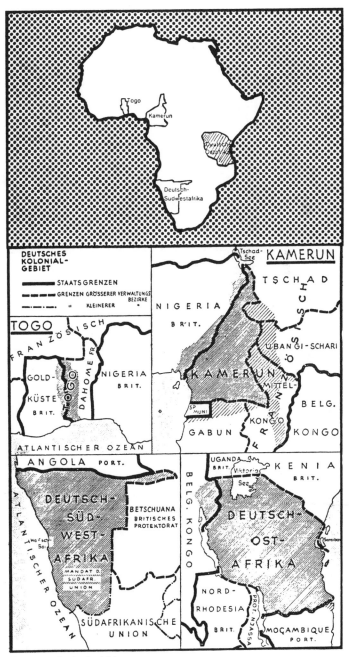

German colonies in Africa

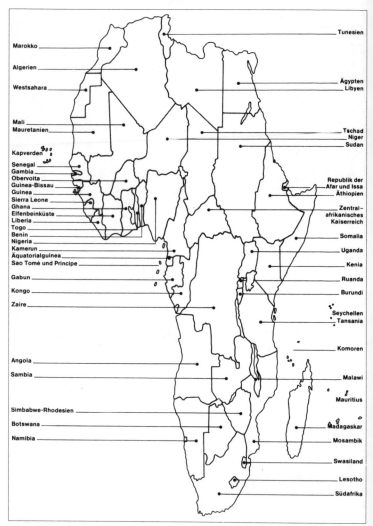

Marokko

Algerien

Westsahara

Mali
Mauretanien

Kapverden
Senegal
Gambia
Obervolta
Guinea-Bissau
Guinea
Sierra Leone
Ghana
Elfenbeinküste
Liberia
Togo
Benin
Nigeria
Kamerun
Äquatorialguinea
Sao Tomé und Principe

Gabun

Kongo

Zaire

Angola

Sambia

Simbabwe-Rhodesien

Botswana

Namibia

Tunesien

Ägypten
Libyen

Tschad
Niger
Sudan

Republik der
Afar und Issa
Äthiopien

Zentral-
afrikanisches
Kaiserreich

Somalia

Uganda

Kenia

Ruanda

Burundi

Seychellen
Tansania

Komoren

Malawi

Mauritius

Madagaskar

Mosambik

Swasiland

Lesotho

Südafrika

Countries of Africa

Walter Rodney writes that the colonial governments imposed head taxes on land, cattle, and people. These could be paid only in the currency of the colonial masters (reichsmarks in the German colonies), so that the inhabitants were forced to cultivate export products or to work on the plantations and in the mines of the whites.[7]

Separation of the races was customary in all German colonies.

The "Native Authority Ordinances" for Southwest Africa from 1907 were the germ of the apartheid legislation still in force today. Africans were settled in ghettos near the residential and work places of the whites, obligatory passes and registration removed their freedom of movement. Prohibition of land acquisition and cattle ownership robbed them of their independent traditional basis of existence. Thus they had to become wage slaves for the whites.[8]

A plethora of pseudoscientific literature and myths artificially magnified the differences between Europeans and the people of the black "race." The rumor of wild "barbarians" and man-eating cannibals was one of the traveling myths propagated in all the colonies, in no cases supported by proof from first-hand observation.[9] The wilder the myths of the gruesomeness of the Blacks, the more easily the crimes committed against them could be justified as educative measures. The German philosopher Hegel based his treatises on the nature of Africans on colonial literature of this type, propagating racist views:

The human body is of an animal nature, but it is essentially the body of a being capable of representation; in short, it has psychological associations. But this is not the case with the negroes, and the eating of human flesh is quite compatible with the African principle; to the sensuous negro, human flesh is purely an object of the senses, like all other flesh. It is not used primarily as food; but at festivals, for example, many hundreds of prisoners are tortured and beheaded, and their bodies are returned to those who took them prisoner so that they may distribute the parts. In some places, it is true, human flesh has even been seen on sale in the markets. At the death of a rich man, hundreds may well be slaughtered and devoured. Prisoners are murdered and slaughtered, and as a rule the victor consumes the heart of his slain enemy. And at magical ceremonies, it very often happens that the sorcerer murders the first person he encounters and divides his body among the crowd.[10]

For Hegel, Africa was "the land of childhood, which, lying beyond the day of self-conscious history, is enveloped in the dark mantle of night."[11] He considered its inhabitants unready for freedom. They were in need of awakening and education by Europeans. Hegel's racism is in direct opposition to the humanistic ideology he is thought to represent. Fanon writes fittingly: "Bourgeois ideology, however, which is the proclamation of an essential equality between men, manages to appear logical in its own eyes by inviting the sub-men to become human, and to take as their prototype Western humanity as incarnated in the Western bourgeoisie."[12] In my opinion racism goes beyond discrimination: it is the economic, cultural, political, and social imposition of one's own interests and interpretations.

The colonizers condemned the colonized to being what they turned out to be, and then criticized them for the way they turned out: the result of inhuman treatment can only be refusal, defense, and atrophy. The colonizers saw these forms of resistance as laziness, cunning, and meanness, and the lazier, more cunning, and meaner they called those who resisted them, the more natural it became for the colonizers to respond with regimentation, whip, and murder.[13]

> The negro is the born slave, who needs his despot as the opium smoker needs his pipe, and he lacks any noble characteristics. He is prone to lying and stealing, is disloyal, and deceitful; and if superficial observers believe they perceive a certain affability in him, it comes exclusively from the limited irritability of his nervous system and the consequent blunted reactive capacity of his will.
>
> . . . I have tried to make an impression on the Massai with forest fires, firecrackers, even with a coincidental eclipse of the sun on 12/23, but I found that the only thing that made an impression on those wild sons of the steppes were bullets of the repeater and double-barrel rifles and by persistently using them against their own bodies, at that.[14]

This is the commentary of Dr. Carl Peters, founding member of the Society for German Colonization (1884) and of the German East African Society (1885), which took over territories, for the most part in East Africa.

German Women in the Colonies

Political diplomacy, military occupation, and defense were carried out exclusively by men. However, German women also immigrated in large numbers to the colonies and stood by their men's side. Martha Mamozai estimates that women made up two-fifths of the total German immigrant population. Most of these women were nurses, domestic workers, and teachers. Many traveled to the colonies to work in the mission schools and stations there, to take jobs in already established households, or to get married. The Women's Association of the German Colonial Society was founded in 1907 as an organization of women for women that facilitated and supported the travel of single women to the colonies. "As to skills, they had to 'know how to cook, wash, iron, and make a simple skirt and blouse.' Best suited were 'country girls' who were already familiar with poultry, husbandry, dairy farming, and garden work."[15] The director of the colonial school for women in Witzenhausen, Baroness Zech, formulated the mission contract for German women as follows:

> Her energy should not take the form of a free, tomboyish nature, but through true femininity she should put the stamp of her nature on the new overseas Germany; she should not merely strive and work out there, but she should be imbued with the spirit of pure Christianity, the high priestess of German breeding and custom, the bearer of German culture, a blessing in the foreign land: German women, German honor, German devotion across the sea![16]

Women remained excluded from important colonial policy decisions. Even when they had to suffer under the chauvinism of their husbands, they frequently internalized it in such a way that blinded them to their own oppression. They participated in oppressing the Africans, and in those cases where German women made reports, they hardly deviated from the descriptions of the male colonialists. "Uncleanliness," "carefree nature," "born laziness" were some phrases frequently used to stereotype African women in order to justify the necessity of a "strong disciplinary hand."

Simone de Beauvoir writes on the combination of racism, sexism, and classism: "If they belong to the bourgeoisie, they feel solidarity with men of that class, not with proletarian women; if they are white, their allegiance is to white men, not to Negro women."[17]

Where German women did not reflect critically on their situation, and this was most often the case, they were not able to positively interpret cultural differences around them and put them to their own use. Having internalized the male projections, they sought fulfillment in the roles accorded them of hardworking, modest wife and mother, receiving in return the privilege of being honored as the "guardian of tradition." The outpost of home and fatherland placed the German woman above every Black woman and man, and this advantage seemed enough to reconcile her to her subordinated role in relation to her husband.[18]

On the one hand, Black women were denounced as "whores,"[19] thereby justifying their rape by white men. On the other hand, German women were far less opposed to the diminution of sexuality and reproduction. Black women opposed the appropriation of their bodies with birth strikes, which the cessation of birth premiums could hardly hinder,[20] whereas it was not uncommon for white women to give birth to seven or more children. "I am not aware," writes Clara Brockmann, in 1910 in Southwest Africa, "not even through hearsay, of any case where a Kanaka woman has had nearly so many offspring."[21]

The German woman is as indispensable today for the propagation of the "master race" as she was in the early twentieth century, and her standing in the white male world continues to be dependent to a great degree on offspring. Any solidarity with a Black woman, in this connection, would have been equivalent to a loss of prestige and power.

In ascribing negative traits, white women were considerably crueler and blinder toward Black women than toward Black men, possibly due to fear of rivalry and to self-hatred. Men were described as ugly far less often and received less contempt. Mamozai concludes, in the descriptions of Black women: "If colored people are all stupid, their women are in any case the stupidest and laziest."[22]

And When You Leave,
Take Your Pictures with You

Our white sisters
radical friends
love to own pictures of us
sitting at a factory machine
wielding a machete
in our bright bandanas
holding brown yellow black red children
reading books from literacy campaigns
holding machine guns bayonets bombs knives
Our white sisters
radical friends
should think
again.

Our white sisters
radical friends
love to own pictures of us
walking to the fields in hot sun
with straw hat on head if brown
bandana if black
in bright embroidered skirts
holding brown yellow black red children
reading books from literacy campaigns
smiling.
Our white sisters radical friends
should think again.   .
No one smiles
at the beginning of a day spent
digging for souvenir chunks of uranium
of cleaning up after
our white sisters
radical friends

And when our white sisters
radical friends see us
in the flesh
not as a picture they own,
they are not quite as sure

if
they like us as much.
We're not as happy as we look
on
their
wall.

JO CARRILLO[23]

Colonization of Consciousness through Mission and "Education"

If the culture-bearing power bears down upon the still largely un-cultured peoples solely by means of such measures as taxation and the concomitant coercion to work, the latter either will be overwhelmed by it or will seek to shake off the power that is working on them. So the mission must stretch out its helping and redeeming hand to them by sowing Christianity and effect in them an inner conversion alongside the external one.

MISSIONARY GRÖSCHEL[24]

Julius Nyerere, president of Tanzania, states, in regard to the function of and content of the colonial education system that it "did not transfer the knowledge and values of Tanzanian society from one generation to the next, but was the conscious attempt to change these values and to replace the traditional knowledge with the knowledge of a different type of society." In all colonies the transfer of skills was supposed to implant

the values of the colonial society and to train [Africans] for service in the colonial apparatus. In these countries the official interest in educa-tion was based on the need for local office personnel and minor civil servants; beyond that, various religious groups were interested in im-parting knowledge of reading and writing and further education to the population as a part of their mission work.[25]

The physical and economic exploitation had many faces: forced labor, the plunder of raw materials, and so on. The psychological enslavement and the emotional/spiritual subjugation of native Africans to the needs of the colonial power were taken over by colonial institutions and mission schools. Often missionaries protested against forced labor, land alienation, and mistreatment of people. In particular the wars of annihilation, such as that against the Herero—whose resistance ended in their near total extermination[26]—led many missionaries to give up their "neutral" position and take up the cause of the oppressed. For the most part, however, the missionaries and the colonial administrations maintained a tacit relationship of mutual support. F. Fabri, inspector of the Rhine Mission Society, the largest in its day, was among those who openly encouraged cooperation between colonial administration and mission, and whose idea of African people was clearly stamped by the racial ideologies of his time.[27]

> Thus the question arises whether the backward state of certain races and peoples, apparently based on a divine decision, doesn't also determine a different place for them in the holy healing place, and whether also in the New Covenant—the universality of Grace in the presence of Christ notwithstanding—in the present time of the world, a number of peoples and nations are and shall be set back until a new era in God's kingdom. . . . For even if it is in truth a sin to God and men to claim, with the supporters of slavery and the Boers in South Africa, a difference in nature among the various human races, it corresponds neither to actual reality nor to the word of God to deny or minimize the effectively existent and far-reaching difference among the various human races. When a negro stands before us, black as ebony, with kinky, wooly hair, compressed skull and receding forehead, in contrast to the massively developed back of the head and the lower portions of the face, the lips expansively protruding, the nose pressed flat—when I behold him, now enlivened by the deepest sensual spark, then again in dull, lethargic indifference, impervious to the rod of the tormentor; to immerse oneself mentally in this sight—and tribes like the African Bushmen and the Australian Papuas present an even sadder and more moving picture—is to be struck with the irrefutable impression: those are not merely the traits of the materialist primeval man disfigured by sin; here lies a fundamentally singular secret, reaching beyond all notations of history.
>
> FRIEDRICH FABRI, 1859[28]

Even where less extreme racist opinions were represented and the basic equality of humans was not cast in doubt, there was, nevertheless, agreement that the "heathen" were to be reeducated.

> We are all of one mind, the missions, too, that the negro soul is not as we want it and can use it. For it is only out of this conviction that we derive the justification for influencing the negro soul and for dislodging it from its previous path of development.
>
> DR. KÜLZ, GOVERNMENT PHYSICIAN, 1910[29]

Protestant and Catholic mission stations were established as early as the beginning of the nineteenth century in Africa. "These early mission settlements likewise formed the basis for the establishment of the school system on the continent."[30] In their educational content they contributed directly and indirectly to the training of children as well as adults in those "virtues" desirable for work in the administration, on the plantations, in the colonial masters' households: punctuality, obedience, willingness to work.

In his mission book, Johann Emonts provides a description for children and adolescents in Germany:

> The poor heathen children grow up practically like the wild animals of the field. They have the benefit of no, or, better stated, a wild, education. Those little wild children become big wild people, that is: mean, evil people, ruined in their manners, and as there is little about them that is good and pleasing they are therefore all the more unpleasant and wild to behold. . . .
>
> . . . First of all the wild heathenness must be taken out of them. It lies deep in their little black nappy heads. They must renounce the heathen manners and customs that they have practiced from their youth. They may no longer watch the heathen dances. They are to stay away from the heathen sacrifices and ceremonies from now on. They may no longer continue to trust in the many magic devices, fetishes, amulets. Their belief in spirits must disappear. Modesty and decency, order and punctuality, love of their neighbor and a sense of justice must be taught to them. It is clear that this is not possible in a few days or weeks. It takes years.[31]

In addition to general "good deportment," education was to transmit also the division of work along gender lines, as it determined the relationship between men and women in German (or European) society. African women were trained in and restricted to typical domestic activities, which formerly fell also in the male sphere of responsibility. Men were favored in admission to schools.[32]

The introduction of wage labor particularly encouraged the polarization of the sexes: as a rule women did not receive paid work (they usually took over the unpaid duties of housewife), so that often prostitution became their only source of money; in cases where they received pay for work on the plantations, their remuneration was less than that of men.[33]

The limitations of educational opportunities concurrent with the favoring of some individuals led to hierarchical structures that undermined the solidarity of the community. Those who could secure a position in the colonial administration system tended to identify with the oppressors, just as some village elders were corrupted through financial cooptation.[34]

> This internalization of one's own oppression beside simultaneous (and usually only apparent) participation in power leads to grotesque relationships. Oppressed women defended the men's world, subjugated peoples, their conquerors. "Us German boys got to stick together!" said a black man in Brazil in World War I, and another, when there was talk of the "new" fascist Germany: "We be some black Negroes, but we got Hitler blood!"[35]

From a Ghanaian by the name of "Bismarck" I learned that this is a quite commonly heard name in his country. Underlying this might be the attitude that Winnie Mandela speaks of regarding her name:

> My father always had the greatest admiration for the German people and their industrial achievements. That's why he insisted on that terrible name "Winifred," which subsequently became "Winnie." He also believed in the Christian names, because of the missionaries. Whenever he disciplined us he would refer to the hardworking and industrious Germans. He wanted us to become as strong as they are. As if I had my fighting spirit from them! But since I became internationally known under that name, I'll have to continue with it. After all, it is a constant reminder of our oppression![36]

The Colonial Heritage

The economic, political, social, and psychic colonization continues today. When in the 1960s most African countries were demanding independent status according to international law, a complete relinquishing by the former colonial powers was hardly possible.

> Through diverse measures, taken both before and after independence, the new states of black Africa remained tied de facto to Europe (primarily to the respective colonial powers) economically, politically, and culturally. Shortly after the founding of the OAU,[37] eighteen of the African states were joined to the EEC by the signing of the first convention of association, in Yoaunde, Cameroon (20 July 1963). The new states took over the social and economic apparatuses—administrative centers, ports, railroads, schools, hospitals, etc.—which were patterned on the needs of the colonial powers and concentrated principally in urban centers.[38]

The reliance on apparatuses already in place facilitated political and economic stability, but also hindered forms of development oriented toward the specific needs of the country. Dragolyub Najman stresses the fact that even today numerous African educational systems are still based on those of their former rulers and should be regarded as unsuitable to the needs of the African countries.[39] In nearly all countries—Tanzania being an exception[40]—the school operates separately from traditional, informal educational institutions of family and ethnic group. It seldom creates a connection between the various cultural orientations and coexisting forms of production, and augments—through one-sided qualification for duties in the administrative sector—the flight from the countryside and unemployment.[41]

Educational content colonizes consciousness in very subtle ways.

> The black schoolboy in the Antilles, who in his lessons is forever talking about "our ancestors, the Gauls," identifies himself with the explorer, the bringer of civilization, the white man who carries truth to savages—an all-white truth. There is identification—that is, the young Negro subjectively adopts a white man's attitude.[42]

A soap advertisement, "for delicate, white skin"

In a variety of ways the idea is transmitted that white skin color is the better skin color and that European (i.e., white) consciousness is progressive thinking. Creams to retard pigment formation are offered everywhere on the African, American, and European market. Fanon wrote as early as 1952:

> For several years certain laboratories have been trying to produce a serum for "denegrification"; with all the earnestness in the world, laboratories have sterilized their test tubes, checked their scales, and embarked on researches that might make it possible for the miserable Negro to whiten himself and thus to throw off the burden of that corporeal malediction.[43]

The cosmetic preparations that work on the pigment material melanin enjoy great popularity even today and are used especially by women. Thus Awa Thiam urges that

> measures be taken against newspapers which publish advertisements for these bleaching agents. They should be boycotted or banned by Black countries. These products should be withdrawn from Black markets. There should be a campaign to spread information about

them among Black women as well as men. Let Black women and Black men wear their black colour with dignity and pride.[44]

Black women were and are the most exposed to oppression and must correspondingly undertake the greatest efforts to attack it. In precolonial society patriarchal structures hindered their full equality.[45] In colonial society the woman was just as exploited as the man. But the man was, however, elevated above the woman by the fortified structures of patriarchy and hierarchy. And, in concert with Angela Davis, we must note: "If the most violent punishments of men consisted in floggings and mutilations, women were flogged and mutilated, as well as raped."[46] They were situated in an additional, direct power relationship to their oppressor.

Racism and sexism, in their multifaceted interaction, produce a situation whose complexity is not often recognized. Thus Awa Thiam rightfully assails Kate Millet as one of those feminists who place oppression of women and oppression of Blacks on the same level. "If rape is to women what lynching is to Blacks, then what do we make of the rape of Black women by Black men?"[47] This is a question not often asked because it implies a very limited and false perception, one which Adrienne Rich describes as "tunnel vision."[48]

Notes

1. Entwicklungspolitische Korrespondenz, ed., *Deutscher Kolonialismus, Materialien zur Hundertjahrfeier 1984* (Hamburg, 1983), pp. 55–56. Hereafter EpK.

2. Detlef Bald, Peter Heller, Volkhard Hundsdörfer, Joachim Paschen, *Die Liebe zum Imperium, Deutschlands dunkle Vergangenheit in Afrika* (Bremen, 1978), p. 19.

3. "Thus the roughly 9.5 million people from third world countries living in the industrialized nations in the middle of the 1970s make up less than .5 percent of the inhabitants of all developing countries. From this it is clear that, unlike a century ago in Europe, emigration can hardly contribute in a significant way to the solution of the demographic problems of these countries." From Jürgen Bähr, *Bevölkerungsgeographie, Verteilung und Dynamik der Bevölkerung in globaler, nationaler und regionaler Sicht* (Stuttgart, 1983), p. 318.

4. Joseph Ki-Zerbo, *Histoire de l'Afrique noire d'hier à demain* (Paris, 1978), p. 218. The figures vary between forty and two hundred million people, according to what peripheral factors are considered. See Gert Paczensky, *Die Weißen kommen* (Hamburg, 1970), p. 179. Many died during the long trek to the coast and under the torturous treatment on the sea passage: "Given that the sea passage lasted two months, we can surmise the mortality rate caused by epidemics. It was horrific. As a way of addressing this problem the Blacks were forced up on deck during the day, despite the dangers, so that they could get fresh air and even work a little. Dances were even arranged, with the threat of the whip where necessary. That was to help raise the morale of the most depressed among them. Nevertheless there were frequent revolts. Crew members were lynched. All the revolts ended in blood-

38

baths, often even necessitating the use of firearms. The leaders were executed in the presence of all, or were drowned or whipped to death. Sometimes their buttocks would be slit with a knife and a mixture of hot pepper and vinegar poured into the wounds. The leader of a hunger strike would be killed and force fed to the other slaves."

5. Heinrich Loth, "Sklavenhandel unter deutscher Flagge?" In *Der Beitrag der Völker Afrikas zur Weltkultur,* ed. Burkhard Brentjes (Halle [Saale], 1977), p. 55.

6. Bald et al., *Die Liebe zum Imperium,* p. 39.

7. Walter Rodney, *How Europe Underdeveloped Africa* (Washington, D.C., 1974), p. 182.

8. Martha Mamozai, *Herrenmenschen: Frauen im deutschen Kolonialismus* (Hamburg, 1982), p. 45.

9. See, for example, William Arens, *The Man-Eating Myth: Anthropology and Anthropophagy* (New York, 1979).

10. Georg W. F. Hegel, *Introduction: Reason in History* in *Lectures on the Philosophy of World History* (Cambridge, 1975), p. 183.

11. Hegel, *Philosophy of History,* trans. T. M. Knox, Great Books of the Western World 46 (Chicago, 1952), p. 196.

12. Frantz Fanon, *The Wretched of the Earth,* trans. Constance Farrington (New York, 1965), p. 163.

13. Jean-Paul Sartre writes concerning the colonizer: "Thus, oppression is justified through itself: The oppressors create and maintain by force the evil that turns the oppressed more and more into that which he must be to deserve his fate. The colonizer can accord himself absolution only by systematically propagating the 'dehumanization' of the colonized, that is, by identifying a little more each day with the colonial apparatus. Terror and exploitation dehumanize, and the exploiter empowers himself to this dehumanization in order to exploit further" (Jean P. Sartre, *Kolonialismus und Neokolonialismus* [Reinbek, 1968], p. 26).

14. Carl Peters, *Gesammelte Schriften,* ed. W. von Frank, cited in Bald et al., *Die Liebe zum Imperium,* pp. 85, 37.

15. Mamozai, *Herrenmenschen,* p. 16.

16. Clara Brockmann, *Briefe eines deutschen Mädchens aus Südwest,* cited in ibid., p. 145.

17. Simone de Beauvoir, *The Second Sex,* trans. and ed. H. M. Parshley (New York, 1974), p. xxii.

18. There were always committed feminists who considered the abolition of slavery and all forms of exploitation as a part of their struggle

against female oppression. In America it was the committed middle-class women of the white women's movement who were in the front lines of the anti-slavery movement. They saw in the oppression of the slaves a part of their own oppression by male domination, which, however, led to an unjustified equating of "house slavery" and slave labor. See Angela Y. Davis, *Women, Race & Class* (New York, 1983), p. 34.

19. Mamozai, *Herrenmenschen*, p. 167.

20. "The native, particularly the Herero, takes the position, after the revolt, that he wants to produce no children. He feels himself a prisoner, expressing this in every job that does not suit him; and he wants to provide no new laborers for his oppressor, who has deprived him of his cherished laziness. Anyone who has had the opportunity to see, especially among the Hereros before the revolt, the characteristically prolific broods, and then looks around today on most farms, the difference would be immediately remarkable. . . . In this regard German farmers have been attempting for years to address this situation by offering a premium, perhaps a nanny goat, for every native child born on the farm, but generally in vain" (*Brief eines Farmers 1912*, cited in ibid., p. 52).

21. Clara Brockmann, *Die dt. Frau in Südwestafrika,* quoted in ibid., p. 156.

22. Ibid., p. 166.

23. Jo Carrillo, "And When You Leave, . . ." in *This Bridge Called My Back: Writings by Radical Women of Color,* ed. Cherríe Moraga and Gloria Anzaldúa (1981; New York: Kitchen Table: Women of Color Press, 1983), pp. 63–64.

24. From *Buch der deutschen Kolonien* (Leipzig, 1934), cited in Bald et al., *Die Liebe zum Imperium,* p. 115.

25. Julius Nyerere, "Erziehung zum Vertrauen auf die eigene Kraft," special supplement in *Afrika Heute,* no. 22 (1967): 4.

26. "At the beginning of the revolt there were about 100,000 Hereros. At the end, according to the last official statistics of the year 1913, the figure was 21,699. These were expropriated" (Paczensky, *Die Weißen kommen,* p. 60).

27. K. Hammer, *Weltmission und Kolonialismus* (München, 1978), pp. 244 f., 251.

28. Friedrich Fabri, "Die Entstehung des Heidenthums," quoted in EpK, p. 148.

29. From *Verhandlungen des deutschen Nationalkongresses,* cited in Bald et al., *Die Liebe zum Imperium,* p. 115.

30. Bikai D. Galega, *Bildung und Imperialismus in Schwarz-Afrika: Historische und sozio-politische Hintergründe* (Münster, 1984), p. 87.

31. Johann Emonts, *Der armen Heidenkinder Freud und Leid. Ein Missionsbuch für unsere liebe deutsche Jugend* (Aachen, 1923), pp. 28, 77.

32. See Mamozai, *Herrenmenschen,* pp. 95, 113.

33. Until the arrival of the Europeans, prostitution was unknown in Africa. See ibid., p. 113.

34. "In another connection, in judging colonialization, I have added that Europe has gotten on very well indeed with all the local feudal lords who agreed to serve, woven a villainous complicity with them, rendered their tyranny more effective and more efficient, and that it has actually tended to prolong artificially the survival of local pasts in their most pernicious aspects" (Aimé Césaire, *Discourse on Colonialism,* trans. Joan Pinkham [New York, 1972]).

35. Mamozai, *Herrenmenschen,* p. 20. Her citations are from Maria Kahle, *Deutsche Heimat in Brasilien* (Berlin, 1937).

36. Winnie Mandela, *A Part of My Soul Went with Him* (New York, 1985), pp. 49–50.

37. The OAU was founded in 1963 as a political umbrella association of the independent states.

38. Galega, *Bildung und Imperialismus,* p. 244.

39. Dragolyub Najman, *Bildung in Afrika—Vorschläge zur Überwindung der Krise* (Wuppertal, 1976).

40. In Tanzania education reform was approached in conjunction with changes in the overall social-political conception. See Nyerere, "Erziehung zum Vertrauen," and Galega, *Bildung und Imperialismus,* p. 248.

41. D. Najman, *Bildung in Afrika,* p. 80.

42. Frantz Fanon, *Black Skin, White Masks,* trans. Charles Lam Markmann (New York, 1967), p. 140.

43. Ibid., p. 111. (See original text: *Peau noire, masques blancs* (Paris, 1952).

44. Awa Thiam, *Speak Out, Black Sisters: Feminism and Oppression in Black Africa,* trans. Dorothy S. Blair (London, 1986), pp. 107–8.

45. Ibid.

46. Davis, *Women, Race & Class,* p. 7.

47. Thiam, *Speak Out,* p. 114.

48. Adrienne Rich, *On Lies, Secrets and Silence: Selected Prose 1966–78* (New York, 1979), p. 299.

African and Afro-German Women in the Weimar Republic and under National Socialism

Defeat and Occupation of the Rhineland:
The "Black Scourge"

German colonial rule came to an end in the very first years of World War I. With the exception of German East Africa the German colonies were occupied by French and English troops. For its role in the war, Germany lost all its overseas territories and was required by the cease-fire agreement to consent to the occupation of the left bank of the Rhine as well as the cities of Cologne, Coblenz, Kehl, and Mainz on the right bank. The Treaty of Versailles mandated the occupation by the victorious powers for a period of fifteen years and the gradual withdrawal of troops within this period, as long as Germany abided by the other treaty conditions (keeping up reparations payments, etc.).[1]

Black colonial soldiers were also among the ranks of the occupation forces. Hence, when the Rhineland was occupied by French, Belgian, British, and American troops, Black soldiers were among them. The largest portion was in the French army, with between thirty and forty thousand Africans, some from Madagascar and Morocco, but for the most part from Algeria and Tunesia.[2] During the war, Germany declined—more from necessity than of its own free will, for England had blocked Germany's access to the seaway—to call Blacks into action. Hence it was easy for Germany to denounce the introduction of Blacks as an "act of inhumanity that was dangerous to the German people." In 1920 Field Marshall Hindenberg wrote in his book *Aus meinem Leben*:

Where there were no tanks, the enemy set black waves upon us. We were helpless when they broke into our lines and murdered or, worse, tortured the defenseless. Human indignation and indictment is directed not at the Blacks who carried out such atrocities, but at those who brought such hordes to German soil allegedly to fight in the war for honor, freedom, and justice. Those Blacks were slaughtered by the thousands.[3]

Hindenburg's comments demonstrate the hypocritical nature of this indictment: he condemns the French for appropriating the Africans for their purposes, but at the same time shows his own bigotry in his remarks about the brutality and bestiality of Africans. The indignation he directs particularly against the French bespeaks more resentment and frustration about the war than any genuine sympathy for the Black people sent to fight the war by the victorious powers. In the final analysis, the German "protection forces" had carried out their conquest in Africa with Black soldiers from other colonies.[4]

Pommerin writes that Hindenburg mentions a few lines later in his book that the Germans were superior to the Blacks in one-on-one combat. From this statement he infers, somewhat paradoxically, "There can be no talk of incipient racism in Germany at that point."[5] To my way of thinking, however, a clearly emerging racism is evident in Hindenburg's vocabulary, which—looking at the colonial period—parallels the language of the German colonialists. When Pommerin says "incipient," he is, in my opinion, underestimating the continuity between racist tendencies before and during the war.

Nationalism and colonial zeal persisted after Germany's defeat. Supporters and members of the German Colonial Society were among those calling for the revision of the Treaty of Versailles, eager to see Germany alongside the other colonial powers.

Generous funds were put up for colonial propaganda as well as for the popularization of pseudoscientific theories that ascribed a cultural, social, national, or national-social meaning to the colonial policy.

Slogans like those about a "people without room," of colonies as a "national necessity," as a symbol of the "national honor," of "Germany's international prestige," of the "right to colonies," of Germans' "civilizing calling and mission" as part of the white race, to participate in the "education of underdeveloped races" were taught in schools, defended in universities in "scholarly" tracts, preached by speakers at gatherings, and disseminated in newspapers, magazines, brochures, and books of all genres.[6]

We Need Colonies!

Whether Center Party man, whether Democrat,
whether bowling club, whether union—
the voices are quavering.
It screams from flier and placard:
We want a colonial mandate.
We must cultivate!

Then the Wild Bills and the Romeos
would have a corner of land
to work off their raring energies.
So, hold fast to the word.
It's about the fight for German Southwest.[7]
We must cultivate!

The black man wants to come back to us,
to the whip, drill, and lover's luck
and Prussian manners.
Let's tear the dark continent piece by piece
from the foreign menace.
We must cultivate!

KARL SCHNAG[8]

In the consciousness of the colonial avengers Blacks remained subhuman creatures to be civilized and disciplined. It is no wonder, then, that the occupation by Black soldiers was felt by much of the German population to be especially humiliating. People of "lower race" and "lower origin" had achieved the right to enter as an occupying force.

"Black Rapists" and "Rhineland Bastards"

Shortly after the arrival of the occupation troops, all political parties, with the exception of the Socialist party, submitted a parliamentary petition calling for the withdrawal of Black Troops.

> Despite the peace accord, the French and Belgians are still using colored troops in the occupied Rhineland territories. Germans feel this improper use of the coloreds to be a disgrace and observe with growing indignation that they are exercising rights of sovereignty in German cultural territories. For German women and children—boys and men—these wild people are a dreadful danger. Their honor, life and limb, purity and innocence are being destroyed. More and more cases are coming to light in which colored troops have defiled German women and children, injuring, even killing, resisters. Only the smallest portion of the perpetrated atrocities are reported. Shame, fear of cruel vengeance close the mouths of the unfortunate victims and their families. At the behest of the French and Belgian authorities public houses are established in the territories occupied by them, in front of which

Advertisement for Hildebrand's German Chocolates, portraying Hermann von Wissman, governor of German East Africa (1895–96)

colored troops crowd in droves, and there German women are exposed to them. All over the world, increasingly outraged voices are being raised, condemning this indelible disgrace. Is the Imperial government cognizant of these occurrences, unworthy of human beings? What does it plan to do?[9]

As "victors," German soldiers in the colonies assumed the right to rape the women of foreign peoples. As a defeated nation, it was now German women who were subjected to rape by the "victors." The parliamentary petition did not attack this unwritten male right to enslave women, but merely propagated the myth of the "disgrace to the race." That was the context of the talk of "improper use" and "wild people." Where were complaints against white soldiers and white German soldiers to be heard? Luise Zietz, representative from the Socialist party, was one of the few who protested against the double standard of morals:

> I want to further point out that the petitioners, who are now justifiably turning against the beastly acts of brutality in the occupied territory, found no word of protest when in Germany our own mercenaries perpetrated such beastly acts of brutality against German women. . . . I refer only to my fervent plea in Weimar to get the women representatives to unite in a protest against the many brutalities and violations of decency by the German soldiers against German women . . . I linked it to a special case, where in Hamburg Noske's troops treated a woman in the most unheard of manner, arresting the woman, beating her terribly, hoisting her skirts over her head and whipping her naked body, knocking her teeth out of her mouth, and abusing her in the most egregious manner. And what did the women representatives whom I asked to join me in a protest tell me? Oh no, we don't want to publicize that . . . we'd better leave it alone.[10]

As for the German soldiers abroad, their behavior during the so-called campaign of the Huns in China is described as follows:

> At that time reports were substantiated that in China, Germans set up bordellos, to which Chinese women were brought and abused by German soldiers. Fearful of being taken to these bordellos or of being raped by the soldiers, the Chinese women jumped into the well, preferring to drown in the water than to be subjected to the brutalities of the German soldiers.[11]

"Jumbo": a poster intended to depict the stationing of Black French soldiers in Germany after 1918

A medal of the Bavarian mint (1920), from a plate by the Nazi graphic artist Karl Gotz. On one side, a long-haired blonde woman is shackled to an oversized, helmeted penis, which is meant to represent a Black French soldier. The caption reads "Black Infamy." On the reverse, there is a Black soldier whose foreignness is expressed with overemphasized facial features and an earring. The words "Liberté, Egalité, Fraternité" are meant to be ironic and are representative of the open enmity directed at Black and white Frenchmen.

The greatly exaggerated stories of the particular brutality of the Blacks and of their uncontrolled physical urges nevertheless had the effect of denigrating and eliminating these male competitors for white women. White women became more inclined to place themselves under the "protection" of white men. One representative of the Bavarian Popular party pointed as laudable examples to America, "where a Negro is lynched if he assaults a white woman, and to England, which before the war required that no white woman work in the presence of coloreds in India or Ceylon, so as not to degrade the woman."[12] Incidents of rape that white German men/ husbands perpetrated on women seemed irrelevant in view of the indisputably more frightful sexual offenses by Blacks.

For a long time, the birth of Black children in the occupied territories was not discussed either in public or in parliament. This was in part because their numbers were inconsequential, but also because it was difficult to reconcile the statements of the mothers with the image of the "black rapist," "for as we know from a later official investigation, only one mother attributed the conception of her child to rape."[13]

That a German woman might voluntarily associate with a French man—and a Black one at that—simply had to be overlooked by the Germans. To the degree that Afro-Germans did come under public scrutiny, the assumption of their particular form of inferiority was undebated, since they counted as "not even pureblooded." For example, a newspaper report in *Germania* in September 1920 carried the statement that it was a well-known fact that "half-breed" children would inherit the defects of both parents.[14] This claim can be traced back to the race theory of Gobineau, who, in his pessimistic conception of history, was known to have interpreted any social and cultural change as an instance of decline.

A Swedish pastor named Liljeblad was the first to become interested in statistics and other official documents on Afro-German children. He traveled to Germany especially to do research. The motive for his investigations becomes evident in his claim that he had met children in Germany with the most varied appearance, including one with black and white stripes on his back. In his essay "The World's Shame on the Rhine," which he published after his visit to Germany, he made bold estimates, based on a birthrate of 1,500 children per year, that by the end of fifteen years of occupation, the total number of Afro-Germans would approach 27,000. The actual number of Black children according to official statistics at the time of his publication (1924) was only 78.[15]

Even if, in order to "conceal any forms of 'fraternizing' between the population of the Rhineland and the occupation soldiers,"[16] Liljeblad's figures had not been published, the birth of Afro-Germans attracted increasing attention. The ostracism of and attacks on Afro-German children and their mothers began not with National Socialism, but as early as the Weimar Republic. In addition to the controversial names "half-breed" and "mulatto"[17] Afro-German children often were called "bastards" unreservedly.

The Society for Racial Hygiene (founded in 1905) began conducting sterilizations for "eugenic reasons" in 1919 for the protection and elimination of "racial diseases." In 1927, the commissioner of the Palatinate informed the Imperial Bureau of Health that considerable cause for concern would arise as these Black children matured. He inquired whether it was not possible to render those children infertile through a painless operation when they reached puberty.[18] At that time there was no legal basis for such medical intervention, and restrictions governing sterilization stated that illegitimate children, who generally had the citizenship of their mothers, required a parent's consent for any such intervention, and only in very rare cases, under duress, was it given. However, it is difficult to prove at this late date how many children were secretly sterilized or allowed to disappear, or who grew up in welfare institutions rather than under the protection of family or other caretakers. In the mid-1920s, the Imperial Ministry had already considered handing over "the half-breeds" to mission societies, with enough financial support to send them abroad.[19] Quite apart from that, it was easily possible to sterilize children under the guise of preventing a "racial disease," as long as no one had them in protective custody.

Protection of the Family and Forced Sterilization: Disgrace to the Race and Colonial Propaganda

In 1928 Hitler wrote in *Mein Kampf*:

> It was and is the Jews who bring the Negro to the Rhine, always with the same concealed thought and the clear goal of destroying, by the bastardization which would necessarily set in, the white race which they hate, to throw it down from its cultural and political height and in turn to rise personally to the position of master.[20]

With the rise of National Socialism, race anthropologists demanded more and more openly that mothers of Afro-Germans not only be granted the right to terminate pregnancy, but that they should be forced to do so.[21] The calls for strict measures for handling those already born also grew stronger. Dr. Hans Macco, in his tract "Race Problems in the Third Reich" claimed: "These mulatto children were either conceived through force or else the white mother was a prostitute. In both cases there is not the slightest moral obligation to these offspring of alien-race."[22]

In contrast to Gobineau, who in his resigned interpretation of the future thought that the demise of Aryans was unavoidable, his National Socialist followers were convinced that the "inferior genetic inheritance" could be weeded out and the master race consciously bred by means of rigorous state intervention in matters of birth control, marriage laws, and sterilization.

Immediately following Hitler's seizure of power in 1933, laws were enacted penalizing sterilization and abortion on demand. At the same time, laws were introduced mandating sterilization for reasons of racial hygiene (eugenics).[23] The calls for an increase in births by white, German, Aryan women and the laws for mandatory sterilization did not represent a contradiction in National Socialist ideology. These laws were different aspects of a single policy intended to bring female reproduction under greater control, thereby ensuring the existence of the racist system.

> The number of degenerate individuals born is dependent primarily on the number of degenerate women capable of bearing children. In terms of racial hygiene, sterilization of the degenerate woman is therefore more important than that of the man.[24]

The emphasis on the virtues of motherhood for German Aryan women was an indirect, coercive means of balancing out the "loss through degenerate offspring" with desirable offspring. It is obvious that only those Aryan women who brought Aryan offspring into the world were glorified. Those who bore Afro-Germans, Sinti-Germans,[25] or half-Jewish children were excluded from the cult of motherhood and were denounced as "whores" in public and often by their closest relatives.

In consideration of foreign-policy interests, caution was exercised not to allow the abuse of Africans and Afro-Germans to go beyond certain bounds. A note of warning from the Foreign Office stated:

> Let us not forget, now that the accusations against Germany over the Jewish question are beginning to abate somewhat, that we must not allow the colored question to provide new substance to the enemy propaganda in the struggle against the new Germany.[26]

In order not to antagonize foreign diplomats traveling to Germany and thereby jeopardize trade relations, a campaign was even begun

Cover for an issue of *Illustrated Film Courier,* featuring Hans Albers in *Carl Peters.* Africans—male and female—and Afro-Germans were hired for title roles and bit parts in propaganda films made to glorify German colonialism. Carl Peters was notorious for his excesses as a colonial officer and was finally disciplined, sentenced, and removed from his position as Reichs-Kommissar. His legend gave rise to a devoted following, however, and he was regarded as a harbinger of the Thousand-Year Reich—one of the "great educators of the German nation." The Department for the Propagation of German Literature announced in a statement of January 10, 1938, that Peters, who had died in 1918, had approached the ideology of the Third Reich fifty years before its establishment. In juvenile literature and even in a movie, this colonial conqueror was presented as a role model for the German youth movement.

against xenophobia.[27] In addition, the small minority of Africans from the colonies who came to Germany with merchant fleets were not to be unduly provoked. For the most part they came from influential families and their participation in the production of colonial propaganda would assure political advantages if a situation should develop wherein overseas territories should come to be distributed by mandate.

As a means of ensuring the facade of tolerance displayed to the outside world, individual Afro-Germans were deliberately granted privileges, whereas the majority were unable to realize their educational and occupational ambitions. The flexible operation of the "Aryan legislation" was to facilitate "in certain situations, when it would seem to serve purposes of foreign policy, the treatment, for example, of an African Negro as equal. Such a waiving of the race law in hiring the offspring of a 'racially alien parent' into the German civil service will yield advantages for colonial policy."[28]

After 1937, it no longer seemed necessary to refrain from sterilizing Afro-Germans because of foreign relations concerns or for fear of protests from the church. In 1933, a study of twenty-seven children in Wiesbaden, carried out by Dr. W. Abel, then a research assistant at the Kaiser Wilhelm Institute for Anthropology, Human Genetics, and Eugenics and later a professor at the University of Berlin, purported to prove scientifically the inferiority of Afro-Germans. In his investigations of Afro-Germans and Asian-Germans, whom he referred to in his study as Moroccan and Annamese bastards, he concluded that these children suffered from early psychoses with above-average frequency and attained their class average in school performance in only 86.9 percent of the cases. Abel linked his investigation results not to the hostile attitudes that marked the children's environment but to genetic factors, thus attributing the responsibility for the racial mixture and poor heredity to the mothers.[29]

Abel himself[30] was the anthropological evaluator for establishing race membership in "Special Commission 3," which was inaugurated in 1937 with the charge of "carrying out the discreet sterilization of the Rhineland bastards."[31]

By 1937 four hundred mandatory sterilizations of Afro-

Germans had been recorded, for which there was never a legal basis. The partially available declarations of parental consent must be regarded with particular skepticism. This, all the more when we note the comment of legation counselor Rademacher:

> Internal administrative measures make it possible to prevent the half-castes from reproducing. The mother can be won back for the German community through mandatory education in a concentration camp.[32]

Notes

1. See Rainer Pommerin, *Sterilisierung der Rheinlandbastrade: Das Schicksal einer farbigen Minderheit, 1918–1937* (Düsseldorf, 1979), p. 7.
2. Ibid., p. 12.
3. Paul von Hindenburg, *Aus meinem Leben,* cited in ibid., p. 10.
4. Martha Mamozai, *Herrenmenschen: Frauen im deutschen Kolonialismus* (Hamburg, 1982), p. 39.
5. Pommerin, *Sterilisierung,* p. 11.
6. Detlef Bald, Peter Heller, Volkhard Hundsdörfer, Joachim Paschen, *Die Liebe zum Imperium: Deutschlands dunkle Vergangenheit in Afrika* (Bremen, 1978), pp. 175–76.
7. The German colony Southwest Africa (Namibia).
8. In *Die Weltbühne* 22, no. 16 (1926), cited in Entwicklungspolitische Korrespondenz, ed., *Deutscher Kolonialismus, Materialien zur Hundertjahrfeier 1984* (Hamburg, 1983), p. 16. Hereafter EpK.
9. Verhandlungen der verfassungsgebenden Deutschen Nationalversammlung, vol. 343. *Anlagen zu den Stenographischen Berichten,* nos. 2676–3076 (Berlin, 1920), cited in Pommerin, *Sterilisierung,* p. 16.
10. Luise Zietz, *Stenographische Berichte der Nationalversammlung vom 20, Mai 1920,* cited in Mamozai, *Herrenmenschen,* p. 291.
11. Ibid., p. 292.
12. Representative Ammann in *Verhandlungen des bayerischen Landtags* (Tagung, 1919–20), cited in Pommerin, *Sterilisierung,* p. 23.
13. Ibid., p. 24.
14. Ibid.
15. Ibid., pp. 25, 28.
16. Ibid., p. 28.
17. Within the initially neutral-sounding word *mulatto,* from the Por-

54

tuguese *mulato,* which had been adopted into German usage as early as 1604, is concealed the idea "that the Black is to the White as the donkey is to the horse, and that together they produce a hybrid that is barren" (Léon Poliakov, Christian Delacampagne, and Patrick Girard, *Über den Rassismus: 16 Kapitel zur Anatomie, Geschichte und Deutung des Rassenwahns* [Frankfurt, 1984], p. 64).

18. Palatinate Commissioner Jolas's document is reprinted in Pommerin, *Sterilisierung,* pp. 92–93.
19. Ibid., p. 32. I was unable to find any information about which countries were considered as sites for deportation and whether such deportations took place in individual cases. One can assume that the children were to be taken to countries of former colonies.
20. Adolph Hitler, *Mein Kampf* (New York, 1939), pp. 448–49.
21. Pommerin, *Sterilisierung,* p. 42.
22. Hans Macco, "Rassenprobleme im Dritten Reich," cited in ibid., p. 43.
23. Laws against voluntary sterilization were contained in para. 226 St. GB; paras. 219 and 220; also para. 218, for abortion, from 22 May 1933. Laws on preventing congenitally diseased offspring from 14 July 1933; "as of 1935 there was then 'eugenic' pregnancy interruption also, formally tied to the consent of the woman, but tied to subsequent forced sterilization" (Gisela Bock, "Zum Wohle des Volkskörpers . . . Abtreibung und Sterilisation im Nationalsozialismus," *Journal für Geschichte* 2, no. 6 [1980]: 58).
24. Bock, "Zum Wohle des Volkskörpers," p. 59.
25. An ethnic group of Central European gypsies.
26. *Stichworte für die Chefbesprechung am 21, November 1933 über die Rassenfrage,* cited in Pommerin, *Sterilisierung,* p. 55.
27. See ibid., p. 54. For the same reason, Hitler ordered anti-French posters withdrawn from circulation that were slated to be shown at the 1934 exhibition "German People and German Work" and conjured up the "Negroization of France." See ibid., p. 64.
28. Ibid., p. 66.
29. Ibid., p. 48.
30. Abel's name deserves special mention here because several investigations from the postwar period were largely uncritically based on his results. For example, Walter Kirchner's study, *Untersuchungen somatischer und psychischer Entwicklung bei Europäer-Neger-Mischlingen im Kleinkindalter unter besonderer Berücksichtigung der sozi-*

alen Verhältnisse (Berlin, 1952). Further attention is given to Abel's investigations in the following chapter.

31. Pommerin, *Sterilisierung,* p. 78.
32. *Aufzeichnung Rademachers zu R. 62669/41,* 4.12.1941, cited in ibid., p. 83.

Our Father Was Cameroonian, Our Mother, East Prussian, We Are Mulattoes

Sisters Doris Reiprich and Erika Ngambi ul Kuo
(ages 67 and 70) Speak about Their Lives

DORIS: We had a sheltered childhood and never felt we were different. When children called us "Negro" or "Negerbabbi," that didn't annoy me. I simply called them something back: one boy named Gabriel, I called "Archangel Gabriel"; one with a round head, "balloonhead"; the boy named Gabriel ran after me, caught me at my front door, and beat the stuffing out of me. I didn't bother him again.

I still remember, once, my blond girlfriend and I—we were around five years old—compared our hands and were amazed that mine were so brown and hers so light. We couldn't explain it. The grown-ups didn't say anything about it either, for them it was obvious. Yes, we grew up just like other children.

At school we were given very preferential treatment. When the school doctor came to our class, we were supposed to undress. I wouldn't, so the teacher picked me up, put a piece of chocolate in my mouth, and carried me up and down the room because I cried so much. I can still see her white lace handkerchief turning all brown from wiping my mouth. I got a kick out of that.

ERIKA: Our mother was aware that boys and men were always after colored girls, just to try them out. That's why she always told us: "Don't let them fool you; you're just like white girls! They think you're something special, and when they've had their fun with you—boom. Watch out!" I went unkissed for a long time out of absolute fear.

DORIS: Me, too [laughing]. My friends and I still believed in the stork at thirteen or fourteen, and wondered where babies came from.

ERIKA: Our father was well liked and well known in Danzig, and so were we.

DORIS: There weren't any other Africans besides us. Once in a while a freighter would come through or a circus with a colored person. My father would bring them all home, and Mother would have to cook a huge pot of rice and stew. We used to love that, especially that babble of voices when they talked to each other in their African languages.

ERIKA: Father came to Hamburg in 1891 as a twenty-year-old with two other Cameroonians, on the Wohrmann Line [a German freight and cruise ship company]. The three of them came from prominent families in Cameroon and, at the suggestion of Kaiser Wilhelm II, were supposed to be educated here.

DORIS: Father was to study medicine, but fainted at the first dissection of a corpse. Then a shoemaker offered to train him. But he put Father in the shop window to have him work. A black man was a sensation at that time; everyone would run and press his nose up against the window. Father never went back there again and became a merchant.

He got married, and in 1895 his first daughter was born; she's twenty years older than we. In 1896 Father purchased German citizenship for fifty gold marks. And when Danzig became a Free State in 1918, his citizenship was changed over to the Free State. Father was loyal to the kaiser and more German than many native-born Germans.

Our mother met Father at the home of mutual friends in Danzig. He was divorced, and in 1914 they got married. Mother's family had quite varied reactions: it didn't make any difference to her brother; he was very nice and later spoiled us children. Her sister took it all right at first, but during the Nazi period she would say: "It's fine for you to come, but I don't want to see your husband and your kids in my home." Of course Mother didn't go there anymore.

Our grandmother lived in a tiny village in East Prussia and was absolutely mortified over her daughter's marriage plans. She didn't come to the wedding either. She had never seen a black person in her life, not even from a distance. After Erika was born, mother sent her mother a picture, in which Erika was posing the way

Our parents

babies do in such photos—her little slip unbuttoned on one side, legs drawn up, she holding one toe bent way back. Grandmother showed up immediately, scared to death that the baby was crippled with a deformed leg. With Father she was very distant at first, but she stayed with us until she died and became bosom buddies with her black son-in-law.

Father was a good family man. He used to romp and play with us. To his way of thinking we were to go first to boarding school and then get married. But we had our own ideas: I wanted to be a fashion designer, because I had a talent for drawing . . .

ERIKA: . . . and I wanted to be a pediatrician.

"We only hire 'Aryans'"

ERIKA: In the fall of 1932 Father was summoned to our school— a private high school for girls—and was asked to take us out of the school. Father was so shocked that he complied immediately. I was almost finished at the time. In looking for a training position afterward, I heard at every turn: "What, you want to work for us? We only hire 'Aryans.'" One good friend who I had been close to from the first day of school dropped me like a hot potato. Later, in Berlin people spat on us in the street and taunted us with "bastard," and "mulatto." It was awful.

Finally, I found a job that I really liked, in a Danzig art shop. However, after four weeks I had to leave, because business associates had threatened my boss that they would stop doing business with him if he kept me on. He was very satisfied with me, and he was really sorry.

Actually, it had already started in 1927–28 . . .

DORIS: But not for us; for the Jews. Two neighborhood boys were already going around in SA uniforms, chasing Jews off the streets and pulling their beards. There were a lot of Jews living in our neighborhood, from Galicia and elsewhere. A lot of them wore pajes [characteristic hair locks worn by devout Jewish men].

Our mother became terribly upset over this and asked the boys' mother if she couldn't train her boys better. But it got worse and worse; for us the troubles really started in 1932. All of a sudden many folks—particularly recent arrivals from the so-called Reich—saw that we were different. As Erika mentioned, they started instigating dissent, thereby hindering Father in his work as a salesman. Merchants were urged not to order from him anymore.

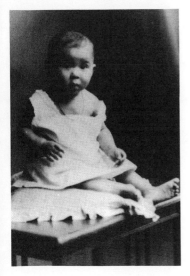

Erika Ngambi ul Kuo

Father with his daughters

A little while later we received an eviction notice for our five-room apartment. We probably would not have been able to afford the rent any longer anyway, because Father's business had gone broke by then.

ERIKA: After that Father worked for a Jewish firm that had been dispossessed. An SS man took over the business in trust and was decent enough to pay our father the weekly commission for re-orders from some of his old customers. That's something he didn't have to do. Besides that, our mother carted a lot of good stuff to the pawnshop. That's how we lived.

DORIS: Times were getting hard. Mother had to look for a new apartment, because as a Black man Father wouldn't have gotten one. We moved into a shabby three-room flat at the edge of town, and even one of those rooms we rented out. I was signed up at a middle school, where I was well received in the beginning. Some teachers remained neutral and friendly, but others made life very hard for me from 1933 on.

Often when I came home from school my mother would notice right away that something was wrong: "What's happened?" And then I would cry, she would cry, we'd hold each other tight. "Oh, people are so crude, to do that to a fourteen-year-old child!"

I had to take part in the course on "Race" and had to listen to statements like "God made all whites and Blacks, half-breeds come from the Devil" or: "Half-breeds can only inherit the bad characteristics of both races."

The teacher made me go with them to the exhibit "Race and Folk." When my mother wrote asking that I be excused from classes like that, the answer came that this was a schoolday like any other and it was the same for all schools. At the exhibit they showed, among other things, retouched photos of colored people in Munich whom I knew, with filed down teeth and weird facial expressions.

They also made me go along on a trip to see a ship, even though I didn't want to. After the trolley ride we had to march behind the flag; of course, I walked with my head down. We had barely gotten there when the teacher called me over, stuck carfare in my hand, and said that I had to go home. "As a non-Aryan you can't march with us behind the flag!"

It wasn't until 1974 that I stopped having nightmares of school. I was in Danzig then and saw that the school had been razed down to the foundation. Since then those terrible dreams are gone. Mother also suffered a lot back then; the authorities even asked her to get a divorce. Most of our friends and neighbors suddenly didn't know us anymore. I don't know how they could bring themselves to just drop us like that. It was really terrible for me when I ran into my best girlfriend, with whom I used to do everything—answer marriage ads and I don't know what other silly things—and she suddenly got red in the face, turned, and walked away. I ran after her asking, "Why, what's wrong?" But she didn't know me anymore. Once when I dropped off some photography work at the shop where she was working, she had to wait on me. She acted as though she had never seen me before in her life.

I was also kicked out of the German Gymnastics League. At some point I received a note from the team leader—a pretty nice fellow, actually—saying that I wouldn't be allowed to come anymore. I was put out of Girls' Bible Circle, too.

In 1936 I finished middle school. From 1936 to 1939 I tried to find work. It was simply impossible. On the basis of my applications I did get a lot of replies, but as soon as I presented myself, it was: "No." I started working in a little one-horse town as a nanny, just to have something to do and so that there would be one less mouth to feed at home. After three days I had to leave because the mayor had seen me. I enrolled in a typing course at the *Arbeitsfront* ("work front"). Once there, I was asked in writing not to show up anymore—although they had allowed me to pay for the course. At home I learned to type on our old typewriter, practiced shorthand I knew from school, and my sister drilled me thoroughly.

Finally I was enrolled at the Polish Business School, but couldn't stay because, of course, I couldn't speak Polish.

The "Adolf period" was the worst that anyone can imagine. You can't just suddenly label people as having a "life not worth living." They couldn't really liquidate us, but neither did they want to tolerate us.

After the war started everyone was drafted for duty; they drafted me as of December '39 as a warehouse worker in a stationery and office supply company. In that unheated warehouse I had to roll heavy rolls of paper. Then I had the good fortune to have the office manager get sick and, thanks to my shorthand and typing skills, I was able to take over her job. The boss had turned me down once before, but this time he had to take me.

My predecessor transferred to the office of the *Waffen-SS* (*Armed SS*), where she was better placed. Two years later I moved to a civil engineering firm. When I first got there the contracts manager did look at me strangely, but hired me anyway—for one hundred and twenty-five marks net; before, I had been earning sixty-five marks. Later I learned that he had thought I was sun-tanned from vacation, since my hair was straight. The boss was married to a half-Jew whom he had taken to Luxembourg to safety. I am indebted today to the boss and the contracts manager for protecting me from all the harassment by the state and allowing me to get anything I wanted—special discounts, grocery cards, and other forms of savings.

ERIKA: In 1938 I married a countryman of Father's in Danzig and moved with him to Berlin. My husband was a wrestler on tour at the time, and I met him when he was visiting in Danzig.

DORIS: The Africans in Berlin kept in close touch with Father; they knew he had two daughters. And when one of them got my sister, they heard there was another one. But they didn't get me. They wrote to Father, who said: "I'm no marriage broker!"

ERIKA: In Berlin I worked in a bookbindery. After the interview I was hired first as a temporary replacement and later taken on permanently. But the harassment I had to take from the junior boss! Right around that time the Germans took Paris. The boss stood up in front of me and said: "Give it to the niggers good!" My colleagues supported me, however, and put him in his place.

"Father was sixty-seven when our
passports were taken away"

DORIS: In 1939, just at the beginning of the war, Danzig became German, in keeping with the motto: "Home to the Empire." Ac-cordingly, we had to surrender our Free State passports. For a year and a half we had no passports at all and of course couldn't go anywhere; afterward they issued us alien passports. This I.D. saved me later on with the Russians.

ERIKA: My husband was stripped of his German citizenship then. Since Cameroon was still a French colony,* he turned to the French consulate and got French citizenship with no trouble. Thus I became a French citizen through marriage. We had to check in with the police every week.

In Berlin we had to put up with a lot. During my pregnancy I had to hear: "Our führer places no value in that kind of children." When our daughter was four years old, I registered her in nursery school, since I was working during the day. After a week I couldn't take her there anymore, because they argued they couldn't subject the other children to having to play with a "nigger child."

During the war my husband got an acting contract in Munich. Our daughter was four then. We had reserved two seats together on the train so that the child could sleep along the way. All of a sudden the compartment door opened, an SA man appeared in the door: "Hey, Nigger, move your butt and make room for the elderly lady!" I don't know where I got the strength to restrain my husband. He weighed a good two hundred pounds; he tore into that SA man like a tiger. The man took off immediately. I dare not think what could have happened. After a while my husband said: "Madam, you can have my seat." But she refused.

DORIS: Father was very supportive of his daughter from his first marriage, as he was of other mulattoes when they had problems. Like for J and M, who had been put out of the swimming pool because the "dear" Germans didn't want to swim in water where "Niggers" swam. In the early days he also got a lot of help through Hindenburg, whom he probably knew from the time before the war, when he was supplying coffee and cigars to the court.

Father was very well liked in Danzig and was an honorary member of the Citzens' Army. Even today the old Danzigers still speak of him with the highest respect. This also no doubt worked in

---

*From 1884 to 1918 Cameroon was a German colony; from 1918 to 1946 it was split between French and British mandate administrations. After 1946 it was under a United Nations Trusteeship until it gained independence in 1960.

his favor when the *Gauleiter* came to visit. In order to get to our house near the old town hall he had to pass through two SS barriers. Father, a tall, imposing person, went up to them and said: "Excuse me, please, gentlemen." The SS immediately let him through, and then again on the other side, too.

Mother and I had been watching the whole time from behind the curtains; our neighbor came running over, white as a sheet: "For God's sake, what's going to happen now?"

Later we were told that the *Gauleiter* had asked what was going on and was told: "Oh, that's an old African from our colony. We all know him." That was all.

Father was sixty-seven when our passports were taken away. He was determined to get out of Germany and go back to Cameroon. Everything seemed to be in order; he was examined and declared "fit for use in the tropics." He just had to go to the colonial office one more time; there they informed him: "You may go if you'll make propaganda for us." His answer was, we were told later: "But, gentlemen, how can you suggest such a thing? I can't promote a country that despises my color."

What happened then, I don't know. Anyhow, after he left the office, he had a heart attack on the street. That was in May 1943.

He never recovered; but we got a lot of assistance from people. Someone brought two eggs, someone else, a piece of bacon or whatever they could spare. Everyone thought that Father had fainted from hunger. The word had gone around that we were getting Polish ration cards, which had practically nothing on them. Trolley cars and other such facilities were also forbidden to dogs, Jews, and Poles.

When Father died in June 1943, the gravediggers took off their hats in dismay, mumbling "the old gentleman." The funeral procession was endless, despite the Nazis.

Many Were Sterilized or Even Carried
Off to Concentration Camps

DORIS: Until Father's death we were pretty much left in peace. Beginning in the fall of '43 the harassment started: for example, I had to constantly return to the racial policy office, where I had to show my passport, and then I could leave. They said it was for our protection because we were colored.

I even told one young man I met that he shouldn't be seen on the street with me. But he refused to stop walking me home after work. One day he was put in jail for it, after having said: "I do my duty, and my personal life is nobody else's business."

Three days later he showed up again in quite good spirits, telling us about a cockroach that had entertained him during that time, how he had let it run back and forth in a crack in the table. None the worse for his detention, he came back to us totally unscathed.

At that time I was supposed to be sterilized, too. They took me to the women's clinic; I cried my eyes out on the way. One of the men, trying to console me, talked to me continuously. Why, I don't know. He took me into the clinic and then let me go. Because I was supposed to have been sterilized, I was especially thankful later for my two children. My daughter has blonde hair and blue eyes, of all things. I would love to have shown her to Hitler and told him: "Here's a German girl, but she's not for you!"

ERIKA: Many colored women were sterilized. Gerda, Hanna . . . Christel's mother hid her in a convent near Cologne. They got her out of there and sterilized her too. Our nephew also. After the sterilization they sent him right home; they didn't even allow him to rest.

DORIS: In 1943 a woman we knew came to Danzig to have her baby, whose father was a mulatto. Everyone in her town knew it, and she was afraid of reprisals. Only our mother could visit her in the hospital, we couldn't be seen there. The staff gawked at the baby anyway because it was so dark. And they were so happy: "What an adorable baby!" Afterward the woman wanted to get married, had an examination, got all the paperwork done, and asked the doctor. She was very happy. But she still had to go to the marriage bureau, where she had to hear: "Aren't there any white men? Of all things, must it be a Negro?" So the marriage didn't come off.

We knew that Jews were being taken to camps. A boat loaded with Jews was blown up in the Baltic Sea; the screams and despera-

Erika Ngambi ul Kuo with daughter, Beryl (mother of Abena Adomako; p. 199)

tion were heard all the way to where we lived. We often heard about mulattoes being taken to concentration camps. Our girlfriend S, a mulatto, and her husband, a Dutchman, were picked up two days later at S's mother's house. They were accused of all sorts of things: "Nigger whore, mixed marriage," and so on and so forth. Anyway, they carted off the parents and grandparents and left the child alone in the house. The neighbors were told they'd better not look after the child, but in spite of that, they came the next morning from Bromberg to Danzig to let us know. Then I went over to the boy's house and often I took him walking up on the embankment bordering the concentration camp. I would pick him up and hope that S could see him if she stretched herself up at the window. S later told us that upon hearing our whistle she would actually pull up at the window and see us.

Then I was stupid enough to ask for permission to speak to her in the Bromberg concentration camp. I wanted to know if I should keep the boy or send him to his uncle in Berlin. One man said to me straightaway: "Let me tell you something, you'd better get out of here as fast as you can so that the same thing doesn't happen to you." That was 1943. Sure, I knew about the camps but I always thought: "But I haven't done anything." And besides that was Bromberg, and I was in Danzig.

S's husband ran away in '45 with a Polish fellow when the Bromberg inmates were transferred to Stutthof near Danzig. The front was moving closer and closer. The two of them came to our place in Danzig deathly ill. We nursed them back to health and hid them in our house until the end of the war. After the war we found out from former prisoners that S had been left lying in a grave in the concentration camp with bubonic plague. The Russians nursed her back to health and one day she turned up at our door.

S's mother remained missing. S herself died in 1953 as the result of a kidney ailment she had contracted in the concentration camp.

Forced Labor and "Watchdogs"

DORIS: Early in 1945 the so-called watchdogs picked me up because of my looks and took me to a shipyard where I had to haul pipes. Passersby who had seen what happened told my mother the "watchdogs" had taken me. No one could find out what was going to become of me. It was awful for my mother. After several days of forced labor we were outside the shipyard gates and there was an air raid. As the low-flying aircraft approached, everybody scattered in all directions, many running away, myself included. First I went to a friend's place, who explained to me that she couldn't let me in because she was just leaving to go to her sister's in Zoppot. Then I spent the day in the arsenal passageway. After checking with neighbors to see that the coast was clear, I went home that evening. The house had an extra cubicle where the door could be concealed with a cabinet. At first I stayed there.

At the shipyard we had had to sleep on some straw on the cement floor and I had caught an awful case of pneumonia. It was a cold winter and I wasn't used to heavy work outside. My mother nursed me as well as she could; we were afraid to call a doctor. Unfortunately I ended up with defective bronchial tubes. When we hadn't heard anything for a while, I came out of hiding. The "watchdogs," a special unit of the army, were rural police who wore beaked caps with crescents and numbers on them. They marched through the streets, rounding up all suspicious-looking people, hunting for deserters, alien laborers, whomever. They were quick to hang their victims, even their own deserters.

One evening I saw something hanging on a tree near Kran Gate. Curious as I am, and near-sighted too, I went up to see what it was. There was a man hanging with a large sign fastened around his neck "I am a traitor." That happened often. When they needed people for work, they just picked up a few who had no papers—I only had a foreign passport myself.

They Needed Us for Their Colonial Films

ERIKA: My husband was an actor and a star at the Ufa Theatre. In the hope of regaining the old colonies after the war's end, many colonial films were made: among others *Dr. Karl Peters* with Hans Albers, *Quax in Africa* with Heinz Rühmann. They needed colored people. We were hired and the wages were good. We got to travel abroad a lot. All the actors and everybody else were very nice to us. They definitely weren't Nazis.

We always dreaded going home. But where were we to go? A war was on, and our roots were here. In spite of everything.

DORIS: Yes, as of 1938 I came to Berlin for the movies. That's where I met the home folks—home folks—that's what we still call each other today. Before that I didn't know any.

During the filming we had a lot of fun. On our breaks the Africans would often get their drums and we'd sing in front of the studios. People would come running from all the productions. They loved to listen to us.

After 1933 hardly any of the Africans returned to Africa. What were they to do there? Who would have paid for their trip? So they struggled along in films or the circus. They'd pose for circus advertisements or for an African film; they weren't displayed as attractions, but they did take on all jobs. If they weren't working on a movie, they would sell smelling salts and other things at fairs, for example. There was always something to do, the old Africans didn't live badly. There were also colored people who were determined to be white and would have nothing to do with us. For example, one woman wouldn't ride with all of us to the filming location.

We earned good money, had fun, and didn't have too many qualms about it. At most it occurred to us once in a while that they could knock us mulattoes off while making a movie, all at one time. But where would they then have gotten other Africans?

One time about two hundred to two hundred and fifty Black prisoners of war were brought in because they needed extras for a film. Black POWs from the United States besides. Those poor fellows were glad to be with us, since they got to eat and play football and were treated well. We also put money together to buy things for them.

Of course that was an isolated case with the movies; Jews were already forbidden to appear. People who didn't go to the camps, however, didn't know all that. We earned good money—twenty-five or thirty-five marks a day for three, four weeks; we got ration cards, heavy labor compensation cards. The work wasn't heavy, we just had to be there, and that was all.

It was pleasant, comfortable: no politics, no Nazis, just happy people. We were all together—young and old Africans, who today are living scattered all over Germany. Many also died during the war years. In Munich, Hellabrunn, Prague, and Babelsberg a lot of films were made. Yesterday a film, *Water for Canitoga,* in which Erika's husband played, was aired again on East German TV.

When I would come back after filming to Danzig, where no other Africans lived besides Father, I didn't miss anything. I could always adjust—one time I'd be black, one time white. But mostly I was a mulatto.

War's End and the Postwar Period

DORIS: Our girlfriend's husband whom we had hidden in our house—he being a Dutchman—was separated from us when the Russians came and sent back to Bromberg. Since Danzig was completely bombed out, Mother and I moved to Bromberg too, going partially on foot and partially by train. We worried about Erika in Berlin and she about us. One day I heard shooting and ran out into the yard. I had just washed off my feet and had on Papa Katlewski's big slippers. A Russian came over the fence shouting "the war is over!" He took me by the hand running out of the yard. Our Dutchman came running behind us and grabbed my other hand. There I was running between the two of them to Wolloschin Platz (Liberty Square). The Russian let me go and started shooting wildly for joy. C and I made tracks out of there. A neighbor woman watching the scene immediately informed my mother: "A Russian has just taken Doris away!" Mother fainted from shock and had to rest for five weeks.

Mother and I were very fearful after the escape from Danzig. People kept us hidden in a room with a cupboard pushed in front of the door. Even though we each had a bed to ourselves, out of fear we slept huddled together in one bed.

Since Mother only spoke German and all of her papers had been burned, the Poles didn't want to believe that she was my mother. "A German, get her out of here," a lot of Poles thought, under-

The family picture that saved Mother's life

The dance troupe "South Sea Magic"

standably. Indeed, they had gone through horrible experiences with the Germans. I found a family picture in my passport as proof, which saved Mother's life. Since we couldn't speak Polish and had nothing to eat, the three of us, with S, started a music and dance group. I, an office girl, had to learn tap dancing and acrobatics. Anyhow, we earned two thousand zloty every evening, enough to eat a good breakfast of eggs and sausage in the morning.

In November '45 we slipped out of Bromberg, got ourselves exit visas written up and surreptitiously stamped at the office. C, the Dutchman, distracted the guy at the office, I did the stamping.

When we tried to use them to get tickets for the trip, we found out that there was supposed to be a picture on the exit visas—so we had to go through the whole thing again. You can't believe how scared we were! The dance troupe carried on, with whites, Blacks, and various foreigners—everybody thrown in together. We needed to have at least ten to perform: often we were as many as fifty and went on tour. In 1947 I met my husband, a Berliner.

He was a musician in our group. In 1948, with my daughter on the way, I was still jumping around and tap dancing like crazy in my sixth month. My dear husband said, "You will not jump anymore, I forbid it." On the same evening a festival was being held in Alu Square in Hannover with the entire Hautevolee. My cousin thought that perhaps with the performance there we could also get some other engagements, so I performed again. My husband waited in the wings until I was finished and then took me home in a taxi. With that, the show was over for me.

I stopped making movies in the early '60s. Leaving the house early in the morning, learning parts at night, it was just too much, and the family got short changed. After *The Little Fixes, Tea Time, The Best Friend,* and many others, I quit.

My little boy played a part in *King Thrushbeard.* One actress stuffed him with so many sweets during that time that for weeks he couldn't bear to look at any more.

ERIKA: We had to check in with the police every week. Since I still had French citizenship, I needed a work permit, and they cut off my food stamp money. "Germans don't get any in France either," they told me. After making an application, I got welfare support.

At that time it was hard for a foreigner, race hatred was definitely still around. In the first place I was not Aryan, and besides, I was a foreigner, so no work.

Later I worked at GEMA [an organization that supervises media distribution rights]; there they said: "Does it have to be a Black?

Erika Ngambi ul Kuo and her husband   Doris Reiprich and her husband

On the set for the filming of *Ten Little Negroes*, Krumme Lanke Studios, Berlin

Erika Ngambi ul Kuo (*left*) and Doris Reiprich's son (*front, right*) in the film *Auntie Wanda from Uganda*

Isn't there anyone else?" In 1947 I applied again for German citizenship. And in 1963 I finally got it. They even asked if I had a receipt stating that I had lost it. What an absurdity! I had to write an essay in German to prove that I could write flawless German. My birth certificate and all my other papers were of no value; I was treated like a foreigner. I know exactly why it took so long: namely because I am legally German and therefore they would have had to pay me compensation.

DORIS: After the war we wanted to get out of Poland and go back to Germany. The Russians offered us free passage to Africa . . .

ERIKA: . . . from Bromberg to Africa! [peals of laughter]

DORIS: Our mother had always been German, couldn't speak a word of French—yet, for her too, we had to apply for German citizenship after the war. It took years and years. Then she had to go to the immigration office to show that she spoke perfect German. In 1957 she became seriously ill, so I called the office: "My mother is seriously ill, she doesn't have long to live, and her one remaining wish is to die a German."—"Yes, we'll take care of it, we'll get right on it," was always the answer. When I was getting ready for the funeral in November '58, the telephone rang: "You can pick up the German papers for your mother." I never went, the papers are still lying there rotting.

ERIKA: Every once in a while we go to the Danzigers' meeting, but not because of the propaganda they're making now. We want to see our friends.

DORIS: After the Nazi period the hostilities toward us quickly tapered off. I can't forget everything from that time, but I'm no longer miserable either. It's past, and I'd prefer not to know anything more about it. Now and again people address me in English, but they don't mean any harm. One day I was sitting on the bus with my little grand-niece cuddled in my arms. I heard one woman say to her neighbor, so touched: "Look, they love their children, too." People can be so thoughtless. She meant it sincerely.

"Nigger Kiss" or "Moor Head" [popular chocolates] doesn't bother me either; I don't think anything about that. In the hard times Father even sold these. And I have never thought of Sarotti-

Mohr as negative either—for us it's like Luisenkuchen or something like that. [Sarotti is a chocolate company that uses the image of a young "Moor" as its trademark. Luisenkuchen are popular cakes.] Somehow I'm past that. But when I think about South Africa, I could explode. There it's like fascism. A colored person has to get off the sidewalk when a white person comes. I would protest down there as much as I could, regardless of what it might cost.

People used to ask me often whether I would marry a black man or a white one. "It doesn't make any difference to me; all that matters is that he's a decent person," has always been my answer. A lot of them say: "My God, after all you've been through, you can't marry a white man."

My husband and I lead a peaceful life. By now we've become happy grandparents, and no one makes anything of the fact that we look different. Everybody likes to come to visit. Our children didn't have any difficulties either, there were other colored children to play with or in their classes. It doesn't matter to children whether they are colored or not, unless something is made of the fact by adults. A neighbor's boy once said to my son: "Hey, you're a Negro." To which he responded cool as a cucumber: "Yeah, I know. So what." And they went on playing; the two of them were very close friends. No, we don't have any more difficulties. In both children's schools we were in the parents' association and in many organizations we were officers. In 1976 we had a white German boy as a foster child, whom we took care of from when he was ten until he became an adult, with the complete agreement of the Child Welfare people. Now he lives in West Germany but visits us as often as he can. We are "his family." Many of our children's friends have come and stayed at our home and still enjoy seeing us. None of the three children has ever made an issue out of the fact that their mother is a mulatto. I have always enjoyed being a mulatto, in the rough period, too, and I have always been able to manage black and white within me. I remember when a coworker once asked me in the '40s whether I was unhappy having to live as a mulatto. My girlfriend, who was white, and I looked at each other quizzically. I said: "No. You know, what I have already experienced because of my background you will never experience in your entire life."

Afro-Germans after 1945:
The So-Called Occupation Babies

MAY OPITZ

After World War II there was hardly any further mention of the Afro-Germans born before or after 1919. They became an overlooked minority, and it was uncertain how many of them survived National Socialism and with what physical and psychological consequences. Klaus Eyferth, Ursula Brandt, and Wolfgang Hawel concluded in 1960: "After World War I some 800 children of colored French soldiers were born. Of those only a very few are still living in Germany. Many seem to have emigrated or to have died early."[1] Surviving Afro-Germans and Asian-Germans—and many other persecuted minorities—were not recognized after the war as politically or racially persecuted groups and were excluded from "compensation payments." Fasia Jansen, the Afro-German daughter of a Liberian man and a German woman, was forbidden under National Socialism to attend school and was made to work in a kitchen where "food" was cooked from garbage for war prisoners and KZ [concentration camp] inmates. In a conversation with Peter Schütt she makes the observation:

> The term "racially persecuted groups" immediately became restricted to Jews, and soon there was no more talk of the other victims of racism, the gypsies, the Poles, and the Russians, nor of us Blacks.[2]

In the '50s the blossoming field of social science attempted to research the situation of Afro-German children born after 1946. The objective of nearly all these studies was to provide assistance in integrating these children into German society and to draw attention to the possible difficulties of integration, such as prejudice and/or social danger signals. Very noticeable is the often moralizing religious undertones of the publicity concerning the presence of this specific group of children. Frequently the titles of the articles themselves indicated the sentimental concern of their authors, as in for example, Manfred Franke's "Responsibility for Our Mixed-Race Children"[3] or Marianne Baumeister's "The Little Mulattoes: A Serious Question for Us All." The latter article ends with the questionable statement that "we must view it as our human and Christian duty to be helpers to these disadvantaged children."[4] While some writers, such as Eyferth, Brandt, and Hawel and Luise von Frankenstein, attempted to consider the social and psychological circumstances that determined the attitudes toward Afro-German children and thus their image of themselves and others,[5] some studies saw a "natural disadvantage" in the actual or perceived difference of the children.

In 1952, an article appeared to this effect in the weekly *Das Parlament* with the headline: "What Has Become of the 94,000 Occupation Babies?" The article reported on committee deliberations in parliament, generated by an SPD [Social Democratic Party of Germany] inquiry, which took up the question of the legal status of the children born out of wedlock. In this report, the situation of Afro-Germans was deemed a "special problem":

> Among the occupation babies, the 3,093 Negro mulattoes form a special group, presenting a human and racial problem of a special nature. . . .
>
> The authorities of independent youth welfare agencies have for years been concerned about the fate of these mixed-blood children, for whom the climatic conditions alone in our country are not even suited. The question has been raised whether it wouldn't be better for them if they were taken to their fathers' countries. . . .[6]

The judgment here, a priori, that Afro-Germans, because of their different appearance, were a "human and racial problem of a special nature," gives great cause for concern. It brought out an attitude that projected onto a putative "problem group" potential impediments to integration. A more constructive approach would have been to focus on the lack of tolerance among those sectors of the population which, because of their conscious or unconscious racist attitudes, were the real problem group, in serious need of pedagogical and psychological attention.

> The fact that the situation of colored children in Germany is cause for special considerations and studies is regrettable. . . . It is obvious that the German public is not yet capable of assuming a posture free of racial prejudice. It would be a weak excuse to suggest that other peoples also have severe race problems. Only a long-term education process will be able to dislodge the tradition that causes us after all this time to believe in the superiority of our own race.[7]

Shipping Afro-German children abroad with the reasoning that the climatic conditions were not suited to them was the easiest way to avoid coming to terms with a situation that had prevailed since the occupation of the Rhineland after World War I.

There were a few successful cases of Afro-German children born after the Second World War being adopted by families abroad. In the above-mentioned parliamentary debate a CDU [Christian Democratic Union] representative was able to report of only one child that the Parisian Red Cross had sent to Casablanca, and came to the conclusion that:

> The mulatto question will remain an internal problem for Germany that will not be easy to resolve. We must make the German public aware of this issue, since mulattoes born in 1946 will be entering school in 1952. Of course we could not think of publicizing this issue as was done in one city at mardi gras time where the parade included a float bearing the sign "Made in Germany." On the float were German children made up as mulattoes.[8]

Investigations by Eyferth et al., Frankenstein, and others show that essentially three prejudices were at work with the so-called occupation babies:

1. Resentment of the enemy occupation forces readily targeted black children, the visible offspring of the "intruders."
2. Prejudice because of the social background of the children. Their mothers were blamed for the children's illegitimate birth and it was readily assumed that as "Yankees's girls," they only got involved with black men for commercial gain. As long as the children were

young this prejudice was leveled exclusively against the mothers; the children were seen as cute and innocent. In the expectation that "the apple doesn't fall far from the tree," the children themselves soon became the objects of this prejudice.

3. Prejudice founded on handed-down colonialist or National Socialist ideologies of race theory, according to which "mixed-race" people were supposed to represent inferior heritage and intelligence.

Even research studies that expressly called for enlightenment and setting aside of prejudices reveal the same prejudice—some clearly, some more subtly—with varying effects on boys and girls. Before going into these studies, we will offer a thematic analysis of race terminology and gender polarity.

The Self and the Other: A Digression on Race Terminology and Sexism

Racism is an ideology that empowers one group to dominate economically, politically, and culturally and to impose its own standards on others. As has been demonstrated in the section on colonialism, racism goes hand in hand with sexism. In the North American colonies, for example, a white woman who married a black man could be remanded to slavery, and this "by law, for the duration of her husband's lifetime."[9]

Today worldwide racism and sexism are evident in the international and sexual distribution of labor and property.

20% of the world's population, most of which is white and living in the North Atlantic region, controls:

90% of the world's income
95% of the scientific knowledge
90% of the gold reserves
70% of the meat supply
80% of the protein.[10]

According to UN publications, women perform two-thirds of all housework but own no more than one-tenth of the world's income and one-hundredth of the private property.[11]

Racism is not a genetic disease. No one is born with racist beliefs and attitudes. Physical differences between people are not the cause of racism. These differences are used as an excuse to justify racism.

(To offer an analogy to sexism: anatomical differences between male and female human beings are not the cause of sexism. These differences are used as an excuse to justify the mistreatment of women.)[12]

How little social power has to do with morphological and physiological differences becomes particularly evident in race classifications. Most of the obvious differences are not based on inherited traits but in their degree of prevalence among various groups. We can assume that in the course of their ethnic evolution, people have never lived in total and constant isolation from each other. Migrations have continually served to obliterate geographic separation and the "exchange of genes during mankind's evolution has led constantly to changes in genetic endowment and thereby to phenotypic change within the races and also to the formation of new races."[13]

With this knowledge, it seems virtually impossible to divide people into "races," and in fact the boundaries are very controversial. "In general, the number varies, depending on the researcher, between six and about forty." Poliakov et al. point out that in contemporary biological measurements, Blacks alone are subdivided into more than ten subgroups.[14] The ideological content of the concept of "race" becomes particularly clear in view of the fact that in Germany "race mixing" is usually meant to refer to partnership between Black and white persons and their offspring.

Since "races" only present temporary results of evolution, there is neither any reason to retain them in their present-day form nor any justification for inventing dangers from racial mixing.

We can assume a human being—regardless of the origin of his/her genetic make-up from different races—represents a system that in its internal adaptations incorporates an equalizing mechanism,[15]

especially in view of the acknowledged fact that the culturally created environment changes faster than people's gene composition.

It was calculated that all people have about 6.7 million genes (inherited traits) in common, in equal measure for racial groups, ethnic groups, ethnicities, and individuals who represent those groups. In contrast to that, the difference in genes between a "typical" white and a "typical" Black—here the concept "type" is taken to be opposite extremes—was estimated at 6 (Glass) to 29 or 30 at most (William S. Boyd).[16]

"Race" is conceivable only as a hypothetical construct and is a concept strongly loaded from the history of its usage. In my view it is critical to break through the myth of a "pure race" and to avoid the term "race" totally, or at least to expose its political content. On this point, I applaud Bishop Tutu, who, in his idea of a society that does not distinguish on the basis of skin color or other traits, speaks not of a "racially mixed" but of a "nonracial" society.[17] Any system that claims to separate people by using group-specific inherited traits and explains behavior and psychological dispositions as belonging to them is inadmissible. Such categorization is based on the acceptance of a "natural, ahistorical, and asocial human being, who doesn't exist."[18] Also questionable is whether biological gender difference can fully account for distinct gender roles.

> Culturally familiar gender polarity rests on constructions that are evolutionarily and anthropologically improbable. As far as the physical body is concerned, dimorphism is so uncommon, and occurrence of intermediate levels of all kinds (even genital) so frequent, that hermaphroditism should rather be placed on a continuum.[19]

"Male" and "female" must be understood as cultural attributes, which receive their particular definition by virtue of one's being born as a woman or man in a patriarchal or matriarchal society.[20] This is not to argue that biologically identifiable differences do not exist between men and women. But still, of the complexity of roles in reproduction, for example, no justifications for domination can be derived. In all patriarchal societies, sexism means power for men, an inferior status assigned to and maintained for women.

> Sexism has always involved the exploitation, mutilation, annihilation, domination, and persecution of women. Sexism is subtle and deadly at the same time and means negation of the female body, violence toward

the woman's self, lack of regard for her existence, expropriation of her thoughts, colonization and usurpation of her body for pleasure, taking away of her own language to the point of controlling her conscience, restriction of her freedom of movement, downplaying of her contribution to the history of the human race. When it says on the gravestone "Mr. and Mrs. Heinrich Schultze," a woman's life is then permanently extinguished.[21]

Racism and sexism function according to the same principle. They use biology to explain differences that are social, in order to classify them as fixed, "naturally determined" phenomena.

There is no scientific basis for the assumption that any particular race is inferior to another, less intelligent, less capable, or of a lesser culture. The myth of racial superiority must be attacked as such. It is obvious that the lack of educational, economic, and equal opportunity for advancement actually sets some groups back.[22]

The point here about "races" also holds true for genders.

Scientific Studies on the Status of Afro-Germans in the 1950s

Two relevant anthropological studies, Walter Kirchner's inaugural lecture, "An Anthropological Study of Mulatto Children in Berlin with Special Consideration of Social Relations" (1952), and Rudolf Sieg's work "Half-Breed Children in West Germany: An Anthropological Study of Colored Children" (1956), have been published.

In both studies, as in other reports on Afro-Germans, loaded terms like "Negro,"[23] "half-breed," "mulatto"[24] were used without analysis of the problems inherent in the terminology. Sieg even spoke of the "effects of bastardization"[25] in his study, and Kirchner explained, with reference to Eugen Fischer,[26] that the "question of the genetic transferral of morphological traits could be studied particularly well in a bastard population." Kirchner's study was conducted with the agreement of Berlin's Lord Mayor Dr. Ernst Reuter, in cooperation with the Central Youth Bureau and the Berlin State Youth Bureau. As "subject" Kirchner indicated:

> With a eugenic objective, this study looks at European-Negro half-castes in Berlin, primarily children of German women and American Negroes who were in Germany in the postwar years as members of the occupation forces.[27]

Despite his apparent belief in the equality of "races," Kirchner clearly reveals racist attitudes:

> It is especially important to emphasize the impossibility of formulating a valuation measurement for races and racial mixture. Gobineau's theory has led to the widespread belief that there are superior and inferior races as such. But the fact is that each race is suited in different degrees for certain tasks.
>
> It is out of the question to regard one group of people as inferior because they are incapable of certain physical or mental requirements due to their racial make-up. Yet it makes sense to point out the variations among races and the consequences resulting from racial mixing, borne most heavily by the half-breed her-/himself. This is the task of eugenics or applied anthropology.[28]

Citing H. Muchermann,[29] Kirchner gave particular weight to the slight differences between people when he spoke of the supposedly justified effort "not to distort the peculiarities of an ethnic group by introducing entirely different racial mixing into that ethnic group." Regarding children, he said that nearly all exhibit a "natural un-inhibitedness" and could require special educational attention.[30]

In claiming that this behavior is "natural," Kirchner was able to disregard completely societal influences on behavior. He also expresses the racist belief that "the decidedly European-looking Berlin mulattoes" were closer to whites than, for example, "the decidedly negroid half-breeds of Jamaica." Kirchner recognized that "racial discrimination in Germany was certainly not an instinctive reaction, as it was made out to be, but had its roots in a politically engendered, historically rooted nationalism."[31] Nevertheless, he based his work totally on studies from the National Socialist period, for example, on Dr. W. Abel's work on "crossings between European and Annamese,"[32] whose results were used during the Third Reich to validate the inferiority of Afro-Germans. It was well-known that Abel considered himself the anthropological expert for "assigning race" in the Special Commission 3, established in 1937, to "discreetly carry out the sterilization of the Rhineland bastards."[33]

Further, Kirchner based his work on studies from the United States that claimed lower intelligence in Blacks. With J. Comas, we can conclude that many of the studies cited by Kirchner, such as that of Jon Mjoen,[34] do not take into account the influence of sociocultural conditions.[35]

Another source that Kirchner used for his own interpretation of the situation of Afro-German children, and the one from which he drew his projection for their future, was F. Franke's edited report (1915), "The Mental Development of Negro Children,"[36] a summary of studies that had been conducted in African colonies. Selecting these investigations with no regard for type, extent, and area of research, Kirchner quoted some of the results that, without exception, claim differences among "races" as proof of the superiority of Europeans. To quote from his examples:

> Whereas the European youth progresses in the development of abilities, the Bantu child was found incapable of making further progress in most directions. The growth of his intellect, which promised so much at first, stopped right at the stage where the European's intellect began to unfold its greatest powers. (Theal)

> The predominance of memory over reflection and the relatively early halt in intellectual development appear to be fact. (Waitz)[37]

Kirchner's findings for Afro-German children studied in Berlin are reminiscent of the results as well as the prognoses from investigations that had taken place in the spirit of colonial conquest, as can be seen in the following quotation:

> As far as racial factors are concerned, we can assume that the advance in development demonstrated by mulatto children will probably stop at puberty. Intellectual ability in particular should remain moderate, according to available studies of American Negro half-breeds. By the same token, we can assume that the strong tendency to be ruled by physical urges, as shown in the mulatto children, will remain present as a negroid racial trait.[38]

Any proof of the untenability of Kirchner's research results is superfluous. His vocabulary as well as his methodology demonstrates the similarity of his research with race theorists from the colonial period and race hygienicists under National Socialism. Studies that ignore, deny, or insufficiently take into account the existence of prejudice and discrimination must necessarily lead to the false conclusion that differences between whites and Blacks are "racially" conditioned.

Rudolf Sieg's anthropological investigations were valuable in pointing out social influences on behavior. From Sieg it was obvious that identifiable differences in behavior and ability and the varying frequency of psychic and somatic illness among white and Black children in a racist environment should be neither surprising nor attributed to biology. Rather, these differences are a result of racism, a kind of "fallout" from the effect of discrimination.

Sieg found that in some children's institutions, staff complained about behavioral and discipline problems among Afro-German children, and that

> in the very homes where there were complaints of discipline problems, the colored children, to a significant degree, named or otherwise indicated "white" as their favorite color, while their Afro-German peers in other homes preferred, depending on the prevalent environmental influences—not elaborated upon here—red, blue, or green, or sometimes "brown" or "black."[39]

With few exceptions, the same children suffered from recurring skin problems with above-average frequency. Upon closer examination of the conditions in the home it was determined that the children in question were not receiving enough recognition and pedagogical attention, and as a result lacked adequate self-esteem. In an effort to gain acceptance, this deficiency manifested itself in conspicuous behavior and self-loathing. "Black" skin—the most noticeable trait of difference in comparison with white children (preferred by the staff)—is the physical organ that proved particularly susceptible to "care-related injuries." Sieg summarized his results as follows:

Among the results of a study of 100 three- to six-year-old racial half-breeds from the postwar period, it was significant that 26% of the half-breeds living in children's homes or orphanages suffered with skin ailments. In a comparison group of white children from the same homes, such ailments were found in only 4% of the cases, while with half-breed children who live with their mothers, no pathological changes in the skin were noted. This indicates that the observed skin ailments occurred nearly exclusively in the institutions, in which there was a lack of pedagogically trained personnel and the affected mulatto children suffered from an inferiority complex because of their skin color. Therefore the author believes that the skin ailments that are frequently appearing in specific homes can be labeled as care-related injuries, as a type of "hospitalism of institutionalized colored children."[40]

In addition to anthropological research on Afro-Germans, surveys and studies were carried out that were intended to give a view of the social connections. The number of so-called occupation babies was estimated at four thousand until 1955, but this figure represents only those illegitimate children who were registered by social welfare agencies. An international organization, the Association for Aid to Children, estimated the total of children of occupation troops to be ninety-four thousand in 1952.

In two conferences (in 1952 and in 1953), World Brotherhood, an "organization for the abolition of intergroup prejudice"[41] had as its conference theme the "problem of German half-breed children." Part of their mission included sending out questionnaires to school administrations and youth agencies, which were to provide information about the children's family situation, their social integration, and attitudes of significant individual and group caretakers. The study results showed that seventy-five out of one hundred children were being raised by their mothers or relatives. External circumstances hindered mothers and children, especially in the early years of the occupation, from maintaining a continuing relationship with the fathers, who as a rule were stationed for eighteen months to two years in the Federal Republic. Military superiors with racial prejudices frequently denied marriage licenses to Black soldiers, "and perhaps many a sudden transfer of a Black soldier is/was traceable to this attitude (if the soldier was not attempting to shirk parental responsibility in requesting a transfer)."[42] Not until 1950, when the soldiers were no longer separated into Black and white regiments, were the restrictions eased; after that, engagements and marriages increased.

Unwed mothers, in most cases, had to provide for their families by themselves. In her investigation "Illegitimate Children of Foreign Soldiers, with Particular Consideration of Mulattoes," Luise Frankenstein refers to statistics of the German Association for Public and Private Assistance, according to which only 9 to 10 percent of all soldiers—but 25 percent of Black soldiers—paid child support.[43]

By law, all illegitimate children had equal status, but for children of foreign fathers, it was often the case that "the legal mechanisms of forcing a noncitizen to fulfill his responsibility toward his illegitimate children [broke] down if the father [was] in a foreign country."[44]

For this reason, the mothers of these children were more likely to find themselves in financial difficulty and so were forced to resort to welfare assistance more often. This was also true for unwed mothers in other countries who gave birth to children of German soldiers and were unable to claim support. "In this regard, of the 8,000 German soldiers who fathered illegitimate children in Norway, only 50, that is 0.6%, make support payments."[45]

The results of the questionnaire that had been circulated by World Brotherhood indicated, on the whole, that there were no noticeable differences of any kind in intelligence or behavior between the Black and the white children, and that the institutional personnel as a rule gave Black children no special treatment: "And this is the tenor throughout: understanding, good, correct, tolerant, and evenhanded in their care, no exceptions, no difference whatsoever, fair, polite, exemplary. . . . The staff member endeavors to make no difference and no fuss. . . . (Munich)." In another part of the study it becomes clear that there was frequently only the appearance of free acceptance of Afro-Germans. Hidden behind the caring, in these cases, was a feeling of particular moral obligation and responsibility. To quote, for example, from the Baden-Württemberg ministry of culture: "The faculty has recognized its equalizing tasks and acted accordingly." For, "if only out of professional ethics, a good teacher behaves exactly the same way with a colored child as with a white child. For how can the child help it? (Würzburg)."[46]

The concluding question, a question that remains unelaborated in the World Brotherhood report—How can the child help it?—insinuates that someone should bear the *blame* for the existence and/or blackness of the child. I am unavoidably reminded of the story about the "Moor" in Heinrich Hoffmann's "Struwwelpeter":

> As he had often done before,
> The woolly-headed black-a-moor
> One nice fine summer's day went out
> To see the shops and walk about;
>
> . . . .
> So one and all set up a roar
> And laugh'd and hooted more and more
> And kept on singing—only think!—
> "Oh Blacky, you're as black as ink."
>
> . . . .
> Now tall Nikolas lived close by—
> So tall, he almost touch'd the sky;
> He had a mighty inkstand, too,
> In which a great goosefeather grew;
> He call'd out in an angry tone:
> "Boys, leave the black-a-moor alonc!
> For if he tries with all his might
> He cannot change from black to white.

On the surface, Hoffmann is condemning discrimination; yet indirectly stated within this condemnation is the idea that it is preferable to be white. The lines "For if he tries with all his might / He cannot change from black to white" are to be interpreted, as Deltgen has done, in the following manner:

The Negro is not to blame for his misfortune; it is not polite to add insult to injury. That Blackness is a stigma and that the Negro is disadvantaged by it remain the inviolate assumptions of this thought process: The poor black Moor does not deserve ridicule but sympathy. Big Nikolas shows the same prejudice as the boys he criticizes: he assigns negative value to the Negro's different skin color.[47]

The punishment that Nikolas devises for the white German boys fits his racist position—he makes them black:

> See, there they are, and there they run
> The black-a-moor enjoys the fun.
> They have been made as black as crows,
> Quite black all over, eyes and nose,
> And legs, and arms, and heads, and toes,
> And trowsers, pinafores, and toys,—
> The silly little inky boys!
> Because they set up such a roar
> And teased the harmless black-a-moor.[48]

The putative blame for the fate of Afro-German children was laid first and foremost, and often exclusively, on their mothers. For instance, in the *Sonntagsblatt* Sunday newspaper (1950) under the caption "Children of Fate: Of 200,000 Occupation Babies, 3,000 Are Mulattoes," this statement appeared: "A large number of mothers of mulattoes must bear the blame for half-breeds coming into a world that harbors such hostility toward them."[49] This reads as though there is shame or sin inherent in bringing a colored child into the world. It was primarily the mothers who were subjected to censure, which was tied in with condemnation of their motives for associating with a Black soldier and of the social milieu in which the woman moved.

Luise Frankenstein's work contains the following descriptions, or more accurately, judgments, as characterizations of different women with Afro-German children:

The mother comes from an uncultured environment.
The mother is red-headed, strong, tall, of above-average intelligence.
The mother is an uneducated factory worker.
The mother comes from a morally inferior family.
The mother is an intelligent, clean, and tidy woman.[50]

In conclusion, she says:

> Our material supports the finding that a bad homelife or the lack of a
> consistent family unit is conducive to the girls' straying; it shows,
> however, that only one-fifth of the girls come from a good environ-
> ment, i.e., a family not uprooted, one that is complete, respectable.[51]

It remains to be seen how Frankenstein measured "respectability,"
"backwardness," or "intelligence," and what it means, accordingly, to "stray." Her condemnation of and contempt for the mothers of black children negates her claim of contributing to the
elimination of prejudice through social critique.

I would like to add that Eyferth et al. concluded that in exclusively working-class residential areas, Afro-German children were
accepted much more freely than in generally more respected middle-class neighborhoods.[52]

The ways in which children view themselves and feel others view
them determine their attitudes toward the world and in this they
are especially influenced by the people closest to them. Mothers
of Afro-German children were themselves experiencing reactions
from their milieu that hindered their ability to develop positive
relationships with their children. Not infrequently, relatives and
neighbors shunned the mother, and new intimate relationships
were also difficult to develop. As has been stated in many reports:

> Neighbors point to the "Nigger whore" and her "bastard." Husbands
> or potential spouses force the mother to choose between them and the
> child.[53]

The above-mentioned article from the *Sonntagsblatt* of November 1950 stated:

> mothers of mulattoes are trying harder than ever to place their little
> Negro half-breeds in children's homes, and there are no means that

have not been tried to turn these children out anonymously or to deposit them on the doorstep of children's homes in remote, unfamiliar cities. . . .

Approximately 70% of all Negro half-breeds are already in institutions, mostly communal arrangements, although a large number of mulattoes are kept in charity institutions, through municipal or state programs, which, however, can provide only limited care.

The author implied that Afro-German children imposed a particular social and financial burden on the community and that it was only in the rarest cases that the mothers wanted to take care of their children. On the contrary; the fact is that all the research refutes this and shows that the majority of the mothers, in spite of, or indeed because of, the hostilities and impediments to their children were especially supportive.[54] Frankenstein reported:

Of 603 mothers, 92 are prepared to give up the child for adoption. In a little more than half of these cases, the mother is concerned not with getting rid of the child for her own convenience, but about providing the child with a better chance in life, e.g., some want to send it to the father or other adoptive parents in America because they imagine America as the paradise for colored people. In such cases the thought of a separation is painful for the woman, but she does not want to stand in the way of her child's happiness.[55]

In 1952, with the enrollment of the largest entering class of Afro-Germans imminent, a few preparations were made to facilitate their prejudice-free integration into the schools. In Bremen, for example,

conferences were held at individual schools, in which each child and its acceptance into the peer group was discussed. The municipal school board returned to the issue again, although less frequently, inquiring about the experiences gathered in the interim.[56]

Even though such measures set Afro-Germans apart as a special group with specific problems, the results of such consciousness-raising efforts were nevertheless able to neutralize this disadvantage. In cities where no such "campaign" was initiated, the number of Afro-German school graduates with diplomas commensurate with their abilities was much lower.[57]

Prejudice and fears on the part of teachers often ruled out recommendations to more advanced schools and had the added effect of preventing an open discussion of racism in the school, often fostering feelings of resentment.

> We found that only a few teachers dared to speak with their class openly about the differentness of their colored classmates. A few, in the course of studying foreign cultures and races in geography classes, for example, quite casually take up the example of the community of white and colored children in their own class and discuss it with the children. But these are exceptions. The school in no way helps the majority of white classmates of colored children to draw a connection from the fairy-tale and picture-book image of Moors and parents' remarks about "wild" men, to the reality of a dark-skinned classmate.[58]

Since loose morals were always ascribed to the mothers, Afro-German girls were not only subjected to racist preconceptions, they were also accused of being inclined toward the mother's "aberrant behavior."

> Not infrequently there are comments like: "She's already just as scatter-brained, superficial, and concerned about her looks as her mother" or, "Sure, she's already starting to look at boys." Such judgments as these pigeon-holed children as already being what people believed their mother to be; yet, in our experience there is hardly anything known about the mothers except the fact that they have a mulatto child.[59]

Prejudices quickly become self-fulfilling prophecies, i.e., people begin to behave in accordance with what appears to be expected of them.

Expectations regarding ability and prejudice about intelligence provide a classic example of this: population surveys by Eyferth et al. showed the presence of a prevailing stereotype that Blacks were more suited for nonacademic and service occupations.

> Occupations that were frequently named as appropriate for girls were laundress, maid, factory worker, and typist. For boys positions as stage performer, musician, car mechanic, and elevator boy were recommended.[60]

At first, access to schools for advanced study was denied Afro-German children inordinately often, although they could prove themselves qualified. Then many teachers, parents, and vocational counselors, in consideration of anticipated difficulties, would attempt to interest the Black children in the occupations where their skin color was in demand or at least was not a problem. In Wiesbaden's journal of the Hessian Youth Circle, an article in 1963, "Half-Caste Children," said uncritically:

> On this point the employment bureau is under no delusions. We are realistic enough to see that the relatively good integration of colored children into public life later is not a given. Even in this city, where colored children are dressed just like others, where they speak the same dialect, where we have been accustomed to them for a long time, even in this city there would be a hue and cry if the city clerk's son wanted to marry a kinky-headed, dark-skinned girl. So, what can we do? We can only recommend that these girls choose nursing, nursery-school teaching, or a similar occupation; for in these occupations they can fulfill their maternal inclinations, and they have the capacity to achieve a degree of independence that very few of these girls have.[61]

When girls and boys are given one-sided information about possible vocations that reflect the prejudices of this society, it ultimately becomes a given that Blacks are going to be grouped into certain vocational fields, which then in turn is explained as the result of supposed inclination and intelligence. One conclusion, for example, is

> that tavern owners often try to employ mulatto girls in their businesses, because they believe that the movie-stereotype of a mulatto or Negro woman, the imagined laxity of the mother's way of life, and the attraction of the exotic, could be advantageous for their "business."[62]

Accommodating existing prejudices can lead to a situation where it is considered an imposition to be instructed by Black policemen/ women, attorneys, doctors, so that the circle of having to prove oneself and the perceived inability to prove oneself is completed.

Notes

1. Klaus Eyferth, Ursula Brandt, Wolfgang Hawel, *Farbige Kinder in Deutschland: Die Situation der Mischlingskinder und die Aufgaben ihrer Eingliederung* (München, 1960), p. 11.
2. Peter Schütt, *Der Mohr hat seine Schuldigkeit getan: Gibt es Rassismus in der Bundesrepublik?* (Dortmund, 1981), p. 152.

3. Manfred Franke, "Verantwortung für unsere Mischlingskinder," *Gewerkschaftliche Monatshefte* [Köln] 10 (1959): 622–24.

4. Marianne Baumeister, "Die kleinen Mischlinge: Eine ernste Frage an uns alle," *Zeitwende* [München] 23 (1952): 742–44.

5. Eyferth et al., *Farbige Kinder*; Luise Frankenstein, *Soldatenkinder: Die unehelichen Kinder von ausländischen Soldaten mit besonderer Berücksichtigung der Mischlinge* (Genf, 1953).

6. *Das Parlament,* 19 March 1952.

7. Eyferth et al., *Farbige Kinder,* p. 109.

8. *Das Parlament,* 19 March 1952.

9. Martha Mamozai, *Herrenmenschen: Frauen im deutschen Kolonialismus* (Hamburg, 1982), p. 14: "The same fate befell their children. This law, conceived actually to prevent white women from marrying colored men, became a trap for women seeking to buy their freedom. To secure them and their children as lifelong slaves, many were married off to colored men by force. In the climate of the general antislavery movement there were, from 1764 onward, even German and German-descended women who organized against white slavery."

10. Klaus-Martin Beckmann, ed., "Rasse, Entwicklung und Revolution," supplement of *Ökumenische Rundschau* [Stuttgart] no. 14-15 (1970): 25.

11. See *Frankfurter Rundschau,* 26 July 1980.

12. Ricky Sherover-Marcuse, *Towards a perspective on Unlearning Racism: 12 Working Assumptions* (Oakland, n.d.).

13. Gerfried Ziegelmayer, *Rassengleichheit-Rassenmischung? Die anthropologischen Grundlagen,* Vortrag im Studium Generale der Universität Heidelberg im Wintersemester 1969/70 (überarbeitete Fassung) (Köln, 1971), p. 181.

14. Léon Poliakov, Christian Delacampagne, and Patrick Girard, *Über den Rassismus: 16 Kapitel zur Anatomie, Geschichte und Deutung des Rassenwahns* (Frankfurt, 1984), pp. 18, 26.

15. Ziegelmayer, *Rassengleichheit-Rassenmischung?* p. 187.

16. K. Saller, "Judenfeindschaft als Erscheinungsform des Rassenhasses," in Rolff Italiaander, *Rassenkonflikte in der Welt* (Frankfurt, 1966), pp. 30–31.

17. See Bishop Tutu: "Gott segne Afrika," in *Texte und Predigten des Friedensnobelpreisträgers,* ed. Freimut von Duwe (Reinbek, 1984).

18. Wilhelm E. Mühlmann, *Rassen Ethnien Kulturen* (Neuwied-Berlin, 1964), p. 133.

19. Carol Hagemann-White, "Thesen zur kulturellen Konstruktion der

98

Zweigeschlechtlichkeit," in Barbara Schaeffer-Hegel and Brigitte Wartmann, eds., *Mythos Frau: Projektionen und Inszenierungen im Patriarchat,* 2d ed. (Berlin, 1984), p. 137.

20. Margaret Mead concludes:

> In every known society, mankind has elaborated the biological division of labour into forms often very remotely related to the original biological differences that provided the original clues. Upon the contrast in bodily form and function, men have built analogies between sun and moon, night and day, goodness and evil, strength and tenderness, steadfastness and fickleness, endurance and vulnerability. Sometimes one quality has been assigned to one sex, sometimes to the other. Now it is boys who are thought of as infinitely vulnerable and in need of special cherishing care, now it is girls. In some societies it is girls for whom parents must collect a dowry or make husband-catching magic, in others the parental worry is over the difficulty of marrying off the boys. Some peoples think of women as too weak to work out of doors, others regard women as the appropriate bearers of heavy burdens, "because their heads are stronger than men's." The periodicities of female reproductive functions have appealed to some peoples as making women the natural sources of magical or religious power, to others as directly antithetical to those powers; some religions, including our European traditional religions, have assigned women an inferior role in the religious hierarchy, others have built their whole symbolic relationship with the supernatural world upon male imitations of the natural functions of women.

(Margaret Mead, *Male and Female: A Study of the Sexes in a Changing World* [New York, 1949], p. 7)

21. Marieluise Janssen-Jurreit, *Sexismus—Über die Abtreibung der Frauenfrage* (München, 1976), p. 702.

22. Otzar Hamoreh, ed., *Internationale Lehrerkonferenz zur Bekämpfung von Rassismus, Antisemitismus und Verletzung der Menschenrecht* (Tel Aviv, 1982), p. 195.

23. In the United States, as a result of the Black Power movement of the 1960s, the term "Negro" was definitely relegated to the category of discriminatory words. See Stokely Carmichael and Charles V. Hamilton: "There is a growing resentment of the word 'Negro,' for example, because this term is the invention of our oppressor; it is *his* image of us that he describes. Many blacks are now calling themselves African-Americans, Afro-Americans, or black people because that is *our* image of ourselves" (*Black Power: The Politics of Liberation in America* [New York, 1967], p. 37).

24. See note 17 to the earlier section "African and Afro-German Women in the Weimar Republic and under National Socialism."

25. Rudolf Sieg, "Mischlingskinder in Westdeutschland, Eine anthropo-

logische Studie an farbigen Kindern," *Beiträge zur Anthropologie* [Mainz] 4 (1956): 65.

26. E. Fischer, *Die Rehoboter Bastarde und das Bastardierungsproblem beim Menschen* (Jena, 1913).

27. Walter Kirchner, *Eine anthropologische Studie an Mulattenkindern in Berlin unter besonderer Berücksichtigung der sozialen Verhältnisse* (Berlin, 1952), p. 1.

28. Ibid., p. 3.

29. H. Muckermann, *Vererbung und Entwicklung* (Bonn, 1947); also, "Das Rassenproblem—anthropologisch gesehen," *Stimmen Der Zeit* 142 (1947).

30. Kirchner, *Eine anthropologische Studie an Mulattenkindern*, pp. 3–4.

31. Ibid., pp. 17, 38.

32. W. Abel, "Über Europäer-Marockaner und Europäer-Annamiten-Kreuzungen," *Zeitschrift für Morphologie und Anthropologie* [Berlin] 36 (1937).

33. Rainer Pommerin, *Sterelisierung der Rheinlandbastarde—Das Schicksal einer farbigen Minderheit 1918–1937* (Dusseldorf, 1979), p. 78.

34. J. A. Mjoen, *Harmonic and Disharmonic Race-Crossing: Eugenics in Race and State*, vol. 2 (1923).

35. Juan Comas, *Racial Myths: The Race Question in Modern Science* (Paris, 1958), p. 15.

36. F. Franke, *Die geistige Entwicklung der Negerkinder* (Leipzig, 1915).

37. Ibid., cited in Kirchner, *Eine anthropologische Studie an Mulattenkindern*, p. 43.

38. Kirchner, *Eine anthropologische Studie an Mulattenkindern*, p. 62.

39. Rudolf Sieg, "Häufung von Hautaffektionen bei Mischlingen in Kinderheimen," *Praxis der Kinderpsychologie und Kinderpsychiatrie* [Göttingen] 10 (1961): 179.

40. Ibid., p. 180.

41. World Brotherhood, "Das Problem der deutschen Mischlingskinder," Zur 2. Konferenz der World Brotherhood über das Schicksal der farbigen Mischlingskinder in Deutschland 1953, reprinted from *Bildung und Erziehung* 7 (1954): 613.

42. Eyferth et al., *Farbige Kinder*, p. 26.

43. See Frankenstein, *Soldatenkinder*, p. 8.

44. Ibid., p. 7.

45. Ibid., p. 8.

46. World Brotherhood, "Das Problem," pp. 23, 623.

47. Florian Deltgen, "Der Neger im deutschen Kinder- und Jugendlied," *Kölner Zeitschrift für Soziologie und Sozialpsychologie* 29, no. 1 (1977): 128.

48. H. Hoffmann, cited in ibid.

49. *Sonntagsblatt,* 19 November 1950.

50. Frankenstein, *Soldatenkinder,* pp. 17, 18, 19.

51. Ibid., p. 21.

52. Eyferth et al., *Farbige Kinder,* p. 76.

53. Frankenstein, *Soldatenkinder,* p. 29.

54. Herbert Hurka, *Die Mischlingskinder in Deutschland: Ein Situationsbericht aufgrund bisheriger Veröffentlichungen,* special issue of *Jugendwohl* (1965). See also ibid., p. 27.

55. Frankenstein, *Soldatenkinder,* p. 28.

56. Eyferth et al., *Farbige Kinder,* p. 55.

57. Ibid., p. 58.

58. Ibid., p. 60.

59. Ibid., p. 67.

60. Ibid., p. 77.

61. *Hessische Jugend,* ed. Vorstand des Hessischen Jugendrings Wiesbaden, no. 10 (Oct. 1963).

62. From *Sozialer Fortschritt, Unabhängige Zeitschrift für Sozialpolitik* [Berlin] 8 (1959): 206.

Helga Emde (age 40)

*An "Occupation Baby" in
Postwar Germany*

I was born in March 1946 in Bingen-on-the-Rhine as a so-called occupation baby. According to the few stories from my mother, my father was stationed in Germany as an American soldier at the time. That was about all I knew of him. My father was very dark, and I came into the world as a so-called mulatto. Since my mother could say absolutely nothing about him, I don't know him and wasn't able to have any contact with him. Nor do I know whether I have any American aunts, uncles, or cousins. It hurts a little that a whole part of my history is in the dark.

I grew up in a time that was still strongly marked by Germany's National Socialist past. My childhood wasn't very different from that of other children except for the fact that I'm Black. I'm the only Black person in the family. My mother believed in an awful saying: "If you say A you must also say B." For her that meant that she had brought a Black child into the world and she now had to own up to it. It was practically a kind of self-punishment. She demonstrated her "owning up" by seeing to it that I lacked nothing. I was stuffed like a pig! Nothing was denied me. In retrospect I really hold that against her. Instead of stuffing me with food perhaps she should have fed me with something quite different. Love, for instance. My sister was a delicate girl, you could almost say skinny. She got what she needed for her development, not just food but love, too. We competed a lot with each other. Neither in my childhood nor as a young adult did I have the good fortune to come into contact with other Blacks in my surroundings. There just weren't any. As a child I only saw Black soldiers, and I ran away from them in fear and terror. This fear clearly shows that I must have internalized the prejudices and racism of my surroundings at a very early stage. Black meant frightening, strange, foreign, and animalistic. For, how else can you explain that I didn't perceive my own blackness as such? That I looked upon a Black man's smile more as a flashing of teeth than as smiling? Of course I wasn't allowed to have anything to do with Blackness. But the idea, the devastating idea of actually belonging to this group was still there!

Black means unworthy of existence. And that's exactly how I felt. I always stayed in the most remote corner; I was shy and timid and felt lucky to be asked to play with the other kids—and how! I felt unworthy of existence. I couldn't afford to be conspicuous or else I'd be noticed, not as a sassy little girl but as "Nigger," "Moor Head," "Sarotti-Mohr." I couldn't afford to be conspicuous at any price, but already I was "big and strong" for my age. I was not supposed to stand out and yet I was noticeable to everybody with my kinky hair and my black skin. Not infrequently people had the audacity, even in my mother's presence, to "marvel over" my hair, that is, to touch it and to give free vent to their delight at the feel of horse hair. What my mother was feeling, I don't know. But it always seemed to me that she somehow felt flattered. Maybe she was getting attention in that way. But we never spoke about it. Almost daily, people marveled at my good German accent and at the same time asked where I came from. Often I considered myself "cute" or exotic, but never as a person with feelings. I had to learn early to take both insult and injury, that is, I had to learn to suppress my feelings, to put things out of my mind and not always be vulnerable and easily hurt. Words like "Nigger," "Sarotti-Mohr," "Nigger Kiss" or "Moor Head"—I heard these terms as a young child and quite frequently.

Sweet tasting insults. For after all, what child doesn't like to eat sweets? I loved them and was always ashamed to ask for "Moor Head" or "Nigger Kiss" in a store. In school I had a girlfriend who always carried around a lot of pocket money. After class she would often invite me for a "Moor Head snack."

Oh yes, another thing: In the school choir they had a song I could not bring myself to sing with them—"Blackish brown is the hazelnut, blackish brown am I, too." As soon as I would hear it I would become flushed with shame, thinking that all the other pupils would point at me. It was torture for me.

". . . as white as I could be"

A white person is beautiful, noble, and perfect. A Black person is inferior. So I tried to be as white as I could be.

When I was about thirteen I started to straighten my "horse hair" so that it would be like white people's hair that I admired so much. I was convinced that with straight hair I would be less conspicuous. I would squeeze my lips together so that they appeared less "puffy." Everything, to make myself beautiful and less conspicuous.

At fourteen I graduated from eighth grade and then took a two-year training course from nuns in a children's home. My time with the nuns didn't do very much to increase my self-esteem. My life was nothing but restrictions, religious restrictions: every morning getting up early to go to "Holy Mass." And shame on me if I was bold enough to ask to sleep late once in a while since my duties started later. Then automatically I was an "ungrateful, spiteful godless little person," who should have been happy at the chance to lead such a good clean life.

Sexuality was, of course, taboo. It goes without saying that you couldn't talk about it either. You couldn't even wear a short-sleeved nightgown in the hottest part of the summer. It was simply a fact that woman is shameless. When I reached puberty the only instruction on sexuality I was given was that from then on I had to keep away from men. As though I had tried to get close to them before!

I felt fragmented, confused, and disoriented, without an identity of my own. And my mother was incapable at this time or at any other time of supporting me, of sharing this experience with me, or of enlightening me. Rather, she seemed glad that I didn't bother her with all these problems. Probably not so much because it was troubling to her, but more because her own prudish upbringing hadn't prepared her for any of this. My fears of being Black and of men were rooted deep within me. What better way to protect myself than with a fat, unattractive body? I ate myself into a regular cage of protection. It was a vicious cycle: I wasn't supposed to stand out—but I was big and fat. Was supposed to be inconspicuous—but I was big and fat and Black. And to top it all off, I was a girl.

My existence in the male world often seemed to me like one long running of the gauntlet. I remember going for a walk with some girlfriends. We had barely passed a bunch of workmen when right away there was the remark: "The Black one, that's the one I want. . . ." Inside, I froze into a pillar of salt. I felt hurt and humiliated, and even now when I write about it I feel anger and hatred toward those men who only looked upon me as a walking sex object.

After my home economics training I worked for two years as an aide in a children's home, and then at eighteen I began my nurses' training.

My nurse's uniform suddenly provided me with an identity and a role. Since childhood I had been trained never to show my true feelings, always to smile and keep my mouth shut. So, on the hospital stations I soon became a ray of sunshine for the patients. There it didn't matter how I really felt. I was simply the little exotic girl. People constantly said things to me about my differentness, and that used to make me feel pretty bad. As long as I was a trainee it was okay, but after my exam I worked in the Frankfurt-Höchst Municipal Hospital and was given only the dirty work to do. I had to clean up but was given no responsibility. They even had the audacity to assign me to frequent night duty, which almost nobody liked. But on the night shift I suddenly became responsible for several stations at once.

On day duty it happened now and then that a doctor on the station would see me and ask if anyone else was on duty. In his eyes I was nobody! So, am I really nobody? I am a German, I was born here, but yet I'm different. A Black woman. A mixture of black and white.

I felt degraded and discriminated against. As before, I had no contact with other Blacks, mostly because I would have preferred to deny my blackness. It wasn't enough that I belonged to a minority; I also felt lonely and isolated. In my own life I repeated the

story of my mother's life in every way. My first boyfriend was a Black soldier, and I had a baby by him. At the beginning of this relationship I harbored very ambivalent feelings: on the one hand I was happy and even proud to have a boyfriend—at least in this respect I didn't have to be an outsider—and on the other hand I had the secret fear of being even more conspicuous. After this relationship was over, I had to "ban" everything Black from my life, at least for the time being.

At twenty-three I got married—to a white man. A year and a half later our child came into the world. We are a very mixed-looking family, with very different shades of color. At last I felt that I belonged and that I had a bit of recognition out there in society. A white man at my side, this could certainly provide me with some security, even if it still meant that only white counts.

With my husband I sought something that I was never able to find, namely solidarity. There was a lot he couldn't understand, simply because he was white. He didn't experience the many subtle abuses and hostilities that his company—and unfortunately my own as well—caused for me. Over and over I would hear from him that I was too sensitive. That's just not a basis for a life together.

And then there were the relatives. My husband's sister, during the course of her psychoanalysis, came to the conclusion that my blackness frightened her and that my personality was too strong for her. Since then I've recovered from the pain that caused me for she was my closest friend for many years.

A good Catholic aunt of my ex-husband and of his doctor-therapist sister voiced the opinion, without ever having seen me, that "I could never be faithful to D (my husband) anyway, because anyone who had ever slept with a 'Negro' just couldn't." So, what am I supposed to say?

Just Be a Housewife and Mother

When my children were still small I began to feel unsatisfied, over-burdened, caged in, hungry for education. My need to catch up, particularly with respect to education, started to become stronger, for practically all of our friends and acquaintances at that time were university students or had already completed their university education. And every time the discussion came up about my needs, I encountered a lack of understanding. Nobody knew how to take what I was saying. Why did I want to further my education? Why go back to school? Why do anything at all to get away from my housewife's existence?

I considered myself ignorant and uneducated. But my friends' answer was that I wasn't ignorant, I knew how to do a lot of things, and I really ought to consider what being a housewife and mother meant. This was their way of trying to "build me up." But actually they were neither supporting nor encouraging me, but rather restricting me to the role of mother. At the same time I was giving them the feeling that they were something special. In debasing myself I was raising the status of my educated friends and offering them the opportunity to do "developmental work" on me. Even my husband didn't take me seriously. For him too I was not an equal partner, but his wife to be shown off, whose presence automatically made him the center of attention wherever we went.

My relationships, with our friends as well as with my husband, really became tense and strained when I finally decided to go back to school. I began by preparing myself in evening and weekend courses for the high-school equivalency exam. Of course I was still working part-time, for we still needed the money. I worked as a district nurse and then later as night-duty nurse in a Frankfurt hospital, and yet my sense of dissatisfaction was becoming increasingly noticeable; I was simply a frustrated housewife and nagging mother.

When the lease on our house on the outskirts of Frankfurt ran out, I pushed hard for us to move back to Frankfurt, as a chance to escape my isolation a little bit. For I felt like I was in a prison, like I had absolutely no contacts with the outside world. My kids had their friends in nursery and elementary school, and my husband could enjoy his little house in the suburbs because he worked in the city and had colleagues from work. After a long hard search—don't forget that I'm not white and for this reason most landlords turned us down—we found a nice apartment practically in the center of town. This move was a real break for all of us: the children went to new schools, in a different environment, and I found a new job in a rehabilitation center for the mentally handicapped, working with people who had just been released from psychiatric care and had to learn to adjust to the outside world again. At the same time I was preparing myself for my exams in the evenings and on weekends. I was petrified of failing and the only words of encouragement that I heard from my husband were that if I flunked once I could take it over again. But I didn't flunk, and as a matter of fact I got the same grade that my husband had gotten when he took his equivalency exam a year earlier. I applied to the university for admission and enrolled. Throughout my undergraduate work my husband could not accept the fact that I had to study too, to do some reading or to write a paper. He would keep me from studying with a very subtle form of "love," often asking me to go for a walk with him, or to sit and have a cup of coffee with him, . . . I was becoming increasingly assertive, defending myself against his "love"—which felt like shackles—and against his feelings of competition. The whole time I was at the university, I worked at least two to three days a week and also during semester vacations. My husband couldn't throw it up in my face that he had to finance my education. Plus I had my household and my children to take care of. Of course there was no question of my husband taking on equal responsibility. Or maybe he did feel responsible but he didn't do half as much at home as I did. Sure, he'd go shopping or run the vacuum cleaner, but that's not taking one half of the responsibility.

Whenever I would tell my mother-in-law about my studies she would only say: "And what about the household?" How could I have gotten the idea that I had the same rights as others?

Suddenly the roles shifted. No longer was I the ignorant little exotic girl, now I belonged to that revered group: university students. And nobody knew how to react. The more equal I became with the others, the more strained our relations became. A couple of friendships soon petered out. Just like that, that quickly. My white sister even said once that I really wasn't entitled to a place at the university and that I was taking the place away from younger people and that in fact I already had a career.

Fortunately, I didn't let anyone deter me. I continued at the university and felt unbelievably good in the role of student because I belonged to "that group," even though I never really had the chance to enjoy my student life. I carried much too much responsibility on my shoulders. The only ones who were happy about my success at university were my children. They supported me in every respect. When I had to study and they were quiet, that in itself was a great form of support.

I was getting deeper and deeper into a crisis situation, a marriage crisis and also an identity crisis. In order to give myself more clarity and distance from these unresolved issues, I decided after completing my teacher's certificate, to take a trip to southern Africa. So I went. On 24 December 1983, I flew to Zimbabwe for the first time, to stay with friends for two months and share their lives.

"I can say 'Yes, I am black'"

Prejudice? Yes, what is prejudice? It's seldom open and direct, but usually very subtle and often covered with a veil of friendliness.

For example, I enjoy listening to music, and it's often hard for me to sit still while I'm listening. But if I express myself, like if I want to dance, then automatically that means: "You've got music in your blood, so you must know how to dance."

Of course I must be able to sing too, because all "Black women" sing fantastically, especially gospels and spirituals. Just think of Ella and Mahalia! And not only can they sing but—in spite of their physical size—they can move to the rhythm.

It was a long journey to find my "self" in this white system of relationships. Alongside my studies I began reading about all kinds of different ethnic minorities, and delved deeply into the issue of National Socialism and the Jews in the "Third Reich." I felt then, and still do, very close to those people.

My circle of friends consists of people of different nationalities. I have since made many African friends. I enjoy being with them, and even seek them out. In their presence I feel comfortable, secure, accepted, and not like a foreigner. But again and again just when I get to feel "at home" with them, I come to the painful realization that ultimately I don't actually "belong" among them either.

The "white world" is more familiar to me. I grew up among whites, although among them also I don't feel like I belong, but am rather a minority. My sons have it easier than I—they are not alone with their differentness; they have me.

An African friend once told me this anecdote: Once when he went out for a walk, he encountered a woman with a child, who excitedly pointed at the "Negro." He leaned over to the child and asked where he was born. —"Here," that is, in Germany. He continued: "So you're a German?" The child answered yes. "You see," he explained, "I was born in Africa, so I am an African and not a 'Negro.'"

He considers the word "Negro" as negative. This conversation really made me reflect and also made me envious, because this Black person was able to refer to his identity in a very natural way.

I have dark skin, too, but I am a German. No one believes that, without some further explanation. I used to say that I was from the Ivory Coast, in order to avoid further questions. I don't know that country, but to me it sounded so nice and far away. And after this answer, I didn't get any more questions either. Germans are that ignorant. I could tell people any story I wanted to, the main thing was that it sounded foreign and exotic. But no one ever believes that I am German. When I respond to the remark, "Oh, you speak

Oliver and Sascha Emde

German so well" by saying "So do you," people's mouths drop open.

It's only recently that I have been able to feel more comfortable in my brown skin and come to terms with my blackness. After a long hard struggle through psychoanalysis, I can say, "Yes, I am Black." I can accept the white part of me as well as the black part and without feeling any breaks between them. Most of all, I am thankful for the unending patience of my therapist who stayed by my side on this rocky journey in the search for my Self, my identity, and my roots.

The Revolutionary

no mother, I tell you I've
renounced your god
—i'm a revolutionary
i know i'm hurting you all, that's the only reason i'm marrying her,
the black girl, who doesn't fit in with us
—i'm a revolutionary
look, i'm leaving her already—i'm going in order to fight. please
take me back, for you all can be proud of me

—i'm a revolutionary
i know what i owe to you all, to you, too, mother, that's why i'm
coming back
—but i'm your son. forgive my revolt.
but from today on i'll choose my underwear, mother.
—that's the price you have to pay.

The Cry

because poverty makes you inventive, i always had things to play with.
and friends. lots. scads.
they played with my things and broke them.
ran away. and i was alone again.
why?
let me in!
i want to belong to you. but they were just gone.
Sarotti Mohr, Moor Head.

why are you ashamed?
who do you feel sorry for me?
why are you torturing me?
Nigger.

let me be like you.
look, i'll straighten my hair,
make my lips thin and put on pretty clothes.
Exotic girl.

i'm a human being, a female person, don't you understand me?
Sex.
you all make me unequal.
housewife and mother.
Nooooo. please, doesn't anyone understand me?
Sure.
all of us. but stay as you are and don't change.
no, no education, where will we be then???
but understand me, i want to be equal.
but please not like us!
you don't belong to us.
HELP they want to stone me and
They're almost succeeding.

Photo R. Kuzelowsky, Kurfürstendamm 216

King Charles

C 6784

Verlag Berliner Künstlerbilder

Astrid Berger (age 42)

"Aren't you glad you can stay here?"

My attempt to tell something about myself should begin with someone else, my father. He is probably the person who had the most significant impact on me, even though I lost him very early—he died when I was eleven.

My father, Kala King, was born in 1895 in Douala, Cameroon, which was at that a German colony. He came to Germany before the start of World War I, and when he got here the German authorities changed his name to Gottlieb Kala Kinger. Here he began teacher's training. His idea—the Germans' idea as well—was that he would return to Cameroon after completing his education. But it turned out differently: during his studies he met a German woman and decided to remain in Germany. Of course, as an African he could never practice his profession; no one would give him a teaching job. So they both decided to go on stage as a dance team in variety shows. They were able to live quite well from this occupation.

I vividly remember my father's stories about this period. Once his wife made him a woman's costume, and he went on stage in one number as a girl and then appeared again in tails in the next. Everyone in the audience said afterward: "Why, that's the young girl's brother." Sometimes, when my parents were in a good mood, they would dance for us.

During the war my father had a relationship with another woman, of which I was the result. I came into the world in Schwerin-by-the-Warthe, in a convent where I was immediately made a Catholic, even though my mother didn't belong to any Christian

denomination. The condition for being able to have her baby there was that I would immediately be baptized as a Catholic.

I spent my first three years with my mother in the GDR. My father visited us regularly. My mother was working and had two other daughters who were somewhat older than I. During the week I lived in a children's home, on weekends I came home. When I was five years old my mother and father agreed that I should live with him; he was quite determined about this. At this time my father was already working in the theater and in films. Soon we moved to West Berlin—my father was considered an undesired alien in the GDR, since he had always worked in West Berlin. I was happy to go with my father, but in the beginning the change to the "West" was terrible for me. Especially when I first entered school, for at that time it was still quite unusual to see a Black child in the school. The teacher looked at me and said out loud: "This is quite an interesting case!" I was a "case," not a person—how was I supposed to deal with that?

Particularly in situations like those it was important for me to have my father. When I'd go home and tell him what people had said to me, he supported me and said: "Those are poor people." He was able to live here very well as a Black person without feeling

Astrid Berger and her father, Gottlieb Kala Kinger

under attack. When people would say things to him about his color, he would laugh and explain things about Africa to them.

But he frequently told me: "You must always have pride in yourself, don't forget that they're pointing their finger at you." And that's how it was. I went to a girls' school and was always the only "foreign child" there. And whenever anything happened, that meant: "It was the Black girl."

My stepmother, because of her experiences as a Jew in the Third Reich, had adopted the position "no matter what, don't be conspicuous." Therefore, she was not very inclined to go to bat for me. With my father, though, I always had the feeling that he wouldn't let anybody get away with treating me unfairly. Because of this, I too am able to protect my daughter very well and stand behind her. It was really important for me to have a person for six years that I could depend on unquestionably—I've never since had so much loving devotion.

During those years we lived with my father's wife, her mother (who, by the way, was very fond of my father), and her sister. Father was acting in films and on the stage, for example, in *Royal*

Highness and *My Three Angels*. He made a good living and we led a pleasant life. Still, I would have preferred it if my father had had the opportunity to teach, as he had been trained to do. The movie scene was not all that nice, and many Africans and Afro-Germans who worked there glossed over their situation and deluded themselves by saying: "They need us." The pay is good, but either you play the naked wild man or woman, or servants' roles. It doesn't require any acting ability, just that you look different. But when you don't have a choice, then you tend to gloss over whatever you're left with.

I even had a couple of roles as a child and later while I was attending the university. That's how I came to play "Little Muck" in *Perlicke-Perlacke,* was a maid in *After the Fall* in the Schiller Theater, and had a part in Giraudoux's *Judith*. During that period I met many of my father's countrymen; it was really like an extended family. I still keep in touch with some of them now.

My father died suddenly at the age of sixty. He collapsed on the stage from a heart attack. I continued to live with his wife, who was extremely strict with me. She'd stick books under my arms as a way of teaching me fine table manners. It was understood that at meals I was to speak only when spoken to. She sent me to high school and tried to raise me to be a "young lady" with piano and tennis lessons. Her ideas of a young lady didn't, however, stop her from having me jump around naked at thirteen as a wild woman in the film *Jungle Vine*. At the time it didn't bother me, because the adults I knew were doing the same thing. It was my first time in Italy, where the filming took place, I was getting 100 marks a day, a lot of money, and was very glad to escape the strict discipline of home for a few days.

At eighteen I started studying music: piano and voice. I married a man who was studying music, and he and his associates encouraged me. I did well and had no problems as an Afro-German. People who study music are outsiders anyway. Besides, there were many Afro-Americans at the time who were famous singers, and they weren't limited to certain parts either.

After nine years of study I was doing well enough to be offered an engagement at the Kiel Opera House, where I was to appear as a

soloist. However, by then I had already decided that I wanted to
have a baby and was pregnant. The salary they offered was very
low, and I also didn't want to make myself financially dependent
on my husband. I would have had to go to Kiel with my baby. The
difficulties of making a career with a child seemed insurmountable.
I declined the offer.

A year and a half later I separated from my husband and decided
to learn a profession with which I could be independent and earn
our living. I sold my piano and took nurse's training—I couldn't

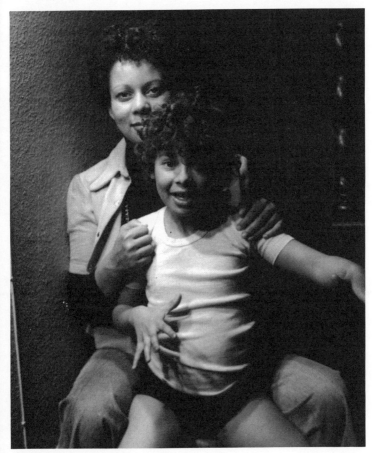

Astrid Berger and her daughter, Julia

have stood having the piano in my life anymore. Today I am still working in this wonderful, but difficult, profession. I've gone as far as one can go in this career and believe that I would do well at anything else I chose to undertake. But I feel really talented only in music.

In the latter part of my life I learned to regard men more critically and discovered that they were in some respects racist exploiters. As my boyfriend that I lived with for a year explained to me in answer to my question why he loved me: "A model or stewardess I can have anytime, but not a Black woman." I left him that very same day.

When my daughter Julia was born, I was twenty-five. Her father is an Italian. The baby and I lived for a while with his parents near Naples. They're lovely people, and we continue to have good relations even after fifteen years. Unfortunately I wasn't able to maintain the relationship with my child's father. I would have loved to have provided Julia with a real family, a family such as I myself missed as a child. Nevertheless this break-up was the right decision for me. I've tried to be a good mother and friend to my daughter and have raised her to be a fearless and proud individual.

I have often felt myself overburdened as a single, working parent, active in the union and politically committed, partly due to the treatment I received as an Afro-German. So often I'm asked questions like "Aren't you glad you can stay here?" And it's extremely hard to tell such a person that I'm German and don't belong anywhere else. By virtue of my black skin I am often in the position of explaining and defending myself, and this has been true for as long as I can remember.

In my professional life, too, I've had to deal with discrimination, more than anything else, because of my color, but not only from patients. For instance, a 350-pound woman, too lazy (though not too sick) to wash herself, once told me: "As a Black hussy you ought to be glad they even let you work in Germany, so come on and wash me!"

But I've experienced so much in my life and done so much that I can also get over one person saying something like that to me.

Miriam Goldschmidt

*"Mirror the invisible /
Play the forgotten"*

Photo: Ruth Walz

Miriam Goldschmidt is an actress of Spanish-Jewish and African descent. She grew up in Düsseldorf and after finishing her studies, she received acting roles working with renowned German directors such as Kortner, Buckwitz, Zadek, and Hollmann and played in a number of cities. In 1971 she decided to go to Paris to work with Peter Brook, feeling that she might experience a more vital form of theater in his acting troupe. Brook accepted her into the International Center for Theatrical Research. He saw it as theater's task to break through the encrustation of language, gesture, and feeling, laying bare humanity's "first nature." Together with the center's multinational ensemble, he also wanted to create a new relationship between actors and the public, a simpler relationship that could bring a person into the world of action, but also into the world of inner feelings—a relationship in which one could find ways of connecting the inner and outer world.

Miriam Goldschmidt mentioned an exercise that the group did together that elucidates the substance of Brook's and the actors' goal of arriving at something essential:

> We stood in a circle, everyone raising a pole from the floor into the air. It didn't matter how different we were, what walk of life we came from, the only thing that mattered was to execute this movement together, to sense who was too fast or too slow, to reach a unity. Here a moment came into being that brought to life the essence of religion, of cult. We often ended the play *Conference of the Birds* with this movement, and when it worked, the audience, whether in Africa, Europe, or the United

States, was always spellbound. A rare moment of common understanding came into being.

For actress Miriam Goldschmidt, this period with the Brook ensemble meant intensive work on herself and, at the same time, on society. They traveled to Africa with the play *Conference of the Birds* and had an extended tour in Australia and the United States that included the plays *L'Os, King Ubu,* and *The Ik*. In Alfred Jarry's *King Ubu,* Goldschmidt played the role of Mother Ubu with stunning success.

In 1980 Goldschmidt left the Brook ensemble to accept an engagement with Peter Stein at the Schaubühne in Berlin, where she has been living since then with Swiss actor Urs Bihler and their two children. She appeared in *The Blacks, Kalldewey,* and *Dibbuk* and performed in Bochum in *Peepshow,* under the direction of Tabori, and in *Titus Andronicus* under Langhoff.

In the 1970s Miriam Goldschmidt wrote a play, which she produced in Basel with Urs Bihler and others. With *Emo and Sanu* she succeeded in communicating to a children's audience the experience she had had with Brook. She considers children's reactions to be an important test of whether theater has an effect upon the audience.

The child's curiosity is international and stems from the need to learn. Curiosity must be satisfied, or else it degenerates and becomes aggressive. . . . We notice that the themes of birth, love, family, fear, jealousy, and death are consistently the central themes among children on the three continents that we played. . . . I'm thinking about the child with no legs in Africa, about the child in the cellar, about the child in the garbage can, about the children who have never seen a tree—the deaf, the mute, the blind, the raped, the abused, the rejected. I think of the children from "good homes"—these are the children I think of. When so many children can, in spite of everything, imagine love, birth, and, above all, fear, then there must be something in common in our relationships, wishes, and possibilities of communicating as people. Here is where I see a path for our theater: the search for strengths and new forms of expression. There I also see a path for teachers and other educators.*

* Quoted in Peter Burri, "Beispiele für aufgehobene Entfremdung" [Models for overcoming alienation], *Nationalzeitung Basel,* 22 July 1974, p. 23.

Miriam Goldschmidt with her son (photo: Ruth Walz)

What Miriam Goldschmidt says here about children holds true also for adult audiences: "Good acting is like a cleansing. It's as though you've been bathed, there is a fragrance about you that you haven't had before, that you've never smelled anywhere before."

A Yiddish Legend * *

As long as the child lives in its mother's belly, an angel with a burning candle stands at its side and teaches it everything there is to learn. When the child is born, the angel blows out the candle. Then the child has forgotten everything.

*   *   *

My angel gave me a mirror
to console me, saying:
"Mirror the invisible
Play the forgotten"
My angel disappeared
and left a darkness
inaccessible to reason
He came back in the shape
of a dog
I gave him the name
Instinct
Slowly I become
that which I have forgotten
Remembering will be my autumn
Knowing my winter

At eighteen I composed a text, that ended
as follows:
"One more step back and
I am with you
Am because I am not
I am over here"

Once I stood by the sea astride
a sand hill
I held the holes
of a baroque flute
—the bequest of my dead lover—
into the wind
Atlantic wind blew

* *Taken from *Theater 1984*, yearbook of the journal *Theater Heute*.

into the flute
it sang
The dead one found space in a hole
He lived
Perhaps I am not an actress
but a hole
Pain makes me round

Racism Here and Now

MAY OPITZ

"Hit Bimbo"
toy, 1950

"Color this black,"
a page in a coloring book

Everyday Racism in Books for Children and Youths

Most of the Afro-Germans born in the 1950s and 1960s, like the preceding generation, grew up without contact with other Black children and/or adults. In spite of the increasing number of African and Afro-American university students, African refugees, and Afro-American military dependents, Blacks continue to be a relatively small part of the population in the Federal Republic.[1] Especially outside of university towns Blacks are still extremely rare, and on the whole most white children probably encounter people of African descent in children's picture books, songs, and games, before they have any personal contact. It is from these fanciful encounters that the first prejudices often arise, foreshadowing actual meetings with Afro-Germans, and having the potential of causing a lasting impression. A look at the image of Africa that German-language children's and youth literature conveys consistently reveals colonial stereotypes and overt or subtle racism. Many of the well-known stories in which people of African descent are described originate in the nineteenth century, during the height of the slave trade and colonial exploitation. Now, as they did then, they disseminate, in unrevised or new editions, the prevailing derogatory stereotype of the work-shirking, ugly, ignorant, exotic, and wild/savage African who is in need of instruction from white Europeans and otherwise unfit for "civilization."

The widespread and popular song of the "Ten Little Negroes" is one of many that serves to teach children about the deficiencies and

128

inferiority of Africans. In this song, the doubly trivialized group, the "*little* Negroes," are brought into a German or European milieu, and in every situation where their ability to fit in is put to the test, they fail. In even the least disparaging version of this song, there is a lone "little Negro" who uses his head and is not doomed to death, but only because he is smart enough to go back to Africa. There he marries and remains. In the versions where return is not mentioned, even the last "little Negro" must die: "They were all gone."

Ten Little Negroes

REFRAIN:

One little, two little, three little, four little, five little Negroes
six little, seven little, eight little, nine little, ten little Negroes.

1. Ten little Negroes, they were sleeping in the barn
   One got lost in the hay. Then there were nine.
2. Nine little Negroes, they went on a hunt.
   One got shot. Then there were eight.
3. Eight little Negroes, they went bowling.
   One rolled to his death. Then there were seven.
4. Seven little Negroes, they went to see a witch.
   One got bewitched. Then there were six.
5. Six little Negroes landed in a swamp.
   One got stuck. Then there were five.
6. Five little Negroes, they liked to drink beer.
   One drank himself to death. Then there were four.
7. Four little Negroes, they cooked a stew.
   One ate himself to death. Then there were three.
8. Three little Negroes, they liked to yell and shout.
   One shouted himself to death. Then there were two.
9. Two little Negroes, they took a trip to Mainz.
   One fell in the Rhine. Then there was one.
10. One little Negro, he was surprisingly smart.
    He went back home to Cameroon and there he took a wife.
    (Popular version)

And when the two have ten children, it goes back to the beginning.[2]

Like ignorance and naïvité, promiscuity and gruesome cannibalism are significant characteristics of African people in adventure stories and comic books. In the hiking song "Negro Revolt in Cuba," said to have sprung up spontaneously in youth groups, the cliché of the bestial wild man is carried to a point that exceeds all bounds of credibility.

There's a Negro revolt in Cuba
Shots ring through the night
In the streets of Havana
Negroes are standing guard.

REFRAIN:
Oomba, oomba, aassa
oomba, oomba, aassa
oomba, eeo, eeo, eehh.

In the streets pus is flowing,
traffic's at a halt
on the corners boys are sitting
feasting on the pus
(Refrain)

And knife-wielding Jo,
a ferocious man-eater,
cuts off just ears and noses
and tries blowing through them
(Refrain)

In the great big tub
the wife looks for her husband,
finding but a few bones
that still bear his scent.
(Refrain)

And the chieftain's sharp teeth
he eats a white cheek
and from an infant's bones
he has a soup made
(Refrain)

Cries pierce the nights
heads roll hither and yon
black Negro hands grab
at gold teeth and more.
(Refrain)

In the thicket and the jungle
human skeletons hang
and the Negroes and the little ones
chew on limbs, smacking their lips
(Refrain)

In the trees bodies hang,
and women stand below,
in anxious anticipation
of the next human meal
(Refrain)

In the rivers bodies swim
with bellies slit open,
the knives still stuck in them
forgotten by the man-eaters.
(Refrain)

When the revolt had run its course
the big, bright sun shone
on the bulging black bellies
too scared even to move their bowels.
(Refrain)[3]

Black people are intrinsically ugly. This message is conveyed especially clearly in the story by Richard von Volkmann-Leander, "The Little Moor and the Gold Princess."

> Once there was a poor little moor, coal-black and not even pure in his color, for his color rubbed off. In the evenings his shirt collar was always very black, and whenever he touched his mother, the prints of all five fingers would be left on her dress. Therefore, she could never stand having him around, and she kicked and pushed him away when he came near her. And it was even worse with other people.
>
> When he turned 14, his parents said it was high time that he learned something so he could earn his bread. So he asked them to allow him to go out into the big wide world and become a musician; he wasn't good for anything else anyway.
>
> But his father thought that he would not be able to make a living as a musician and his mother became very angry, answering only: "Idiot, the only thing you can be is something black!"[4]

The "poor" child—as though being black were not enough, his color rubs off—becomes a chimney sweep in the end. But he cannot get a journeyman's license. At his examination the fact comes to light that the black of the "moor" doesn't come from cleaning the chimney, but from the "blackamoor" himself: "So, to their horror, everyone discovered the truth about him."[5] Having been chased away, he soon finds employment with a couple, where all he has to do is stand on the back of their coach "so that people would see right away that they were well-to-do people." Even here he gets chased away, when the "master" discovers that the little moor's color rubs off. The consoling words of the well-to-do gentleman's wife are significant:

> Of course it is a great misfortune to be a moor, and especially if his color rubs off. But he should not despair; rather be good and have courage, then in time he would become just as white as other people.[6]

Indeed, through conscientious practice on the violin that the woman gave him upon his departure, the "moor" gradually becomes whiter over the course of his travels. When he meets the pretty Gold Princess one day, and she spurns him as a suitor because of his appearance—now a "mousey gray"—he berates himself for his futile efforts for her favor, which he cannot possibly win: "You wanted to marry the Gold Princess? How stupid can you be! You shouldn't be surprised that people laugh at you."[7]

When he meets the beautiful woman for the second time, she has now fallen to the rank of Tin Princess and is only exhibited at carnivals. Because she refused to have someone else choose for her, and was very particular and turned her nose up at one suitor after another, her gold chipped off little by little, until she was nothing more than tin. Now here she stands, punished with ugliness for her willfulness, while the "moor," who strove to accommodate himself, was appropriately rewarded, in that in the meantime he had become a splendid figure of a white man, who for quite some time "had been without a speck of blackness." The story, a lesson in racism and sexism, ends in the predictable admonition "that much in life is fleeting, beauty as well as ugliness, and that everything depends on what lies underneath."[8]

Volkmann-Leander's story is like the song of the "Ten Little Negroes," which is modeled on Frank Green's "Ten Little Indians," written in the mid-nineteenth century. More recent stories, tales, and travelogues evoke similar racist and sexist stereotypes and in just as blatant a fashion.

Characters also are usually presented in such a way that boys identify with the white male protagonist, girls, with the white female secondary character. Blacks, regardless of the setting, appear as more or less insignificant marginal characters. Very often they appear as houseboys or maids, hunting crew or animal keepers.

Brigitta Benzing, who made a critical analysis of four hundred books for children and youths, comments: "Africans in these books are merely a part of the exotic scenery."[9]

The relationship of Blacks to whites is almost always one of dependent and unquestioned subordination. Beyond the personal level, such relations are further carried on with the uncritical acceptance of relationships of dependency between industrialized and still underdeveloped countries. In every case master and servant relationships are presented as inevitable—biologically determined and with a permanence independent of each other, rather than as the result of historical and social forces. By the same token, white heroes appear in the role of well-intentioned missionaries and development experts, bent on bringing the African people out of their antediluvian existence, a task that requires great capacity for empathy and sensitivity:

> Dear Reader, have you ever tried to imagine how a person from the Iron Age would react if he suddenly found himself in the middle of the twentieth century? We don't know what he would think and feel, but we can be pretty certain that he would feel anxiety and confusion and do everything wrong. But in reality there are still many people living on earth today who can be compared with Iron Age people.[10]

> There is still much to be done. The United Nations and the great industrialized countries are helping with money and teachers. With these funds, hospitals, schools, factories, power stations, and roads are being built.[11]

In fiction, nonfiction, and textbooks, history and current events are depicted such that the plunder and subjugation of so-called

". . . so now you see what they do with all the stuff we send to the Third World" (*Bild am Sonntag*, December 12, 1980).

third world nations are not treated thematically. Thus the seeds from which racist and paternalistic feelings of superiority toward people from these countries develop are planted in the minds of white children.

By playing up the ostensibly selfless assistance currently being provided by "first world" nations,

> the moral reflection and reversal on the part of the former colonial powers is glossed over, giving the impression that investments in the "Third World" benefit the people there; there is no mention of the fact that all the profits revert to the metropoles, their products are produced without exception according to Western market interests; no mention that road planning, school construction, etc. serve neocolonial purposes exclusively: the rapid opening of areas of raw materials, the formation of a national bourgeoisie in schools and universities, which oppresses its own people in the desire for foreign capital and its concomitant privileges.[12]

Misinformation that begins in the nursery with myths, half-truths, and lies continues, for example, in the one-sided reporting of the mass media, ultimately rooting itself deep within the collective consciousness of society. Gordon W. Allport writes about the origin and function of prejudice in society:

> At the core of every differentiated and layered society lies the possible temptation to achieve economic, sexual, political, and status advantages through the intentional (or even unintentional) exploitation of minorities. In order to enjoy these gains, prejudice is disseminated by those who stand to profit from it the most.[13]

Viewed in this manner, prejudices serve to stabilize the existing system. They mask as well as mediate existing dependency relationships for the benefit of those who hold power.

Afro-Germans between Self-Assertion and Self-Denial

> A man who has a language consequently possesses the world expressed and implied by that language.[14]

Not only numerous adventure books but also numerous textbooks present people from Africa as "Also-People" of a "Leftover

(Third) World."[15] The positive image put forth of their own "First World" in these books depends on devaluing the cultural forms of people in impoverished lands, whose language, religion, and art are held to be inferior to their own.

For Black children growing up in Germany, such presentations make it difficult to assume a positive approach to their African heritage. Subtle feelings of inferiority are conveyed to them, which stifle the development of a positive self-image, unless such negative concepts are balanced out with a positive side. In Fanon's words:

> I begin to suffer from not being a white man to the degree that the white man imposes discrimination on me, makes me a colonized native, robs me of all worth, all individuality, tells me that I am a parasite on the world, that I must bring myself as quickly as possible into step with the white world.[16]

As a rule, Afro-Germans grow up with white people as their care-takers and often find in the course of their socialization precious little opportunity for identifying positively with people of African and/or Afro-German/European heritage:

1. Afro-Germans usually do not appear in the children's and youth books that they read. When people with black skin are presented as characters, they are almost exclusively Africans in the above-mentioned stereotypical roles. For girls it is even more debilitating, for

   people in children's picture books are mostly male—policemen, soldiers, firemen, showmen, construction workers. Where women are engaged in any occupations at all, they work in service jobs, in farming, in trade, or in a school. While picture-book boys are active in sports, picture-book girls tend to be sedentary, doing handicrafts. Based on an investigation of the 112 most widely read picture books in nursery schools in Bonn, Cornelia Hagemann of the Rhineland Teachers' College found that it is with picture books that the young child first begins learning about a male-dominated world in which men are active and women are passive.[17]

2. Positive identification with an African heritage is further encumbered because in occidental culture "black" symbolizes evil and the undesirable. In this way, a stigma becomes attached to the most visible sign of difference—skin color.

3. In school, the history of Blacks is seldom thematicized, and when it is, then it is often only by connecting it with and emphasizing European history. In the treatment of American history, for example, usually no mention is made of the fact that half of the Americans who drafted the constitution of the United States were slaveholders, and that, by decree (the Dred Scott decision of 1857), Blacks were excluded from the fundamental rights put forth in the constitution.

Only in the exceptional German textbook does African history begin before the "discovery" of the continent by Europeans.[18] Thus the idea is perpetuated that Africa has no history of its own, or at least none worth mentioning.

4. The connection between German colonial history and the history of Africans and Afro-Germans in Germany has, to my knowledge, thus far not been made in history books. Much of the prevailing reappraisal of National Socialism is limited to focusing on the mass extermination of six million Jews, while completely ignoring the persecution and extermination of other "minorities."[19] Those crimes that do receive attention are not infrequently (mis)interpreted as the catastrophic result of Hitler's tyranny and are not looked at within the broader context of German history. Essays of school students reflect this very clearly:

"Tens of thousands of Jews were gassed. I don't know why, but Hitler always had something against Jews." (Seventeen-year-old vocational student)

"Hitler wanted a pure German people with blond hair and blue eyes, even though he himself had dark hair and dark eyes." (Sixteen-year-old vocational student)[20]

Such compartmentalization and suppression of historical facts make it virtually impossible to really come to terms with existing social structures. With regard to the colonial period, such crimes and mass murders can hardly be excused, for then there was no "Hitler" whose dictatorial rule could be blamed. To date, no one has critically examined this period. "On the contrary: due to the idealistic enthusiasm of the colonial perpetrators and writers, only a kind of euphoria remains from the few years of German colonial activity."[21] Although German history books do indicate which powers, acting from which strategic motives, struggled over spheres of influence at different periods and in different places, they do not say by what means, with what consequences, and at whose expense those conflicts were carried out.

5. It is not just the representatives of extreme rightist groups who attempt to depict the presence of foreigners and the rise of bicultural families as a danger to the German people. Leading politicians and respected scholars also speak of "domination by foreigners," "infiltration," and "social explosives." Up to now the Federal Republic has not regarded itself as an immigrants' country and refuses civil rights to many "foreigners" who have been living here for several generations. It thereby prevents the evolution of a multicultural society and takes pains to codify "guest worker status" for people from other cultures. Apart from the irony of this phrase (guests are not usually "invited" to work), foreigners are explicitly and implicitly expected to leave the Federal Republic as soon as their labor is no longer needed. Although the Federal Republic was and will continue to be dependent on foreign labor for its industrial growth,[22] no preparations were undertaken for the social integration and accommodation of the women and men recruited from neighboring European countries.[23] Integration is still perceived of more as a one-sided process of foreigners accommodating themselves to German society than as a reciprocal process of mutual rapprochement in which German society must also find a new identity, one not based on exclusion and separation. Turkish kabob, Greek gyros, Italian pizza, Indian and African teas have long since become a regular part of everyday life in the Federal Republic. Nevertheless the people who have made these and other enrichments possible through their contribution to cultural diversity are regarded with caution. Of course, blatantly racist comments denying the rights of people residing here are rarely made aloud. However, comments like those of CDU [Christian Democratic Union] representative Spranger reveal that the myth of the German people as an ethnic monolith is alive and well:

We must take seriously the legitimate concerns of the German population. This is especially true for those people who are concerned about their own identity, because they fear becoming a minority in their own country.[24]

Afro-Germans, Asian-Germans, Sinti-Germans, and other "hyphenated Germans" seem not to count as part of the German population to Spranger. For the groups in question it means that in spite of their

German citizenship and their having grown up in German society, they are neither wanted nor recognized in this society. Because they appear to be foreigners they are most often treated as such—as people who do not really belong in this country.

They're People Like Us

No! We really don't have anything against Blacks
My wife and I
why, we go every year
to Africa:
That simple culture, the carefree life
that's really something else
and they dance
just great

We really believe
that all people are the *same*.
No one should be discriminated against,
just because he's *different*.

That Africans
are at a different
stage of development
is clear, of course

Well yes
you can see
how little
they're able
to control their famine
it was like that with us too, once
overpopulation and all

We've got to stop
pumping
those millions in development aid
every year
into the dark continent:
What do they do with the money anyhow?

Buy arms and
beat each other
over the heads.
And the way they treat their women!
terrible!

Naw! first they've got to
learn to be
reasonable.
Else they'll multiply
like flies
and just want to
live off us.

I mean, as much as we may love them
we haven't got it all that good ourselves.

MAY OPITZ

Afro-German

You're Afro-German?
. . . ah, I see: African *and* German.
What an interesting mixture!
You know, a lot of folks, they still think
    mulattoes, they're not
    as smart
    as whites

    I don't believe that.
    I think: with adequate education . . .
        You're really lucky that you grew up *here*.
        With German parents, even. How about that!

You planning to go back?
What? You've never been to Papa's country?
    What a shame. . . . Well, if you ask me:
A background like that, it sure does leave its mark.
Me, for example, I'm from Westphalia,
and I think
that's where I belong . . .

Lord have mercy! All the suff'rin' in the world!
    Be glad

you didn't stay in the bush.
        You wouldn't be where you are today!
I mean you're really a smart girl.
        If you work hard in your studies,
        you can help your people in Africa: That's what
        you were predestined for,
                they'll sure listen to you,
    but for us—
        it's sort of a lower culture . . .

What do you mean? Do something here. What d'you
wanna do here? Ok, ok, it's not all smooth sailing. But I
think everybody ought to sweep his own doorstep first!

MAY OPITZ

Afro-German

. . . hm, I see.
You can be glad you're not Turkish, huh?
I mean: this harassment of foreigners is just awful,
        do you get some of that, too, sometimes?
". . ."
Yeah, but *those* problems I have myself.
I don't think you can blame everything on color,
and as a woman, it's not easy anywhere.
Fr'instance, a girlfriend of mine:
            she's pretty fat
            she's got all kinds of problems!
But you seem to be pretty relaxed.
Anyway, I feel
        that Blacks've held onto
        such a natural attitude toward life.
Whereas here: everything's pretty much gone to pieces
I think I'd be glad if I were you.
            We really can't be proud
            of German history
and, after all, you are not that black.

MAY OPITZ

Identification and Self-Valuation

Attitudes of Germans toward Various Groups of Foreigners			
	POSITIVE	NEUTRAL	NEGATIVE	NO RESPONSE
Spaniards	26	55	15	4
Yugoslavians	24	53	19	4
Greeks	24	56	16	4
Italians	19	51	26	4
Portuguese	14	61	19	6
Vietnamese	13	56	26	5
Turks	8	40	48	4
Persians	7	50	38	5
Black Africans	7	55	33	5
North Africans	6	55	33	6
Pakistanis	5	48	42	5

Survey by INFAS (1981/82)[25]

From the time they are children, Afro-Germans realize that their bicultural background is seen as unusual. Moreover, they find themselves confronted with the fact that, to many people, their African appearance signifies cultural backwardness and a number of other characteristics deemed undesirable.

By virtue of their appearance, they are forced to grapple with their identity in German society, a society that essentially considers itself white. At its worst, this means internalizing the racism directed at them, which then leads to self-contempt and self-denial. Many Afro-Germans are quite familiar with the desire to be white, a childhood fantasy dating from the time they realized their differentness, or the desire to emigrate or to flee someday to a country where they will no longer be conspicuous, no longer have to go through life as an exception. Many Afro-Germans respond to the racism of their society by attempting to adapt to societal stereotypes that determine the image of Blacks. They allow themselves to be forced into the roles of the affable, spirited, funny, wild type who add flavor to the lives of white people.

The exotic sells well everywhere. The Berlin newspaper *Zitty,* which considers itself an alternative paper, offered a title page in October 1982 that could not have been a more telling example of German racism. Below the headline "Blacks in Berlin: Beautiful and Coffee-Brown" is an African man in a tigerskin. A white woman embraces him from behind, but all that can be seen of her are arms and hands with red-lacquered nails; the African himself is pictured without a head. The article was part of a series entitled "We're Getting Some Color," which ran for several issues.

Longings for a different, idyllic world that promises totally different enticements from one's own have long been acted upon and exploited by every commercial sector, especially the field of tourism. It is not by chance that a company like Hapag Lloyd Lines lures travelers for its cruises to Africa, India, and Indonesia with slogans like "Encounters with the Poorest of the Poor."[26] This advertisement speaks to all those who regret their loss of emotionality and connection with nature and encourages them to effortlessly consume those lost qualities somewhere else. A desire for the unusual and the different is frequently projected onto Afro-Germans. For them this means being put under the pressure of expectations that have nothing to do with them as individuals or their identity. To the degree that they attempt it, Afro-Germans only rarely succeed in meeting the expectations of those they seek to impress. Apart from their appearance, they have little that is exotic to offer: they speak perfect German, have German names, and/or have no direct connection with Africa or the United States, and live a very normal everyday German existence.

The "In-between World" as Opportunity

The racism in Germany, which is mostly covert, affects Afro-Germans' self-perception and perception of foreigners such that they see themselves as living in an in-between world. In the course of their socialization, Afro-Germans develop a special instinct for recognizing both the positive and the negative sides of special treatment given them as a result of their African or Afro-German background. They cannot totally wipe away either the African or the German part of their background or make it unnoticeable. Any attempt in that direction is ultimately doomed to failure. Illusions of making themselves over can only be sustained through repression and isolation. The desire to be white or to be perceived as exotic would force them to push everything Black or, better, everyone Black out of sight and to remove themselves from contact. To say "I am Afro-German" would then mean "I am not really Black, not like the others who really have problems and/or are really backward." Such repression does not change the expectations of others. It merely prevents access to solidarity with other Afro-Germans—bringing only the advantage of ensuring a position of singularity due to isolation on all sides.

In those cases where Afro-Germans do not accept the external imposition of what seems to be a contradiction, that of being *both* African and German, a self-awareness can develop that necessitates no such fragmentation. The path that Afro-Germans take depends in the final analysis on their individual potential and interests and on their willingness to connect with each other.

In recent decades Blacks all around the world have managed to win more respect for themselves, forcing the world to come to terms with the issue of racism at a more honest and fundamental level. This has not been without its effects, particularly on younger Afro-Germans. In contrast to the generations of war and postwar babies, they will have an easier time locating other possibilities and finding the courage to make their situation and interests visible in German society.

Exotic

After first blackening me up
they dragged me through the mud
wanting ultimately to make me black
absolutely uncalled-for
                    to look on the dark side.

[Exotik

nachdem sie mich erst anschwärzten
zogen sie mich dann durch den kakao
un mir schließlich weiß machen zu wollen
es sei vollkommen unangebracht
                  schwarz zu sehen.]

                  MAY OPITZ

Notes

1. Exact figures are not yet available, since the census does not register color or national origin.

2. Cited in Gisela Fremgen, ed., *. . . und wenn du dazu noch schwarz bist. Berichte schwarzer Frauen in der Bundesrepublick* (Bremen, 1984), p. 39.

3. Florian Deltgen, "Der Neger im deutschen Kinder- und Jugendlied," *Kölner Zeitschrift für Soziologie und Sozialpsychologie* 29, H. 1 (1977): 124–25.

4. In Richard v. Volkmann-Leander, *Träumereien an französischen Kaminen*, 2d ed. (Bremen, 1969), p. 163.

5. Ibid., p. 164.

6. Ibid., pp. 165, 166.

7. Ibid., p. 171.

8. Ibid., pp. 173, 174.

9. Brigitta Benzing, "Zum Afrika-Bild in deutschsprachigen Kinder- und Jugendbüchern," in *Schule und Dritte Welt Nr. 45. Texte und Materialen fur den Unterricht,* ed. Federal Ministry for Economic Cooperation (Bonn, 1974), p. 10.

10. K. Olson, *Aus Njagwe wird Peter,* cited in ibid., p. 13.

11. Robert Clayton and John Miles, *Zentral- und Ostafrika: Eine Geographie und Völkerkunde für junge Leser,* vol. 9, cited in *Die Menschen sind arm, weil sie arm sind,* ed. Jörg Becker and Carlotte Oberfeld (Frankfurt, 1977), p. 128.

12. Wolfram Fromlet, "Die Menschen sind arm, weil sie arm sind. Die 'Dritte Welt' im Sachbuch für Jugendliche der BRD" in Becker and Oberfeld, *Die Menschen sind arm.* p. 128.

13. Gordon W. Allport, *Die Natur des Vorurteils* (Koln, 1971), p. 242.

14. Frantz Fanon, *Black Skin, White Masks,* trans. Charles Lam Markmann (New York, 1967), p. 18.

15. See Karla Fohrbeck, Andreas J. Wiesand, and Renate Zahar, *Heile Welt und Dritte Welt: Schulbuchanalyse* (Opladen, 1971).

16. Fanon, *Black Skin*, p. 98.

17. FU-Info, "*Bilderbücher: Männer aktiv. Frauen pasiv*" (Berlin, 1982), p. 14.

18. Europe is apparently still undiscovered.

19. I put the term *minorities* in quotation marks here because those with power impose the status of "minority," "marginal group," or "outsider" through the exploitation of their power.

20. Dieter Bossmann, ed., *Folgen eines Tabus: Auszüge aus Schüleraufsätzen heute* (Frankfurt, 1977), quoted in Jörg Becker, "Die verpaßten Chancen der Erneuerung, Rassismus im deutschen Kinderbuch," in *Das Gift der frühen Jahre,* ed. Regula Renschler and Roy Preiswerk (Basel, 1981), p. 201.

21. Gert Paczensky, *Die Weißen kommen* (Hamburg, 1970), p. 52.

22. "The economies of all highly industrialized Western European nations will continue to be dependent on foreign workers in the future, as can be concluded from the prognoses for economic developments and for labor needs" (Cappenberger Discussion, *Ausländerpolitik im Zielkonflikt* [Köln, 1982], p. 52).

23. "In this phase, economic interests alone determine the extent of the recruitment and thus the scope of the employment of foreigners. The consequences of introducing a large number of foreign laborers were not considered in the planning and remain completely ignored" (Ministry for Workers' Health and Social Affairs of the State of North-Rhein Westfalia, *Leitlinien der Landesregierung NRW zur Ausländerpolitik* [Düsseldorf, 1981], p. 21).

24. From *Ansprache des Parlamentarischen Staatssekretärs im Bundesministerium des Innern.* Carl-Dieter Spranger, in *betrifft: Ausländerpolitik,* ed. Bundesminster des Innern (Bonn, 1983), p. 92.

25. INFAS, *Meinungen und Einstellungen zu Ausländerproblemen—Endbericht* (Bonn/Bad Godesberg, 1982), cited in Georg Tsiakalos, *Ausländerfeindlichkeit—Tatsachen und Erklärungsversuche* (München, 1983), p. 104.

26. Peter Schütt, *Der Mohr hat seine Schuldigkeit getan: Gibt es Rassismus in der Bundesrepublik?* (Dortmund, 1981), p. 39.

Laura Baum (age 22),
Katharina Oguntoye (age 27),
May Opitz (age 25)

Three Afro-German Women in
Conversation with Dagmar Schultz:
The First Exchange for This Book

DAGMAR: "To be beautiful"—What does it mean?

KATHARINA: Yesterday as I was passing by three guys, one of them said: "Hey, look out: Black!" Immediately I was aware of this as a rejection of Blackness, on the one hand, and on the other hand, that there was also an idea of—"Hmm, how about that!" I didn't react to it at all, because I was too busy trying to understand this two-sided thing.

LAURA: Recently I ran into two drunks. As I was going by, one said to the other: "Hey, look!"; the other said: "Charcoal lighter—hope it burns." To which the first one responded: "Hey, she's good looking!" and the other answered: "But she's not European."

As a colored woman you're mostly viewed as exotic, it fits the usual stereotype found everywhere. With men it's different, I think.

KATHARINA: Since we're not perceived as European, internally we develop this feeling of being different.

Awhile ago you were talking about your mother, who felt that if you develop more toward the African side, and therefore look more African than European, then people like you less. I remember how a friend once told me that I surely looked more like my father. (She neither knew my father nor had she ever seen a picture of him.) I vehemently refused to accept that and was inwardly very confused about having repudiated it so strongly, for I know I resemble my father and have always been sort of proud of it.

It might have been like the situation with those three guys: I resisted being pigeon-holed like that, but at the same time I felt bad, because in doing this, I separated myself from African-looking

women. African women don't fit the European ideal of beauty; for
them there's only the role of the "exotic beauty." And I didn't want
to be seen like that. It really enrages me that this society makes it so
hard for me to regard African women as beautiful. Words don't
really exist for me to describe African looks with regard to African
women or myself without these inferior standards of beauty. It's
not my brown skin that is considered beautiful, but my light-
brown skin. . . . With my broad nose it was a similar situation: on
the one hand I rejected it because it made me look more African,
and on the other hand, rejecting this part of myself made me feel
bad, because I like broad noses on people.

MAY: For a long time I carried with me an image of myself as
being ugly because I look African. Fortunately, I overcame it at
some point. I'd even like having a broader nose. I think broad noses
are fantastic.

However, it really depressed me when I found out in Kenya how
terribly important it is there (at least as important as here) to have a
thin nose, straight hair, and, if at all possible, not to be too dark.
They have creams to lighten the skin, and on important occasions,
women try to straighten their hair with hot combs.

I met two sisters who felt more uncomfortable in Tanzania than
here—they felt more stared at and more marveled at there precisely
because of their lighter skin color.

KATHARINA: It must have been really frustrating to be conspicuous again just when they both thought that finally in Tanzania they
wouldn't stand out anymore. . . .

MAY: Yes, their father thought they should decide between a life
here in Germany or in Africa, and that in any case, in Africa it
would be easier for them. Both of them disagreed, saying that in
Tanzania they were always, though unintentionally, the center of
attention.

KATHARINA: And actually, that has nothing whatsoever to do
with you yourself, but only with how light or dark you are.

DAGMAR: You once said that you now perceive of yourself as
beautiful and that this wasn't the case before. Do you know how
and why that changed?

KATHARINA: I was an ugly duckling, but everyone knew I'd turn out to be a swan. I had no idea how—I was so short and fat and had a short neck, but everybody kept telling me: "You'll be a beautiful woman." Was it different with you?

MAY: Yes, the dumb thing was that when I really could have used it, nobody told me I was beautiful. It changed though when I fell head-over-heels in love. Then everything was just wonderful, and I saw myself as beautiful, too. But I never actually looked at myself in a mirror somewhere and decided I was pretty. I think it came more from an inner feeling. I felt good, and the world was all rosy. For the first time people told me that I was pretty—women, too.

KATHARINA: How you feel about yourself also has a lot to do with how often you get compliments like that.

MAY: That's true; it's often like that; when I'm feeling blah and look in the mirror and think: "My God, *no way*," then nobody else has any reason to tell me I look good.

LAURA: During puberty I felt absolutely ugly. So ugly that I actually had a complex. I was afraid to go out in the street, and I felt really uptight.

MAY: Recently I saw some pictures from back when I felt so ugly. I was rather surprised but I found myself to be really pretty.

KATHARINA: With me it was just the opposite. I feel like I looked ugly in those pictures and can't understand at all how people could have told me I was beautiful. Maybe it was due to my sunny disposition and didn't have much so do with my outward appearance.

MAY: I was never really told I was pretty, but I felt like I belonged. I sensed that others liked being with me and found me fun to be with. Maybe a number of things figured into this. For example, my parents never allowed me to wear clothes that were "in." I always had to wear hand-me-downs from a distant cousin who was three times fatter than me. My grandma would just put an elastic band in them and then thought they were "pretty." I went around in tents. I also couldn't wear long pants and I always felt kind of shut out, especially since in those days it was very important to wear jeans or corduroys and not plaid pleated skirts.

LAURA: With me it was just the opposite—my mother always dressed me up. I often heard people say that as a child or teenager I was described as pretty. During puberty, when I felt so ugly, I was amazed to hear that. Most of the time I got: "Well, she has a pretty face." With time that became more frequent. I could never really believe or accept it, for when I looked at myself in the mirror, I'd get ill. Now I don't hear "pretty" any more, but "beautiful." In the beginning I was pleasantly surprised, because people attributed something to me that I myself didn't even see. And slowly I'm finding out that I am beautiful.

KATHARINA: It's also really a question of what beautiful or ugly is. I find that I often perceive people to be attractive only from a distance, because I find them to be ugly in the way they express themselves.

DAGMAR: The word "beautiful" does have a different meaning from "pretty" or "good-looking." Is that related to what you were just saying?

LAURA: That brings to mind my reaction when people would make it clear that my color, compared with being white, had an "exotic" attraction for them, a foreignness, but not quite as foreign as black. I get this "beautiful" thing at school. A student said to me that mulattoes were especially beautiful people. She finds white pale, but very black, on the other hand, not good either, because she can't recognize faces, they're "too dark." This mixture is seen as the most desirable thing a person could want.

KATHARINA: I can't take that seriously. In the summertime Germans lie out in the sun and try to get as brown as me. In this case it's considered positive to be a different color. Otherwise it isn't positive. I'm very skeptical whenever I hear something like that.

LAURA: It also means that people evaluate each other using purely external factors. That then gives a stereotyped or ideal image of colored women as singing, dancing, laughing, and being otherwise erotic and exotic. I stopped feeling good when I realized that a certain kind of behavior was also linked to this "beauty"; a kind of behavior that's not German or European. That is, rather than a cool and relatively calm temperament, another very specific kind of demeanor was expected instead. That bothered me, and I didn't want to fit into those conceptions. Sometimes it was nice, but, in general, it wasn't.

KATHARINA: Would you rather be white?

LAURA: I wouldn't say that; but I wish I didn't have this status of uniqueness.

DAGMAR: You just said that it's nice sometimes. What were the nice parts?

LAURA: It has to do with my self-confidence, which wasn't so well developed before. The status of uniqueness provided me with a kind of affirmation that often satisfied me when I was feeling bad about myself. While I wasn't acknowledged as an equal, I still received a boost from it. It was kind of nice, although I felt sort of ambivalent about it.

MAY: There's a lot involved in this "beautiful" thing. Actually "beautiful" has more the connotation that people find you interesting because of your color and because they expect that there's an exciting story behind it. A lot of people assume that I have a particular relationship to Africa, even when I explain that I've never lived there. They tell me that they were in Africa, took a drumming workshop, and are fascinated with how Africans dance. . . . I always wonder why they're telling me this. When they really realize that I don't speak any African languages and can't dance like an African, their interest quickly disappears: "Oh, then you're already Europeanized."

LAURA: I haven't had such extreme experiences as that. Often I do notice disappointment, but a certain interest too. People see that it's not so wonderful as they'd pictured it. But there always remains a little piece for them to fantasize about. I've often picked up a feeling of inferiority among such people and that they quite consciously idealize me and my "specialness," into a fantasy. That kind of stuff I don't need because for one thing I'm not a fairy princess and I don't come from someplace with strange creatures and smells . . .

It often happens that when people ask me my name and I answer: "Laura," I get reactions like "But that's not an exotic name at all." Frequently they look at me with such a well-meaning smile that it's clear that they weren't seeing *me* at all. For example, when somebody would address me with "Hi, Trixi," and I'd answer that I'm Laura and not Trixi, they'd say, "Oh, you mulatto girls all look alike." Always these generalizations and mixing us up. . . .

KATHARINA: That's always made me suspicious. I really only ever believed my friend Karin when she said she had seen a woman who looked like me. Otherwise, I never believe for a moment that someone else looked like me. When the "Afro-look" came in, giving credence to the idea that everyone who wore an Afro looked alike . . .

LAURA: Right. Angela Davis or Joan Armatrading . . .

KATHARINA: I actually thought that I looked like Joan Armatrading, and if others who knew me well said it, that was fine with me.

DAGMAR: How do others see you—how do you handle it?

MAY: It often happens with me that people have their own expectations and ignore what I say. When I tell them that I grew up here and have spent my entire life here, the question still might come afterward: "Yes, and when are you going back?" Crazy. Now and then I have the feeling of not belonging anywhere; on the other hand I've grown up here, speak this language, actually feel secure here, and can express myself as I want. I share a background with these people here even if they don't accept me. "Yes, I'm German," I say, perhaps out of spite, to shake up their black-and-white thinking.

KATHARINA: Often I really want to get people away from the narrow-minded attitude that German is just blond and blue-eyed. There are so many different types of people here.

MAY: I often used to think I had to justify my being here. In the meantime, I've realized that I'm bold enough to just ask if there's something wrong when somebody looks at me curiously. Often the person will recognize his rigid way of thinking and the audacity with which he asks the most personal questions.

KATHARINA: In my experience, people of mixed heritage always have special positions in groups. I think we also bring part of it upon ourselves, because we are noticeable and have to deal with both our African and our German parts. As a result, we develop an agility that's not required of a white child. In a seminar, for example, a woman spoke to me, saying that I must have already learned to express myself well in groups some time before then. I'm not expected to be able to speak German well, but I simply present myself the way I am. Then that counts as being intelligent.

LAURA: Yes, that happens a lot, People think I'm a foreigner. If I speak flawless German, I get this "admiration."

MAY: The way they speak to you is sort of paternalistic or patronizing. They take on this attitude automatically. As soon as they see me, they think I can't speak German. I remember a baker that I used to go to often. Each time he would explain every little thing with extravagant gestures. Once he even explained how the weather was . . . I just laughed.

KATHARINA: Continuously playing this same old game makes it hard to make real contact with people. When someone acts like that, I pull back.

LAURA: Well, on the shopkeeper's level you can more or less accept it, get angry about it, or laugh; nothing will change. Now and then I say: "I'm a German." Otherwise, when I meet people I've often made a point of saying that I'm no different from anyone else and would prefer that they have no special expectations of me on the basis of how I look. After we've gotten to know each other better, people often acknowledge having had certain expectations of me, but as a result of my speaking to them about it, we've managed to reach a level where we can change this.

MAY: That always gets on my nerves. No matter where I go, I know some guy is going to say something to me—especially at parties: "Well, where do you come from?"

LAURA: Only from guys, not from women?

MAY: With me it's mostly guys. Recently at an ecology party a guy came up and asked where I was from. I answered, from Münster. So he hounded me until I finally said that my father was from Ghana. Then he said: "I have a fiancée from Rwanda, and you remind me of her." I wasn't the least bit interested; he even dug a picture of this fiancée out of his pocket. I didn't look anything like her. He clung on to me until I abruptly said I wasn't interested in talking with him.

Recently another guy came on to me like that: "Where do you come from? Where were you born?"—"I come from Münster and I was born in Hamburg." Finally, to his satisfaction, I did reveal where my parents were from. But then he wasn't ready for the third degree I gave him: "And where do you come from? And your father? And your mother?" The guy was visibly taken back, but he answered very obediently.

LAURA: That reminds me also that people often attribute things to African men and women that are missing in themselves. I'm often confronted with the sexist view that Africans are uncivilized and have a primeval sense of rhythm, know how to vent their feelings better, because they aren't so restrained by standards as Europeans are . . .

KATHARINA: They just project these images onto people without looking closely.

LAURA: And the image is continuously disseminated by the media.

KATHARINA: And primarily by the entertainment industry—the clincher is the *Zitty* magazine caption "We're Getting Some Color."

LAURA: We're getting some color, fun; action as opposed to gray, as opposed to drab, as opposed to white, as opposed to boring.

MAY: In May there was a national conference in Münster of all groups involved with development politics. I had previously written an article on neocolonial thought patterns and neoracism, and I handed it out in my workshop. The people found it so good that they urged me to send it to the local newspaper. The article was written from various perspectives: what I find objectionable in others, in my workshop, and in myself. Among other things I wrote that, earlier, in a frame of mind of the-whiter-the-better, I had stressed: "I'm not black—I'm mulatto." The article was adopted and in the introduction it said, of course: "M.O. questions our thinking and our dealings, as a member of the solidarity movement, and as a mulatto." When I saw the introduction I was very disappointed; after all, it's an alternative newspaper, and the fellow is very politically committed to development and has written several really good books on South Africa.

DAGMAR: How do you see the question of not belonging and being appropriated at the same time?

KATHARINA: When I was between fifteen and twenty, I often had the experience of being thought of not only as an African or American; every possible nationality claimed me. For example, a Sinti gypsy once came up to me and asked if I were Sinti and was quite disappointed that I wasn't. The same thing happened to me with a Filipino, with a person from Grenada, with some others. They all thought I was from their country. I felt strangely appropriated.

MAY: People try to classify me right away: from north Africa, from South Africa, from Argentina or Hawaii or India—depending on where they had just been on vacation, so that they think that I'm typical for that place.

LAURA: I haven't experienced that here yet except that I'm taken for an American. But to people in the GDR I was from Africa or Cuba. In the GDR it was clear that I wasn't of North American origin; that's rare there.

KATHARINA: It's a weird feeling when every possible culture lays claim to me. That's how I got the idea that I could pass for this one or the other; actually I'm nothing—I fit in everywhere.

MAY: Before, I used to think I didn't belong anywhere, because I stood out everywhere. I thought, I can never be just me; I'm always walking around in this skin color. Then the idea of a country like Brazil, where the population is mixed, consoled me; there, without being particularly conspicuous, I could be accepted. That gave me a feeling of internationality.

KATHARINA: I know that feeling, but it's difficult too: I'm not a Sinti, nor am I from the Philippines or Grenada; I can't pass for one of these nationalities because I don't know what it feels like to be from there. It was clear to me that I feel like a German and feel the closest connections here: to my language; to my growing up here. At a certain point that became what I've identified with. The options for identification offered me from being appropriated by other groups were very confusing to me; sure, it was exciting to feel international, but it also took too much out of me.

MAY: It's basically two different things: the one, being judged from outside; the other, feeling that you belong to a group.

Another thing that comes with being judged or appropriated is, for example, Turks complaining to me about their trouble with

Germans and not even seeing me as a German. Even though I can understand their problems, I'm still not a part of them. Since I've come to understand this conflict, I feel more conscious of being a German and also recognize the differences that are there, despite everything we have in common due to discrimination.

KATHARINA: I was always against being equated with Blacks and thereby being separated from Germans.

Once I was with an Afro-German guy in an American disco. On the one hand I found it was great that only Afro-Americans were there, but on the other hand I felt like I was in a ghetto where I couldn't move and behave freely because I was too unfamiliar in the milieu. I would have had to join them entirely—and I just want to be the way I am.

MAY: How do you mean, be the way you are?

KATHARINA: For example, I was ready to get to know Blacks as an Afro-German, but I immediately pulled back when they wanted to claim me.

MAY: I resist being appropriated just as much. Sometimes I find that Africans are appalled that I've never been to Ghana and can't speak any African language. Then I try to explain to them that there are other things that are important to me. But when they refuse to understand that, I pull back fast, because there's nothing I can do about the situation.

KATHARINA: An African fellow once told me he thought my hair was wonderful. I was rolling it in those days, so it was very straight falling in big curls; it looked very nice. He felt I'd have the best chances in Africa and asked if I wanted to go to Africa—to him, that seemed the most natural wish. On the one hand he admired my smooth hair and my being European and, on the other hand, he felt that I belonged in Africa.

LAURA: To get back to the feeling of "home": In the GDR it was made crudely clear to me that I was a foreigner and that I am not viewed as a German. In the smaller towns it's very strong, but in East Berlin, too, people would often turn around to look at me: "Hey, look." I have no feeling of "home," because this pressure from outside was so great. I speak German. That's the only thing I have to identify myself with. To be a German is for me a definition that others give to me through an ID card and a language, but in principle I don't feel like anything, not even international. This summer in Paris I had the feeling for the first time that I wasn't conspicuous, that no one was turning around to look at me or giving me a special smile, just because in Paris there are so many people of African descent. That was very important for me; I simply felt integrated—on the street, in the subway—even without being able to speak the language.

Here I don't have a feeling of home, because, for example, sales clerks are always saying to me: "You speak German so well!" I'm constantly getting confirmation that I'm not German. Somehow that also seems to have bad effects on me, and it's certainly related to my move from the East and to my moving X number of times within the GDR. I wasn't tied to any place; I did live in East Berlin for ten years, but in spite of that there isn't much that ties me to it, at most my relationships with friends, which also shaped me. That's my real identification, the things that formed me; there's nothing national about it.

KATHARINA: Recently in a flower shop another woman again said to me: "You speak such good German." I answered that I grew up here, and she said so sweetly: "A German girl," and that really made me happy. She didn't get irritated over my answer, and it didn't embarrass her, instead just affirmed me.

DAGMAR: How do you feel about color as part of your identification?

KATHARINA: I wouldn't call myself white, but then again it's not correct either to say I'm black. But sometimes I feel like a white person.

LAURA: I don't actually consider myself white, but there are situations in which I'm not conscious of, or nobody makes me conscious of, being colored.

MAY: I remember a dream where I had on a black skirt and a white blouse. I was hopping around like in a game of pick-up-sticks. I remember distinctly that I was white and had a horse's tail.

Afterward I wondered whether that was perhaps because I usually see only white people around me. My color only registers when people mention it to me. Have any of you had that happen?

KATHARINA: Not as a dream, but as a fantasy.

LAURA: No, not really. But I have thought about why I'm proud of being colored. I don't want to be white or black either, but I do want to be colored. Surely that has to do with the advantages I get out of it.

MAY: In elementary school I got a lead role as a devil in a play. Everybody thought I'd be ideal for the part, because I wouldn't have to wear any make up. I put my heart and soul into playing that devil's part. But later when we wanted to do a play where everybody was a worker in the heavenly bakery, I suddenly got scared that I wouldn't be able to be in it. I thought: "Oh gosh, a black angel, that doesn't fit." I was really glad when I found out I could be in it, too.

KATHARINA: I remember as a child talking with others about my color, that my color looked like coffee with cream. I thought that was a very pretty color, and so did the others.

Until I was about ten, I didn't perceive myself as either white or black. I felt like a normal little German girl; in Africa, too. There I did see the African part of me, but also the difference from people in Africa—for them I was "Eubio," the European—because I looked different. In Africa I felt like a German, because I didn't connect German with skin color. Of course, I also had African relatives and was glad that I belonged to them. It would never have occurred to me to feel in any way different from my blond-haired Norwegian friend.

There were English and German kids and a family with four Afro-American children. Since nothing was said about it, it seemed perfectly normal to me.

The first reactions came in Heidelberg; to white people in Heidelberg I was something different. Then I began to worry about what I actually was. Not only had I been in Africa, but I was born in the GDR besides. For example, they would say: "You speak standard German," because I didn't have a southern German accent. I even had Afro-Czech and English cousins. From this connection I gradually moved from preferring to consider myself a German to being an Afro-European. In the meantime that has changed also, for there's actually nowhere in Europe where I can feel at home.

LAURA: Because you're always viewed as a foreigner?

KATHARINA: Yes. I think my consciousness as an Afro-European still doesn't give me a feeling of belonging. I can still be pushed out.

MAY: I actually find the term "Afro-German" or "Afro-European" quite good. I am declaring that I look different, perhaps move differently, too, also in some respects think or feel differently based on my background and the life situations conditioned by it, but I don't want to be put into a black or white compartment.

KATHARINA: I used to have such a strong desire to consider myself a "normal" white person, that I just acted as though that were the case. This need to fit in still remains subliminally within me. Although I am now consciously dealing with my blackness and place a positive value on the word "Negro," I nevertheless don't like to lie out in the sun to get darker. When I look pale, I feel less foreign and can move more freely.

MAY: I also used to think I would be less conspicuous if I were lighter. Now I'd like to be black, plain and simple.

KATHARINA: Then you could pass in Africa.

MAY: No, not for that reason. I used to wish that, when I was thinking I don't fit in anywhere, but that's nonsense. For a while everybody said I belonged in Africa with my father; they asked whether I didn't want to get citizenship, take his name, and move there. I felt really shut out and was aware of my differences with respect to Africans—I don't speak the language, I don't know or don't accept much about the culture.

KATHARINA: You're more different there than here. For a while I had the idea of just disappearing into the Afro-American community somewhere in the United States and finding a home there.

DAGMAR: Why do you always say "disappear" or "be absorbed," rather than to be "taken in"?

KATHARINA: Because of a desire to finally disappear, to finally cease to be an exception.

DAGMAR: What does it mean to be an exception?

KATHARINA: As a child I often felt like I was a mean child—people were so nice to me and I was always defensive and arrogant.

I enjoyed it most when I could pull my friends into it, like when someone new came into the class and then asked a dumb question.

I really played it up; in those days I used to wear llama sweaters a lot and would always be asked if they came from Africa. Those typical Latin American sweaters that were "in" then, and that everybody was wearing, were suddenly from my grandma in Africa; and I would just generally exploit those stories. People even believed it, and the others really got a kick out of it.

MAY: In elementary school they often asked me where I came from. And I would tell this one friend the craziest stories from Africa.

Once we had a student exchange with Israel, and the Israelis were with us for two weeks. On a class trip a German family came up behind us and thought I belonged to the Israelis. They thought everything was so wonderful here. I acted like I could barely understand German and when they tried to teach me the word *squirrel*, I really played dumb.

KATHARINA: Walking a tightrope between making fun and exploiting an advantage! On a job I play on the fact that I'm of a different color and kind of pretty, in order to get what I want or because it's simply the most pleasant way for myself and others. If one of my colleagues says something against the way I do my work, I smile at her. Then she doesn't say anything else.

DAGMAR: That reminds me of situations when I've played the feminine role; if I can get my way with someone by smiling, then I'll sometimes smile, although I really don't think it's good to play along with that sort of thing.

KATHARINA: Yes, at my job I've often consciously pretended to be naive, in order to avoid being bothered with things that didn't have to do with my color.

At school in the GDR I had a definite advantage over my schoolmates.

DAGMAR: Do you think that teachers were somewhat afraid of being viewed as racist if they punished you?

LAURA: Yes, but there was another side, too: I did have an advantage, I was something different and wasn't taken as seriously as the others.—"She's different anyway, there are other expectations of her and she is also more intelligent. She has to struggle with her environment more, thus she is more critical and more argumenta-tive."

KATHARINA: There's also a form of pity underlying this kind of thinking.

In school I often thought underprivileged children needed such pity much more than I did. For example, there was a boy named Giovanni: he was Italian and lived in a children's home; he was always taunted with "Dago," and no teacher gave him any consid-eration. On the one hand, he couldn't be himself, because he had difficulties with his environment; on the other hand, he also caught it from the teachers and their own prejudices.

LAURA: I was once chosen for the "Physics Olympics"; when I went in they asked me with well-meaning smiles whether I hadn't also been in the "Math Olympics." I didn't like saying no.

Along with all of that I heard how the teachers used to talk about me: "She's such a cute girl."—"Yes, and so intelligent." Appropriately, I became unbearably arrogant.

KATHARINA: With me it was more that the teachers did their best not to show me favoritism. "You needn't come here flashing those big eyes," one said to me once. Actually I thought it was good that they didn't want to single me out.

DAGMAR: That's one explanation; another one would be that they couldn't bear your being better than the others.

LAURA: In school here in West Berlin they don't make such a personality cult as in the GDR. Here there are so many individu-alities that you have to be really outstanding to be recognized. And the teachers don't expect anything special of me.

MAY: Being an exception here isn't generally associated with high expectations of intelligence and performance. Hence, Afro-Germans aren't privileged in schools and other situations.

LAURA: Right, here I'm not privileged.

MAY: I remember a biology teacher who I'm certain couldn't stand me because of my color. His manner of handling subjects having to do with race brought out all his racism, and several schoolmates then emulated him in his prejudice. It was terrible for me, especially since biology was my favorite subject. I got A's on practically all the tests and always got a C as a final grade. When I spoke to the teacher about it, he justified the C's with notes he had made about me on the side. I couldn't do anything about it. At some point in high school it suddenly got better; I don't know why.

DAGMAR: Considering everything you have talked about, how would you name yourselves?

KATHARINA: Whether I think about it or not, whether I argue about it with others or not, it doesn't change the fact that I have African characteristics—my looks, a way of expressing myself, or, for example, that way of holding my hand—you hold it exactly the same way, it's nice.

Because of the time I spent in Africa I'm conscious of the parts of me which were alive there and simply don't exist here in Germany. Because nobody wants to get to know them here, especially not my friends. I think about why that is, and I believe that racist structures prevent us from talking about it. Furthermore there's a lot of unacknowledged fear underlying this.

MAY: Yes, and there's no natural name for us as there is for Afro-Americans; in Germany everyone just talks right around it: half-breeds, coloreds, mulattoes, Blacks, or Negroes.

For me it's even uncomfortable to say the word "Negro"; it has a negative connotation and is used negatively.

KATHARINA: My father, grandmother, and other relatives that I met during my stay in Africa—and whom I like—are Black. I don't want to separate myself from them; that's why I define myself as Black. I call myself "Negro" only rarely or more as a joke.

MAY: For me it's hard, too; for one thing, because Africans sometimes have an offensive way of "proclaiming" their "negritude," and for another thing the word "Negro" itself has all sorts of meanings: "Negroes" are everyone who's a little darker, regardless of what they look like or where they come from, they're all lumped together. Furthermore, in a lot of sayings "Negro" stands for slave and other such things. When I was riding to Berlin recently, the driver, filling the gas tank at the last station before the GDR border, said: "All the FRG drivers fill up here one more time so they won't have to fill up with the *Negro-gas* in the GDR. Or, a friend of mine told his brother: "I'm taking your car today, you can get some other Negro to bring you home." But when a kid says: "Look, Mommy, a Negro," I see that as something different.

With terms like "colored" or "Black" it's similar. For myself I find "colored," for example, not particularly negative; for a long time I was able to identify myself with that more easily than with "Black," because it doesn't obliterate the difference from Africans. One South African in my study group, who counts as "colored" in South Africa, doesn't like the word and finds "mixed" better, which I again can't accept for myself. To say "Negro" to her is still more strange for me, since I associate certain characteristics with that. She has straight hair and looks more Indian than African.

Since then, in the course of our discussions, the term "Afro-German" has come into being.

KATHARINA: I wouldn't want to use the term "Negro" as a designation either, but I would consider a discussion about it important. I'm tired of separating myself from people in Africa, just because here people are always using expressions like "black as a Negro," "You can find yourself another Negro."

MAY: I agree. I'm also reminded that my lighter skin was an advantage when I was going out with a Black guy. Maybe that's why now I'd like to be darker; believe me, I can do without people finding me beautiful and interesting because I'm dark but not too dark. With him I rarely got into a disco, whereas alone I'm a little exotic attraction. On the street, people stared at us shamelessly, and I got a bigger share of comments than usual. They also thought I didn't understand German. In general I experienced the environment as much more hostile and had a much stronger feeling of being Black.

KATHARINA: You probably also allowed yourself to get involved more than I would; I considered my lighter skin as an advantage with which I could also support Africans. If I didn't want to be stupidly stared at with an African in a disco or a café, I immediately addressed the waiter cooly in the most elegant German. Then no one would bother us anymore.

LAURA: I've always felt very comfortable with Africans and Afro-Germans, since I wasn't the sole exception anymore. When I walk down the street with a white boyfriend, I get scrutinized from head to toe.

How do you interact with each other?

DAGMAR: You once mentioned how, when Afro-German women get together, insecurity and maybe competition arise, perhaps because you aren't the sole exception anymore. Is that one of the reasons why there's been so little contact until now among Afro-Germans?

LAURA: When I meet African women on the street, they usually smile in a spontaneous and friendly manner; but not so with Afro-German women; first comes an appraising look and then maybe some other response. I often have mixed feelings, possibly out of competition, I don't know. With Katharina I didn't feel that way, but that's very seldom.

KATHARINA: Yes, but you did look at me pretty critically.

LAURA: I know, I felt terribly insecure, too.

MAY: I found you to be a little cool, too.

DAGMAR: So, what did you think in that situation?

LAURA: "Oh, that's May! Boy, she looks great!"

KATHARINA: But there's always that kind of appraising look among women; I don't know if that's the reason why we didn't speak to each other and get to know one another better. It's easier for me to make contact with colored men; then the competition in a group doesn't come into play. When I met you, Laura, I had ambivalent feelings, too; on the one hand I wanted to show solidarity with you, and on the other hand I thought, if she sees me as a competitor, that'll make me angry and I'll act that way.

LAURA: In the GDR I met women of color, too, and it was always much harder to get together with them than with others. First, due to all of us checking each other out, but then, too, because others mixed us up so often: "Oh, you all look so much alike." They simply didn't want to acknowledge that we had different names and were different women. That's happened to me often, mostly with men. I remember I was in an adult ed course with a colored woman, she was my height, but otherwise we didn't look alike. People we knew called us both by the other's name; I thought they were all crazy. Between that colored woman and me there was definite competition; it still bothers me how it was between us. I knew her only slightly, before we were in that class. We had gotten into a conversation once at a party, and I took down her address. I asked her if we could get together sometime, but she never had time. Then when we got into the same class, I approached her again. But she couldn't find anything better to do than to turn people against me and tear me to pieces. In the beginning I didn't know anything else but to do the same thing until I ended up avoiding the whole thing.

KATHARINA: A conflict between two white women is no different from one between a Black and a white woman.

LAURA: Oh yes it is, because you can only have competition between two similar people—or if it's about color. I'm never in competition with white women.

KATHARINA: I always am. For example, in school I considered my color an advantage, in the same way that others could express themselves well, or were good with figures. As a result things just got competitive. But when I meet Afro-German women, something else happens: I sense a pull, I think we could really have something to offer each other, but then we just pass right by one another. I remember a ballet dancer who avoided all contact with me. At first I thought it was because she was two years older than I or had an entirely different life style. In Heidelberg, for a while I constantly used to run into a colored woman with fascinating green eyes. She always kept her distance. I was afraid to initiate an acquaintance with her for fear of competition.

DAGMAR: Over what or whom do you compete?

KATHARINA: Primarily it's about affinity and recognition, maybe about your own identity also.

MAY: I've experienced that, too. I remember one colored woman I thought was incredibly beautiful and whom I didn't have the nerve to speak to, out of a mixture of respect and a feeling of inferiority. In that connection the thought occurred to me that I consider my color a plus, in addition to the fact that perhaps I really am good looking.

I haven't had any conflicts with Afro-German women; there also weren't any around my age. At school there was a girl four years younger than I; we ran into each other once in a while but we never spoke to each other, even though I would have liked to. I didn't want to speak to her just because of her color, I wouldn't have liked that myself. Because I'm doing these interviews now, I spoke to her recently, and this time it was great. With her I needed a reason, whereas otherwise with people who seem pretty nice, I find a way somehow. But it's really exciting meeting Afro-German women. Recently I met a South African woman in a study group on South Africa. We found an incredible number of parallels; she grew up with various foster parents who were similar to mine—we were both amazed and excited.

May Opitz and Katharina Oguntoye (photo: Dagmar Schultz)

Ellen Wiedenroth (age 30)

"What makes me so different in the eyes of others?"

I'm German, and I'm dark. But then not all that dark either. I've often looked in the mirror and asked myself what distinguishes me, what makes me so different in the eyes of others. Inside I am German because of my German environment, school, my home— just German. And yet it was always made clear to me that that is exactly what I am not. But why? It's all based on externalities.

For brown skin, the German language only has terms borrowed from eating and drinking, like "chocolate brown" or "coffee brown." If someone tries to place me on the color scale, I could be classified as "coffee-and-cream brown." Does that even exist? Oh sure, in people's perceptions there's an unlimited number of shades and corresponding labels. *What you people have in common is divergence from the generally unspoken norm—whiteness.*

But no matter how many nuances are defined, it always comes down to the same thing: You are branded (no, marked) as non-white. And in the final analysis, all the various shades are of no importance whatsoever. "Nonwhite" is essentially "black."

Identifying all those shades is so clumsy, not least because it is intrinsically dishonest. "Black-white": this tediously contrived differentiation breaks down to this opposition. Color is not seen as value-free. "White," the "abstraction" of all colors, is equated with purity (hygienic and moral), with wholeness. "Black," by contrast, the "subtraction" of all colors, stands for dirt, for evil as such, for menacing nothingness.

Around here it isn't proper to denigrate a person openly. But that's easy to get around, since built right into the color symbolism is a subliminal denigration of Blacks, which is in this way all the more effective.

Given the black-white matrix in people's minds—you are placed on the nonwhite side and you are classified as an "also-person." After all, Blacks are "also" people. The fact that this must be said implies that it is not obvious. Pointing out the different shades of nonwhites is lovingly intended. For that's how the message is transmitted: "You aren't all that dark, you're 'just'— . . ." I'm not all that dirty, evil, or threatening, but just a little bit. Surely no harm is intended. And if now and then I open my mouth and defend myself against such classification, okay, then I'm hypersensitive, I can't be talked to. Okay, okay, I had wanted to stop talking about this point a long time ago: I am Black—and not dark-, light-, or any-other-brown.

"I intend to set things in motion"

Since I'm no longer on the defensive and can say: "This is who I am, accept me as a person," only now that I acknowledge my "differentness" can I act accordingly. Today I own up to being a German—and being Black. My very existence is a thorn in the side of this country. But today nobody bumps into me and my appearance without my being prepared. Today I'm the one who does the bumping, I intend to set things in motion. In this society a thinking and relearning process is necessary, to afford me and people like me a life of equality—if not today, then tomorrow.

I believe we must not disappear individually into white society, but that we have to work as a group against discrimination, we must learn to defend ourselves together. Often I'm speechless or unable to react, and I believe a lot of us have learned to keep our mouths shut.

Those soft tones that are continuously drummed into us are the things that make life hard. It starts with the well-meaning inquiry about how I happen to handle the German language so well. It continues with the German last name that I as a woman must have come by through marriage. It goes on with painful compliments

about how beautiful such an exotic look is, ending with the conso-
lation that, after all, I am not s-o-o terribly dark.

Everywhere the same thing—in the job market, in the search for
a place to live. Always I have to identify myself, prove, two times,
three times, that I'm German, prove my right to exist. "Oh, we
thought you were a foreigner." Foreigners are different; they are
singled out; they are—as I said—"also-people." Whoever falls
outside the pale just doesn't belong. To be Black and to be German—there's something wrong about it, there's something peculiar. Black Germans are excluded from our thought-patterns, they
don't even exist in the consciousness of most West Germans. And
we have to start at exactly this point. Others must take note of us;
they must come to grips with our existence; they must experience
us as a reality.

Protected in a "Sterile" World

Right after I was born I was placed in a children's home for a short
time because my mother had to earn money. She then tried to find a
foster family for me, because children's homes aren't considered
good for small children. The first family didn't work out; then I
was put into another one, where I stayed until I was seven. I only
have vague memories of these families.

My mother didn't want to leave me with other people any more,
and it happened that an older friend she had worked with offered
to take care of me. She raised me as a grandchild. A year later my
mother, the woman, and I moved in together.

I really don't have any recollections of being isolated during that
period. It wasn't until I went to school that it began to dawn on me.
My first teacher used to deliberately belittle me in front of the
others if I was noisy or didn't have my homework.

My mother's sensitiveness showed in her reactions whenever I
told her about such things; I think she always thought it was
because of my color but she never uttered a word about it. Color
was not an issue.

In my surroundings there weren't any other Black children at

Ellen Wiedenroth with her mother

all. The people in that suburban environment were always quite curious about who I was and what I did, but I didn't encounter any real problems. At most, I was picked once to recite a poem for a parents' meeting. It was pretty scary standing in the spotlight. I can't say positively that I was chosen because of my color; it was just something I felt.

One decisive experience I recall was of a boy in elementary school shouting "Nigger, Nigger!" after me. I had never heard the word, but just the sound of it . . . I was very hurt.

I cried the whole day, without being able to say a word about it. When I was finally able to tell my mother, she started crying, too, but still without explaining it to me. I had expected her to help me and console me, and that it would all go away. But my mother couldn't deal with the situation at all. I stopped crying; I was just perplexed.

I thought to myself that "Negro" must be something terribly negative, and I still continue to have a strong reaction to that word. Nor can I fathom how anyone can use it in normal speech and think that its completely neutral.

As long as I was growing up in my mother's home I was secluded and sheltered from the outside world. Mother took great pains to avoid addressing and discussing problems if at all possible. The deception of not being different could only be maintained by ignoring the reality. Problems were brushed off outside the door like shoe dirt. Inside was our "ideal world."

My mother was very anxious about me, therefore I was never left alone. It was a major accomplishment for me even to walk by myself to and from school. That was scrupulously drilled into me, and I was really afraid to deviate from the path. I was hardly ever allowed to visit girlfriends, because I would have had to go by myself, knock on the door or ring the bell by myself and say: "Here I am."

So my playmates were books, puzzles, and dolls. No, I didn't have it bad. I had everything: a home, lots of toys, pretty clothes, and good grades. I was always among the best in my class, and achievement brought me recognition.

My books took me out of myself to faraway lands and bygone worlds. I went crazy over Egyptian art. The people were beautiful. I also longed for such long beautiful shiny blue-black hair and often thought about how I could get hair like that. My own hair was nothing by comparison. It always had to be rolled up and continually cut. It was subdued and I with it.

As a child I had no fantasies about wanting to be white. When I noticed at puberty that skin color was very significant—although this remained unarticulated—I thought: "Ooh, if only I were Black! If I'm supposed to be Black, then why am I not?" That was my problem.

Yes, I had a sheltered childhood, but I became depressed, brooding a lot and at some point felt I couldn't go any further.

I said goodbye in a letter to my mother and thought daily about death. I wanted to jump off the balcony, but each time fear restrained me; I might have to go through life as a cripple. My mother found the letter when I had already pushed aside the thoughts of suicide and had admitted to myself my all-too-great fear of such a step. But I hadn't destroyed the document of my despair, for the despair persisted as always. My mother was hurt. How could I even think of such a thing, how could I do such a thing to her, after all she'd sacrificed for me? I was ashamed.

In Search of My Black Identity and a Country

As soon as I extricated myself from my mother's secluded world, a wave of cool rejection slapped me square in the face.

My evolving consciousness of being marginalized caused me to seek out more contact with Blacks. The myth of international Black solidarity became my guiding principle.

In the academic world I met many Africans, with whom I got along well right from the start. Something united us that didn't need to be named. Here I had found what had been so lacking in my life up to that time, namely a niche where my Germanness or non-Germanness wasn't an issue. Blackness opened me up to a new level of community with people. I experienced openness, friendliness, unquestioned acceptance. I was "sister"; I belonged. Out of a passive attitude grew an active one: I wanted to be Black.

With my first friends I focused squarely on going with them to their country. But what always made my ears prick up was the statement by Blacks: "You must go to Africa, there's no racism there. In fact, when you come, you'll get special attention." Then I thought, there you are, something special again, you get better treatment because you're European. I listened in silence, unable to respond.

For a long time I wanted to emigrate. I wanted to go to an African country, to a place that promised me an identity, a little piece of an ideal world. The United States was out of the question as a place to immigrate to, for I didn't want to jump straight from the frying pan into the fire. I took several trips, moving around in northern and western Africa. Particularly in Liberia I had a decisive experience that forced me back to the realization that I am not an African, that I couldn't become a Liberian just like that, or slip into another skin and wipe away my past. I viewed my arrival in Liberia as the first step in getting adjusted to the African continent; I wanted to become acclimated there. By the time I left, however, I was completely frustrated and felt my foundation had been shaken. What had happened?

I lived with the aunt of my fiancé at the time, because the family didn't consider their house good enough for me. I didn't quite understand, especially why I was never once allowed to go there during the day. They placed a high value on custom and protocol. I never was subject to such constraints in Germany. I went along with it all, more out of interest than out of any identification with it.

On a walk along the beach I watched some kids apparently looking for something valuable in a garbage heap. They shouted at me: "white lady, white lady," and once again I was marked and felt branded. I had believed I could take on a Black, an African, identity. This time it was shouted at me that I was white.

I didn't know what to think, nor could I talk about it with anyone. Much later I found an explanation for this incident: my bearing, the observed distance, had given me away. In that scene I had walked by with too much distance, on the one hand, and on the other, too interested to be a local person. My behavior had marked me as a European. Since Europeans are stereotypically white, in that moment I became a "white" person. "White" was a social category, in this case, no different from the classification of "black."

Later I thought I could find my paradise in Hawaii. There, there are so many mixtures—Asians, Europeans—you can't classify people. I thought: "Oh that's great. There you'll fit in." But soon Hawaii was out of the question, as I realized that everything there is Americanized. America has never been a point of reference for me.

After that I put aside my plans of emigrating.

A new stage in my search for myself began. I was no longer searching for a mystical home somewhere outside West Germany. At first I didn't know what in the world I was looking for. In time I came to the conclusion that, if I didn't want to simply survive, but to actually live, I ought first to go after that here in Germany. In the final analysis I'm at home here. This is my home, even if so many of my fellow citizens think my home should be a place where I outwardly resemble the other people. Home is an inner point of reference. It means familiarity, custom—but also security, a feeling of certainty, refuge; it represents a feeling of belonging. I have a

172

right to all of this. I will not be denied my home. "Homeless"—the deadliest expression of abandonment, of rejection.

In Search of My Father*

ELLEN: My first boyfriend was an African. I had never imagined myself with a white boyfriend; that was quite clear to me.

I didn't say anything about it at home. But when my mother found out about him, she went half out of her mind. She wanted to prevent any further contact with him, so we only met secretly. It never came to an open conflict because I moved to another city to attend the university anyway.

MAY: Didn't your mother ever explain to you why she found it so terrible that you had a black boyfriend?

ELLEN: Instead of an explanation, she said that my father had been very undependable and had left her in the lurch. At some point, she decided that he would never cross her doorstep again. Most likely she saw all other Blacks as representations of my father. I had certainly figured on difficulties from outside because of my Black boyfriend, but from my mother . . .

When I moved out, that shut the door for me; but I never dared to sever all contact with my mother. The first few years my mother wanted to maintain contact with my father by force, you might say. She wanted him to see how I was developing, and she thought I should have the chance to get to know him, too. My father didn't take any of that very seriously; he wrote now and then, but not regularly. I myself never wrote to him. For a while my mother had his picture up, but at some point it disappeared without an explanation.

MAY: As a child did you ever imagine visiting your father?

ELLEN: Actually, not until I left home after high school. I had many African boyfriends, sort of as substitute for my father. In talking with H and C, I noticed that with us Afro-German women the search for a father and the search for Black men often con-

*From a conversation between Ellen Wiedenroth and May Opitz.

verged. I never wanted a white boyfriend; blackness and being a man went together, as far as I was concerned. Once I realized that, I wanted to get to know my father.

Through charitable organizations in the United States that offer tracing services, I initiated the action. When that yielded nothing, I put the matter aside. When I got a free flight to Jamaica two years ago, I stopped over in New York for two weeks and started searching more seriously. Thank goodness there weren't too many men with the same name as my father in the phone book, and I found him pretty quickly.

I was very pleased that his whole family knew about me. And my father showed me around with a certain fatherly pride and thought I was there to stay.

His children, however, refused to get to know me. I saw them once briefly and then never again. Maybe they thought of me as a threat, although I wasn't about to make any demands. But my father felt I should remain in touch with all my relatives, half brothers and sisters from then on, for when it came to dividing up his estate. . . . I didn't want to think that far ahead.

MAY: Did you want to stay in touch?

ELLEN: Yes, I did. But not in the sense of thinking I had now found my family. I got along best with my grandmother, my father's mother. But as things turned out, so far I've only been writing to my father and his wife, with whom I also get along well. He doesn't write anymore himself; his wife writes instead. He made that arrangement with my mother, too, thinking nothing of it. That was some nerve!

I hadn't told my mother beforehand that I was going to visit my father. Afterward she accepted it pretty well. She just said she could understand if it was important to me, but she wanted to be kept out of it. Only then did it become clear to me what difficulties I had gotten myself into. My father was determined to see my mother again, but she didn't want that. I thought, "Here I am right in the middle!" At first I was demanding that my father visit me here and see how I was living. But what if he objected to being prevented from showing up at my mother's door?

How We Deal with the Experience of Fear

MAY: At a meeting of Afro-Germans today someone was worried about security for the event, because he feared that neo-Nazis might show up. I, too, had thought about it earlier, especially because this meeting was publicly announced in the press. Fear seems to be a central topic for many of us.

ELLEN: With me, too. In the final analysis any xenophobia is directed at us, too, and I believe that if neo-Nazis see that there's a group such as ours, it could become dangerous.

MAY: Neo-Nazis are also talking about "half-breeds," too—I even read something by them about it once.

For a while fear really got the better of me. Especially when I was working for my thesis, I learned about the things that had gone on—in Berlin and Hamburg in particular. At the time I was considering moving to Berlin and got quite worried about whether I really ought to do it. I finally did move there, but the fear of neo-Nazi uprisings took its toll on me. In Osnabrück there were two guys with swastikas on their leather jackets standing in front of me at the railroad counter. When that dawned on me I went for cover.

ELLEN: Fear blocks me from even dealing with xenophobia. I just don't want to know anything about it. If I had any more information than what you just get every day, then I'd be even more frightened. One suburb of Mainz is a neo-Nazi stronghold, where their national organization is based. So, sometimes I'm really afraid to be in Mainz. It always depends on my mood, but ultimately I feel helpless.

MAY: With our color we are always visible. We're even different from children of binational relationships that are white.

ELLEN: Yes, we're walking targets. We can never "submerge," without that threat either. I can't ever "just walk around."

MAY: H says the same thing, and I was shocked when she said that it used to be impossible for her to go outside without a mask—in the truest sense of the word. She always had to make up her eyes, polish her nails . . .

Maybe many didn't come to this meeting, either, out of fear. Being a loner can definitely have its advantages.

ELLEN: For sure, but I don't like to concern myself with that issue.
MAY: I always come back to these questions in reference to solidarity: How far do I want to go? For example, in looking for a job,
when it says: "No foreigners." Up to now I've never taken one of
those jobs, even if I had the chance because of my German citizenship.
But how long can I afford to do that? The same goes for discothèques,
when the sign says: "Off limits." That applies to Blacks, but generally
not to women. Usually I don't go to such dives, but how far does my
friends' solidarity go? What's my position when my friends go anyway? And what are they saying to me when they do?
ELLEN: Many of them hurt you without intending to, with their
good-naturedness, with their "goodwill." Sure, through years of
experience—I'm speaking now only about the negative ones—some
things can trigger an uptight, agitated reaction in me. Like, I can
usually tell when a person is striking up a conversation with me out of
simple-mindedness, out of ignorance, that I've had a hundred times in
the same form. Those kinds of incidents follow such a stereotypical
pattern. It's not the ignorance or narrow-mindedness of an individual
person, but the fact that I have to constantly be subjected to the same
stupid, uncomfortable situation. That's what upsets me most.
    And then I get angry and it's like I'm paralyzed. I can't shake my
bad mood. I've learned to swallow my feelings in these situations so
well that I usually can't even get my mouth open when I'm on the
verge of choking on something. In situations like that I have a hard
time asserting myself.
MAY: Always justifying, explaining, fighting your way through. For
my academic program I wanted to do an internship at a center for the
physically handicapped in Munich. I presented myself there and was
told afterward that I essentially could do the internship, because they
were looking for people, but that they would require me to do an
interview with the people I would be in charge of. I was very surprised, because I knew that this wasn't normal, and I wondered
where the "reservations" and "safety precautions" started. With a
person with a punk hairstyle? With a Japanese? With a Spaniard?
How black do you have to be to warrant an interview?
    When I recounted this incident to some other people, they thought

it was rather inconsequential, trivial, wasn't worth getting upset about. Nevertheless I didn't want to work there at first.

ELLEN: I once had a discussion with a friend about the varying degrees of discrimination. She has problems with being fat and thus often perceives herself as unfeminine, because she doesn't fit a certain standard of beauty. People often harass her, so she thinks she experiences discrimination just like I do. I think you can't compare them so easily and put them on the same level. There's so much mixed in together. When I add it all up it's unfathomable. And she thinks she can reduce the unfathomable to being fat in our society.

MAY: Sometimes my friends don't perceive me as Black at all, and they often try to trivialize things that are important to me.

For example, if I get upset over figures of speech like "Find yourself another Negro!" I'll get an appeasing "You're right," without their really reflecting on it. Then I feel like a little kid being patted on the head to pacify me.

I'm really afraid of bumping into my friends' racism and thus also into the inevitable question: Who are my friends actually? How far would they go for me? I could cry, because I realize that basically I'm probably all alone.

ELLEN: Now and then I try to think back to situations that I've found problematic. Once I realize what was wrong in that instance, I can't get along with the people involved anymore. That's why I'm friendly with so few people. I'm always prepared to keep my distance.

MAY: I'm very careful and skeptical, too, and prepared to be dropped. Before it gets to that point I usually pull back. So, being Black means, now and then, feeling alone among friends.

ELLEN: As far as that's concerned, I have a mask, too. I give the apperance of going through life in full control. Sometimes I can actually feel myself, right when I'm stepping out of the house, pull my shoulders back and take on a perfectly erect bearing. I can't walk relaxed at all. Walking through the street like that, I'm unapproachable.

MAY: For a while I actually practiced walking erect. That was during my school days, when I felt I wasn't accepted or taken se-

riously on several different sides. I built up a facade of "Nobody can
do anything to me." An erect bearing is also a mask for us, that can't
be seen through so easily; this posture is supposed to be typically
African.

ELLEN: Right, exactly; "we're born with it" . . . [laughter].

Corinna N. (age 26)

*Old Europe Meets Up with
Itself in a Different Place*

"You were conceived in the woods, that's why you've always been so wild," my father used to say to me. "You know, in those days a fellow couldn't take his girl up to his room. We liked each other, but circumstances didn't allow us to stay together. Your mother's family didn't want a colored child in the house."

That's how I ended up in a children's home outside Stuttgart right after I was born, where I stayed for six years.

I don't remember much from that time. Blobbie was important to me, Blobbie, my dreamy brother, blond curls, a real angel face. With him I shared the little that we had.

Then people would come who'd look at me wanting to adopt me. People I liked right off, since they were the same color as me. Not one adoption ever worked out, although a lot of people wanted me. My father refused to give his consent. Even when his best friends offered to take me, he refused. I never understood that, since he thinks a lot of them even today, and my mother would certainly not have been against it, if Father had wanted it.

Then children would come who looked just like me. I'd stand by their beds and stare and think, they're like me. I looked different, that I knew: *why,* I didn't know.

Afterward I found out that it was a private orphanage. At first I was in a small orphanage, later we moved to a bigger one. When we moved, we were all very excited. I still recall vividly that we weren't allowed to play with the new toy they showed us. At night we climbed out of bed to look at it in the playroom. We got caught and had to get under the cold shower one by one. To avoid the punishment I hid in the hallway where there was no light. Luckily, I got away with it.

Around the home was a wall, but we never got out and didn't know much about our surroundings. In each room there was an older child of the orphanage who watched us and had to keep order.

Everything relatives gave us we had to share with the other children. One day I got some boots for winter, and Blobbie didn't have any, just sandals. Since we were the same size, I gave him my boots for the whole winter and went around in sandals myself. This happened without any words, since I didn't talk most of the time. Later I found out that at age five I was at the level of a three-year-old, in my speech development, also.

Our greatest delight was climbing onto the older kid's bed to look at postcards. I was absolutely fascinated by these cards and tried never to cause trouble, so I could get to see them as often as possible as a reward. Even more often we would sneak into the kitchen to snitch fruit. We never got enough fruit. Our diet consisted mostly of gruel, and fights often broke out since the bigger kids would take our food away from us. When I went to live with my parents it took a whole year before I could hold solid food in my stomach. I just wasn't used to it.

One day they didn't let me play with the other children; I had to stay in a separate room with Blobbie. I had a visitor. After a while someone came for me. I felt that something special was happening. We went into the director's apartment; there was a couple sitting there—my future parents. I went straight over to them and sat down by my mother. She asked me if I wanted to call her Anna or Mama. I said Mama right away and did not budge again from her lap. I didn't pay much attention to my father. Later they took me for a walk and bought me a soft drink in a restaurant. When we were there I met a dog for the first time in my life. I screamed and climbed up on a table, which made the dog bark even more, which frightened me even more; they had to drag me away.

The fact that things were changing for me became evident on my birthday. For the first time I was allowed to sit at a round table in the dining room, and there was cake and a red tote bag from my parents. It was a wonderful experience for me, and I adored my red bag. For the first time something belonged to me alone, and no one took it away from me.

It was a year and a half before my father and my second mother got married, so that they could adopt me.

From the Orphanage to My Family Home

When I finally went to live with my parents at age six and a half, I was very attached to my mother and less to my father. Most of the time I was scared of him. We got along fine when we would wrestle with each other. I always felt that he never took me as I was and was constantly making demands I couldn't live up to. My parents disagreed over methods of child-rearing—whether it should be African or European. My father was very jealous of me whenever my mother gave me a lot of attention. As I was in nursery school all day, my mother dotingly devoted the three hours before bedtime to me. That would cause my father to burst in, yelling: "Who are you married to, me or her?" So my mother was constantly divided between us. Even so, I sensed that she was more on his side, and so frequently I had both of them against me.

When I was eight or nine, my mother told me that she wasn't my real mother. I remember it to this day: I was sitting on my parents' couch and the news shocked me. The whole time I had been under the impression that she was my real mother. After that there was a barrier between us as far as I was concerned, a breach of trust. From then on I would ask at intervals who my mother was and why she had given me up. I never felt I was told the whole truth, but that I was getting only one side of the story.

At twenty-five, with my husband's support, I set all gears in motion to find out where she lived. When we found out, with the help of a friend, I got in touch with her. She comes from a middle-class family in a town where the people are careful not to draw attention to themselves. She could not assert herself against her father, who seems to have been a tyrant and didn't want a colored child in the family. Between my father and her there was apparently no substantive relationship either, since he went to England to study after I was born. Her brothers and sisters knew nothing of my existence. She went through her pregnancy in Stuttgart, in order to keep it a secret in her hometown. Her family had a well-known business there.

My first day at school, when I was six and a half:

I was sitting in my seat, unusually quiet. Generally I was not a child to sit still for even five minutes. Then she came in, the teacher, gray-haired, plump. She came straight over to me and smacked me in my face. "But I was being quiet," I thought, "I was quiet."

"This child isn't ready for school," they said.

After this first failure I was enrolled in school at age eight. This time, it worked out—but not for me. I was difficult. I was a loner, but the class did its share, too. I was unfortunately the only colored child in the class. The others took advantage of that, of course, and taunted me: "Do you come from monkeys?"; "You must have fallen in some cocoa"; or "Can I touch you? Can I see if your color rubs off?" For me as a child that was dreadful, and I always struck right back. How was I supposed to defend myself against so much ignorance? One day something awful happened, I got beaten up on the schoolyard by twin brothers just because of my color. The teachers looked on but didn't intervene. I had to get stitches in my head at the hospital. My opinion of teachers sank to zero forever.

Fortunately, these problems got better when we moved from our blue-collar neighborhood of Neukölln to Friedenau. My color became less of an issue, and I also made friends in my class at school.

When I was eight I inwardly divorced myself from my parents, since I didn't feel comfortable with them anymore. When I was ten or eleven, I began to go off by myself for days on end. At first just building huts in the woods and dreaming about being an Indian. Later I wanted to go to America and Brazil, since lots of colored people of all shades lived there. The obvious idea of going to Ethiopia didn't occur to me, since I strictly rejected my father during that time.

If only it wasn't so cold tonight. I'm numb already. The next freight train that comes by, I'm jumping right on it. I'll light myself a cigarette, just don't inhale so deeply, or else I'll get sick. Funny, you feel braver with a cigarette, and when the red glow of the tip flickers in the dark. How long have I been sitting here? Nearly two hours at least. I guess I ought to move a bit, my legs are chunks of ice already. No, better not, there might be guards here making their rounds. I don't want them to find me, now that I've prepared everything so well. Running away because of an F, it's crazy. I can't stand the nagging from my parents. Child, you won't amount to anything if you don't do well in school. Do you have homework? As if I asked every day when they come home from work: Did your boss promote you?

By now they'll probably have found out that I've run off, at 12 o'clock at night. I can just imagine them standing at the phone and not understanding why it won't work. They won't figure it out that fast. I'm not a fool; it was a good idea, cutting the cable in the phone socket and screwing the cover back on nice and neat. Yeah, they'll look, and will have to go to the phone booth to call the pigs and friends to find out where I am. It serves them right. But it's taking a long time for the next train to come, maybe I should have put it off till next summer. If it just wasn't so cold. Rubbing my hands together doesn't help much either, they still hurt from the cold. Better check my gear. Five hundred marks to get to Brazil, that ought to do. Not much food. A blanket, a knife, a flashlight, and my little notebook. Good thing I didn't leave that at home, I don't want them to know what I've been writing about them. Sitting here now in the bushes by the tracks, it all seems so lousy. Two years ago I was also on my way with a backpack, dressed as a boy, like now. It's supposed to be easier as a boy, nothing happens to them; that's what you read in adventure stories. As if girls didn't have enough problems, too, taking off on their own. I wish I were a boy. Don't bring that up again, don't think about what happened two years ago! God, how did I get through that terror. . . . You ought to be able to turn off your thoughts, they just keep going through your head.

I remember exactly how I set out, a heavy ski jacket, wool cap, and backpack. With an ax in it, so I could cut wood better for the hut in the woods. It was night already, I went down the Ku'damm, that big boulevard—it was already all lit up—and stopped in front of a

bookshop with children's books in the window. I noticed this sort of
middle-aged man standing by a car, who kept looking over at me. I
made like I didn't see him; I had a good spot where I could watch him
through the store window. I don't know what made me stand there so
long. And then I said to myself, you've got to go; it's not good, him
staring at you. Get out of here! And then I left, and all of a sudden he
was next to me, babbling at me. I stopped. I could have run, but no, I
stopped. "What are you doing out on the street so late?"—"I was at my
grandma's and I'm on my way home"—"If you want I'll take you
home." I didn't say a word. My heart was pounding. I couldn't even
think straight; only one thing was in my head: You're dressed like a boy,
you look like a boy. Nothing happens to boys, you know that, nothing
happens to boys. I got in his car. What make was it? I don't remember.
If I was really a boy, I'd have noticed what make the car was; boys
always notice the makes of cars. We drove off, first down Ku'damm.
"Where are you headed?" he asked me. "Broadcast Tower," I said. "I
have to go to the Broadcast Tower," trying to sound like a boy. "Neat
car, really super, it's got a lot of horsepower." "Yeah," he said, "good
car." And then I was struck speechless when I heard his question: "Are
you a boy or a girl?" Like a bullet from a gun: "A boy, of course. A boy,
man!" making my voice a little deeper. Then it got quiet. I stared hard
straight ahead. Don't look at him; evidently he went for the line about
me being a boy. With my feet I checked to see that my backpack was
still there. My hand was on the door-handle—When we get to the
Broadcast Tower I'm getting out, quick. In a daze I sat next to him, fear
mounting inside me, strangling me. "Is it much farther?" I asked.
"Nope," he said, "just down this street, then right." I started sweating.
Keep a clear head, if something happens, jump out. How in the world
am I going to get out of this, I was a fool to get in. I want to get out of
here, and in one piece. Finally I saw Broadcast Tower. A feeling of relief
came over me; but, no, he kept on going. Me, terrified: "But there's the
Broadcast Tower, that's where I have to go!" He paid no attention to me
and just kept on driving. Inside me everything was churning up; what
am I going to do, I'll never run away again; I'll take anything: home,
schoolwork, tutoring, everything. I just want out, out. Suddenly I felt
his hand on my leg. "Are you really a boy?" I didn't answer, I had lost
my tongue. Scared out of my mind I sat rigid as a board. Every muscle

in my body was tense; it dawned on me that outside there weren't any more houses, just road and woods. I squeezed up against the car door to get away from his hands. They came at me anyway, roaming upward, then he felt my small breasts. Now it hit me, now he knows I'm not a boy. He laughed: "Running away, huh, honey?" And then he stopped all of a sudden, in the middle of the woods. It's all over, he's going to kill you, do something bad to you. He came closer, his hands on me, my heart racing like crazy. And then, as though another person was inside me, in a very normal voice, calm, "Wait, I have to pee." I opened the door, threw myself on the ground and rolled down the embankment. I lay under a bush and listened, straining to hear if he was coming after me. I couldn't make out the noises anymore. "He's coming," I thought to myself, "he's coming after me; quiet, there was a noise." I darted up like a streak of lightning and took off toward a grassy path, running, running, always with the feeling he was running after me. A full moon, I became aware of it as I was running; shit, he can probably see me. My lungs were stinging something awful, fear drove me on, run, run. I remembered my backpack, my backpack is still in the car. In my head I went through the equipment I had in it. Nothing that could identify me. Again and again I stopped, slunk down in the weeds to hear if I was being followed. I was scared, terribly scared. I couldn't identify the sounds and took off again to safety. As morning broke, I eventually calmed down. I didn't know where I was. I liked it here by the water with the high grass.

Now here I am again, running away. Take a deep breath, girl, it's starting to get boring waiting for the train. I'll smoke a cigarette first and read my journal with my flashlight. If my folks ever read this they'll put me in a mental hospital. Maybe I should throw away the notebook, better yet, burn it. No, I'll keep it and slam it on the table at them when I'm big. And strong. On to Brazil, I'll work hard there until I have enough money for Monaco, where I can get an operation to make me a boy. Then I'll be really strong. Read about it not long ago in the paper. Monaco, a little state like that in the south of France; men go there to get themselves changed into women. To become a woman by choice, they're out of their minds, they ought to be glad to be men. 'Cause boys

have a lot more freedom. Found out all about it. They cut everything off
of them and turn it inside, then they really look like women. It's great,
they can change me there, too, even though my mother says it doesn't
work with women. I know it works; I haven't been praying for it every
night for nothing. I think I hear a train. Yes, here it comes, not going so
fast either. I'll take the next car, good, the next one. I think it's going
faster, I'd better jump or else it's all over. Missed again, it's going so fast,
I'm scared. Shit. There goes Hamburg, there goes Brazil, too. Fall isn't a
good season to emigrate anyway. Next year for sure, in the summer; I'll
steal money for the ticket to Hamburg. I'll spend the night here, just roll
myself up in the blanket and sleep under the bush. Tomorrow I'll go to
P's. I'll stay here awhile and then go home. Too bad, but I have to. On
the third try I'll make it to Brazil—or America, I think as I fall asleep
and dream I'm in the forest swinging from vine to vine. Maybe I'll go to
America, too, and start a revolution.

Boy or Girl?

My greatest dream in those days was to go to Monaco to have an
operation to be turned into a boy. The value of being a man was
constantly held up to me by my father, so that I could only feel
complete as a boy. This idea affected me to the extent that I only
had confidence in myself when I was wearing pants. In instances
where I was forced to put on a skirt, I would stick a pair of slacks in
my schoolbag just before leaving the house, to change clothes in
the next doorway. Due to my performance in school my family
situation got worse. When I was able to fulfill my father's expectations, I was a real Ethiopian, his daughter, his flesh and blood. At
such moments it made me happy that Father acknowledged me as
an Ethiopian, since I couldn't speak his mother tongue. How I
hated myself for being a "mulatto," a foreigner to my own father
and a foreigner to my German environment. This was because of
my color; otherwise there was no difference.

From the time I was in middle school, I used to get together with
colored kids away from my parents' home, with "mulattoes" like
myself. The only thing that bound us together was our color, but
we never spoke about it directly or about our problems. It was

simply checked off—father African or Afro-American? Most of them didn't know their father. When I was with Africans, now and then it bothered me being a "mulatto," something like sitting between two stools. I couldn't ever belong to one side or the other. How was I supposed to feel? You're not taken seriously by anyone. Just as the Germans feel sorry for you being colored, the Africans do too. That was even more of a shock for me. For a while I hated mixed marriages, since we children have to live our entire lives always between two stools. Now I claim myself as a German, since the culture that you grow up in does count, and although you might know about another part—you've visited the country, know the history, the food—that's all.

Father

I'm not your reflection
I sit between two stools
you are not a nightmare
nor the unknown
for you I'm an
unkempt garden
you look into the dark
seeking your image
I'm not your anchor
don't want to be
my face is a crack
a crevice
I see, I am still one
what are you?
your face is scratched
splintered
anchor yourself

like a tree I bend
toward the left, toward the right
I stay and bend
so I won't break

what do you want to play
in the dark night

you are entwined
by your gloomy thoughts
from your ass
the devil's tail grows
like a snake
you creep toward me
want to see your mirror image
splinters fall toward you
I am behind it
your flesh and blood

My father used to tell me lots of stories from his home about battles, kings, and his extended family. My father had problems with his color and didn't get along too well in German culture. I had to bear the brunt of it. I was constantly hearing that I had to do better in school than the Germans, since that was the only way they would acknowledge us. For me that was a big burden, it stayed on my mind, weighing heavily on me.

As I said, I learned from my father that a boy was worth more than a girl. He also treated me like a boy, for the most part. I became like a boy to please him. But that couldn't go on once I reached puberty. To find my identity as a colored person was, by comparison, not so difficult. Through my father I continuously came into contact with Ethiopians. Furthermore, my mother was then working at a French isntitute that ran seminars for French Africans. After school I went there practically every day and met lots of Africans. I soon knew where the countries were located, and their cultures also became more familiar to me.

My father and I are very different. After a while I stopped letting it bother me when people would make remarks about my color. Ignorance stinks, I always say. Later, I didn't have any more problems in school either. But those were replaced by others, like when I had a colored boyfriend and we went apartment hunting together: all of a sudden the apartments were gone, "We don't take foreigners," was the line, and our "But we're Germans," fell on deaf ears. If I got caught riding the subway without paying, I'd have to listen to racist epithets, although they had my German ID card in their hands. Yes, and then the usual "Where ya' from," answer "Berlin," the other one stares, you see the wheels in his head turning, "Okay, but where ya' from?" Today I no longer answer such questions. I am German but I'm not either. For me it was hard because of my childhood, but also because of the circumstances and my father, who still gets upset and fusses about the Germans and puts all the blame on them. You run into idiots all over; that's why you shouldn't think right away it's because of color.

Ethiopia

When I was seventeen I went with my father to Ethiopia. It was great not being noticed. I looked like everyone else. I met his family and traveled with them around the country. I was accepted and shown off.

For six weeks I was in Ethiopia and I often cursed the fact that I had gone along. We stayed with an uncle of my father's, his mother's youngest brother. He had been a judge under Haile Selassie and, after the Marxist coup, had refused to stay on in his office. Not a stupid man, he took to raising cattle. He sold the milk twice a day in the surrounding area. The whole time during our stay in Ethiopia I was uncomfortable. I was constantly reprimanded by my father for not behaving properly. Like, it made me sick always having to greet people with kisses and visit relatives and friends twice a day, who stuffed you like a pig. After a while I made friends with the servants, who lived in back of the house in the most abysmal conditions. But good by Ethiopian standards. Two boys and two girls, the youngest was ten years old and had to work ten hours a day. Now and then they got beatings from my aunt. For me it was inconceivable to have people living in cold, damp little rooms, while they themselves had a house and money. As I found out, the girl was loaned out as a servant by her parents, and that was quite customary there. Her parents weren't in the position to feed their children. They placed great importance on the boys' well-being; they were expected to go to school and get an education. With girls it was just the opposite.

Although our family is Christian, the men and women ate separately, except for me. As a guest from Germany I was allowed to sit with the men. We drove around Ethiopia with my uncle and since one of my uncles was a bank director, I had the pleasure of opening up banks with him in the provinces. I liked the country, from what I saw of it; it was only with relatives and friends that I had difficulties. I looked like them but thought differently and didn't speak their language. Always the same accusatory questions; I felt ashamed and guilty because I couldn't speak their language, even though it wasn't my fault. I didn't force myself. Tebebe, my cousin, was already over twenty and told me she never wanted to get married, because then she wouldn't be free. I understood that completely, I saw how matter-of-factly husbands cheated on their wives. Even communism doesn't help that—women belong in the kitchen and with the children. Liberation from your parents' home means getting married or going abroad, as far away as possible from clan and dogma. In retrospect I was glad I didn't grow up in that conservative, stifling system.

New York

For a year I've been living in New York, where my husband received a fellowship as an artist. The dream of going abroad that I've held onto since childhood has finally come true. I've always been interested in Black history in America and tended to idealize anything black. I was totally convinced that Blacks would never do me any harm and that I could, for example, come and go in Harlem. However, I've grown out of putting everything black on a pedestal or excusing everything or deluding myself. I want to see not only the skin color, but also what a person is made of.

New York opened my eyes to the fact that my color doesn't protect me from everything. I can't move entirely freely in Harlem or the South Bronx, since the people can tell that I'm not from there. New York, it's a melting pot of all the nations of the world. This melting pot and Americans' informality with someone new are fascinating to me. The feeling of being a stranger goes away very quickly here. The staring, the ignorant questions "where are you from, where are you going?" don't come up. It is more full of life, more optimistic than Germany: for the first time, a country for me.

Old Europe meets up with itself in a different place—in New York. I've met people here who have accepted me so naturally, with a degree of interest that I've never experienced in Germany. In New York for the first time I'm taking a more serious or more conscious look at German culture through my encounters with German Jewish and gentile emigrants. I'm reading the German classics and pursuing yet-unresolved questions about the Third Reich. It's only through an extended stay abroad that much of the German culture that I grew up with is becoming clear for me.

New York

You are my day, you are my night
in you I go walking, my Babylon
if death is in front, if death is behind
therefore I laugh
my Apocalypse
my burning blackness
no fright, no fear
and if someone asks
I'll laugh
in you I go walking, my Babylon
let them shake their heads
one doesn't believe in Christ either
until hearing Mozart's Requiem
I need my black hole
my burning Babylon
let the canyons be high
the nights even darker
in between, the people
knife at their throat
death is ahead, death is behind
therefore I laugh
knowing I am alive.

Angelika Eisenbrandt (age 33)

*"All of a sudden I knew
what I wanted"*

My family lives in E, a town near Kassel. I grew up there with my sister and brother in my grandparents' home. My brother and I have the same father, a U.S. soldier whom we don't know. My sister has a white father. All three of us were born out of wedlock. My brother had it easiest, because he got the most support. I had the greatest problem with the things adults said. At one girlfriend's house it was always: "Angelika, you have to go now, we're having company."

It wasn't until about the time I started school that it became apparent that my brother and I looked different. When we played with other kids in our yard or in the house, it wasn't noticeable. When company came, we were cleaned up and our hair fixed up. We were always supposed to look pretty and cute.

Sometimes my brother would put my sister down. He would say she was different from us and that we were a pair. I didn't understand it and it made me cry. Later I sensed more and more that I looked different, and my grandma always dressed me in only certain things. I wore only light colors, white and yellow. "Red," she said, "you can't wear. It doesn't go with your skin color." I didn't say anything. I just got angry. Once I had a pair of red plaid pants. I thought they were great and looked good on me. My grandma took them away.

My mother didn't involve herself in any of that. She was completely worn out after working all day. Starting at four in the morning she cleaned in a bakery, then she came home at seven, and from eight she worked in a photo lab.

Angelika Eisenbrandt
with her mother

It's funny, but afterward, when I was on my own and while I was married, I bought only red things without even thinking. I still adore that color today.

I never understood why Grandma didn't let my brother and me get inoculations. She said we had different blood and that it could be dangerous for us. Only my sister got shots. Later, my brother got a shot for a ship voyage, and nothing happened. I was absolutely amazed.

I think our grandma loved us, but she had difficulties with our being different. She was always afraid that people were talking about us. But when my daughter S was born, she was really disappointed and said: "She's not dark at all." With toddlers she could apparently accept the color, but as they got older it was harder for her to accept.

While we were in school I never went out with other kids, to discos or the like. I would have been allowed to, but I lacked the self-confidence to go out by myself. And my girlfriends weren't so great. My sister took me along sometimes, and it seemed completely normal that she went out and got along okay. I enjoyed it best of all when my brother took me with him. Back then I worshipped him. I thought he was out of this world. It was just within the family that he got on my nerves. Everybody admired and spoiled him. The really unfair part was that if he wanted something different to eat than what was cooked, he got it, but we didn't.

My mother was a photo lab technician, and that's what I wanted to be, too. She took the matter in hand and got me an apprenticeship outside E. But after four weeks I was already homesick. I gave notice and then was out of a job. When I looked for a new job, first alone and then with my mother, it was just awful. Time and again they told me the job was already filled or they had changed their minds. I had the feeling of not being accepted because of my color. I didn't even apply as a photo lab technician anymore, because there weren't any openings for that in E. Later I found a job as a salesclerk. But not until the woman from the employment office went there. By myself I wouldn't have gotten the job. Afterward I thought: "They had to be prepared for who was coming." That was awful for me. I worked there for two years. I actually wanted to stay for three years, but when I met my husband I stopped. That was also difficult because I didn't get along with the manager.

I met my husband through my sister. He was a friend of her boyfriend's. The first time I had a conversation with him I liked him. Possibly because he was six years older and more experienced.

Many people told him he couldn't marry me because there would be all sorts of problems, for example in looking for a place to live. He said: "That's not true at all." That made a big impression on me.

As time passed I thought my husband had married me because he wanted something special. He wanted someone he could show off. That's how I perceived it after a while, especially when he would say things like: "Fix your hair in a different way. You know, like Blacks who have that real woolly hair." But I thought short, straight hair was sharp. He wanted me to look African so people could say I was unusual.

I had gotten married to get away from my mother. When she and I started living together we began to have strong conflicts. Before that I had even looked forward to our living together because I had been with my grandma for most of my life. I thought: "Now I finally get to have a relationship with my mother." In the beginning, when I was still in school, it did work out quite well. We talked to each other a lot and were very close. But later when I wanted to talk about my problems at work and made more demands on her, it started to get difficult. Although I was working, I had to hand my money over to her, and whenever I wanted to buy myself something I had to ask her first. We lived together for six years. In the beginning and also later my sister lived with us. She didn't have such a good relationship with our mother, but she was allowed to do more than I was. She was more forceful in her demands and got her way, while I would keep asking a thousand times. Today she has a better relationship with Mother than I do.

My mother is a woman who has trouble showing her feelings. When I was still living at Grandma's I knew I was loved, for Grandma, and Grandpa too, were kind and gentle. Then when I had to deal directly with my mother, I thought she didn't love me. In spite of everything I'm very fond of my mother and I love her.

Through my sister S I have come into contact with other women and I see that there's still so much I haven't done or don't understand.

At a parents' meeting for the nursery school, many unfamiliar terms would come up. I would sit there thinking: "What are you people saying now?" If I wanted to contribute something, I couldn't. I often went to the nursery school by myself to talk with the teacher. She was very supportive, showing me that I was quite a capable person.

Then when I initiated a project with other residents to beautify our neighborhood, I had a real victory: in collecting signatures I had to go to one of these political types who was a good talker. I thought I'd never get him to sign, but I refused to be intimidated and kept on talking. All of a sudden I knew what I wanted. It was a great success! Later we worked together on a brochure in our group, and it went very well, although I always have trouble expressing myself in writing.

In my second try at schooling, I finished the secondary level of education. It was hard and they all said that working women with children never make it. But I took that as challenge to make it.

I had to work while I was in school and again while S was in nursery school. I often argued with my husband over things we wanted to buy, but since my stamina never held out, he usually got his way. Now I live alone with my daughter and feel very good about it.

I still haven't completely gotten past problems with my color. I've noticed that some people take it almost as a joke when I say something. They laugh even when I mean it seriously.

At my daughter's school I hear over and over again how unusual I look. Then they ask S with surprise: "What is your mother? She looks so different." It's pretty hard for me to walk across the playground at recess when I go to meet S at school. But S doesn't have so many difficulties.

Julia Berger (age 17)

*"I do the same things
that others do"*

My father is Italian, my mother Afro-German. When my mother
was in nursing school I lived for three or four years with my
grandparents in Italy. And yes, I was always spoiled and got everything I wanted.

People did notice that I looked different, but everybody always
said: "Oh, isn't she sweet!" One day my mother just came and took
me back to Berlin. At five I was enrolled in school and already had
one year of school in Italy behind me. At first I still spoke Italian as
well as German, but since then I haven't kept it up. When my
mother used to tell me I had an African grandfather, I would
always say: "But that's not true. I come from Italy." Since then I've
come to understand what she meant, but I had only known my
paternal grandparents.

I had little contact with my father, although he too lived in
Berlin. He owned restaurants here. I used to wish all the time that
my parents got along better and that we could all live together. We
never did live together, but now I understand why my mother
separated from my father. He had a girlfriend and a child with her,
too. In Italy they always wanted to keep it a secret from me that I
had a half sister. She must be ten years old now. I would love to see
her, but I don't think she knows I exist. Nowadays I get to see my
father more often.

Now I don't think of myself so much as an Italian anymore, but
more as a German. I do the same things that others do and have
lots of friends. And no one says to me: "We won't have anything to
do with you because you're brown." At school I never had any

problems either, except for one time. A boy said: "What are you doing here anyway? Why don't you go back where you came from." Another time, in elementary school, a girl told me: "I'm not going to play with you. You're a mulatto." So I said to her: "So? And your father's an alcoholic." I don't know why she said that to me. Maybe she was very unhappy and wanted to hurt someone. But she came to the wrong person.

Teachers treated us like everybody else, too. After I went on a trip to Africa I had to give a report in school about it. They all thought it was wonderful, and I got a good grade. When I go to discos I see a lot of people who look like me. It's not a rarity in Berlin. I don't know if their parents are Africans or Americans. I don't bring it up. There's one girl in my school, too, that I speak to; I don't have any inhibitions about it. But when my friends say: "I saw your sister," I don't know how I'm supposed to react, so I

answer: "Fine. Show her to me." But it doesn't bother me. I've never had kids shout anything at me. But sometimes strangers ask me if I speak German. Yesterday, while sitting in a café with my mother someone asked us that. Then people are usually very surprised that I speak such good German. When I'm out with white Germans that hardly ever happens.

Mostly I'm taken to be half-American, and then when I say my grandfather was African, they are very surprised. I have no desire to be white anymore. That's just the way I am. I have to live with it and I don't find anything negative in it.

My friends do ask where I come from, and then I have to tell my story for the umpteenth time, but I'm not looked upon as a foreigner, neither in school nor anywhere else.

One time I was at a career counselor's office and was telling him I wanted to be a travel agent. He asked me if I knew I had to send a photograph with the application. Sure, I said. He felt I would come up against people who wouldn't take me because I'm brown or because they don't take foreigners. So I said: "Look, I'm not a foreigner."

I thought it might be difficult because of my school record. But I really believe people don't react that way. So many foreigners live in Germany, it's become quite normal now. We're not living in some bygone era; they just can't do that, refuse people jobs.

In Africa I had a pretty hard time. The people were nice, and I liked it. But I don't think I could live there; I'm just accustomed to life here. And I've never lived in a village.

When I went there I had thought that people would be darker, but I wasn't prepared to have them shout "white people" after us. They said: "Toubab," which means stranger. It was meant to be friendly and kids would laugh and wave. I had thought they would take me for one of their own.

Here they shout "black girl" and there they shout "white girl" . . . Where does one really belong?

Abena Adomako (age 23)

Mother: Afro-German
Father: Ghanaian

My color is black. Therefore I'm perceived as a foreigner—African or American. I'm always being asked how come I speak German so well, where I come from, etc. This quizzing gets on my nerves. Most of the time I answer provocatively that I'm German. In spite of my unequivocal answer they continue: How? Why?

I am African, but I'm German, too. African in appearance, German in thinking, behavior, and the way I move: in those respects I'm European.

Africans are described as sweet, dumb, naive, and dirty. My mother and grandmother grew up in Germany as Afro-Germans.* In order to escape prejudices against Africans, they brought me up to be especially clean and neat and to perform especially well at school and in my profession. I had to be better than the others or at least at the top of the group.

Whenever I go to Ghana to visit my relatives, the first period is a time of adjustment for me. Then I'm simply absorbed among the many Africans, even though I still stand out because of my European ways. Ghana! I'm at home, but it's not my home, and still I feel comfortable!

It used to be that when I would see lighter "mulattoes" (Afro-Germans), I would be envious. I thought, their color is prettier, just like a suntan, and they are more easily accepted in this society. I

---

* Grandmother Erika Ngambi ul Kuo talks about her life in this book. See "Our Father Was Cameroonian."

Abena Adomako with her parents

wasn't aware that they have problems precisely because the double identity black/white is immediately visible from their skin color.

During my childhood I only knew a few other Afro-German children. There was one boy in my class with whom I didn't have any particular relationship, but I would have liked to know what he thought and felt. Among the kids in our neighborhood there was another Afro-German girl. Later when she was going out with a friend of mine, I began to wonder: Am I too dark to be someone's girlfriend? I can't blame everything on color. Maybe I just wasn't the right type; but it still makes me wonder.

At that age I had no opportunities at all to go out with boys. Some of my friends already had boyfriends, but I could never join in the discussion and felt very excluded. One of them even said I couldn't get a boyfriend because I was too dark. I kept hearing that until I actually had my first boyfriend. I often think today that, while I was accepted and liked, boys were afraid to become too close to me or too friendly for fear that some kind of obligation or complications would develop. For example, that it would be too difficult to take a really Black girlfriend home.

I also had a hard time because I couldn't be involved in the other kids' pranks. If I was one of five or ten kids going around ringing doorbells or something, I would always be recognized. Be careful, behave yourself, I was always told from the time I was little. And that's how I handled myself until I was about seventeen.

In all families good behavior and upbringing is the goal for the children; with our family the struggle against prejudice was an added factor. Not to be conspicuous in a negative way, at any cost. Always be polite and nice to everyone, that is, a "good" African. That's how you are, and that's what's expected.

During adolescence, when spin-the-bottle and get-acquainted games between girls and boys started, I felt my exclusion. Usually I was made the guard for people's purses and coats. Even today I have a sensitive reaction if someone tries to put those kinds of jobs on me.

In 1980 I went to London as an *au pair*. There my consciousness of my background and color was strengthened and developed. I felt very good. Among the many different nationalities I wasn't noticed anymore, so the burden and stress of having to appear superior and cool, and the feeling of always being eyeballed and harassed were gone. To be able to move freely in the street, in the subway, among people, was a liberating feeling. The question, who or why you are something other than you appear to be, the problem of being Afro-German, simply wasn't there.

I learned to fully accept my own color. I no longer wanted to be lighter. I am Black. Abena and everything that entails, that's me.

Back in Berlin the pressure and stress situations started all over again, the gawking, the hypocrisy, the inferiority. My environment demanded the well-behaved, good Abena it had known before. If I had previously been quiet and introverted, now I was lively and assertive and self-assured. I talked endlessly and exchanged my conservative clothes for second-hand pieces. My behavior was contrary to all the expectations of my family and friends.

After returning from England I went job hunting. I had been trained as a foreign-language secretary and was now making applications in writing and by phone. They ask for statistics: age, nationality. In my head wheels started turning. Can I show up there with my Berlin accent and my skin color? Did the inquiry about nationality arise because of my last name, Adomako? I go to one of the many interviews. Brilliant machinations take place to hide xenophobia and prejudice. So I write and telephone umpteen-hundred times to find a halfway neutral person who is prepared to hire me. When I'm finally hired, it continues; I sense the prejudice of colleagues and superiors.

"You wrote that incorrectly." Doubts about my ability. Africans just can't do that. But I learned this profession. Then I no longer know who's right. It's a circle, and I continue to fight my battle.

In recent years here in Germany I've lost some of my strength and self-confidence. And so the idea and desire arise to go away to a place where people are free of prejudice and I can cross the street without being the foreign object. People say to me, "Go away for a while, then you'll miss 'home.'" That may be, but better a little homesickness than to be unhappy at "home."

It's the time for discos, cafés, and relationships; get dressed up, go out, go dancing; for me that means stress from beginning to end.

1. Getting dressed up: I'm forced to look well groomed and clean. Why? There's the prejudice about poor, sloppy Africans, or the opposite—chic, chic, she must be for sale. So what to put on? I pick the neutral, least exciting or sexy look.

2. At the disco: there are the looks and the whispers from men and women, and the pressure on my date of being observed also; or is it even enjoyable being the center of attention?

3. Dancing: it's generally claimed that people of African background can dance better. I go to the dance floor with the special attention of the crowd on my "little number." No matter what I think to myself—that I danced well or that I'm not feeling so "up" today—I always get praise.

4. The "come-ons": all women get approached, but toward me there's no holding back. I consider the manner in which it's done to be vulgar and debasing. "Everybody knows what a Black woman has to offer a man." First of all she's a sexually attractive woman, second, a woman with character. I enjoy hearing the compliment that I look good, but in my case isn't it more of an insult?

Wherever I show up there are reactions, but I would prefer not always to be conspicuous. I'm not the type to show off, as is so often expected of me.

In order to protect myself from undesirable suitors, I had to build a wall around myself. Being harassed by pimps and dirty old men—that's not my idea of a life! Mistrust and caution all the way; so I appear hard, cool, quiet, conscious of suppressing any possible enticement; then I'm left in peace. This tough façade carries over to everyday situations. It's difficult for a really nice guy to get through to me, and I can scarcely recognize his sincerity. At that point I unconsciously begin testing him. I can hardly explain why it's like this, maybe because I want to know whether, in spite of prejudice and opposition from outside, he would stick by me. But all of this only makes me unhappy.

Even if my experiences sound harsh sometimes, this is how I've learned to deal with my situation and to find a way to myself and to self-realization. More and more I'm finding the courage to let myself be noticed, the courage to step out, and the courage to show my body without hiding myself behind high-necked blouses or white shirts in shame. That's important to me.

I have to assert myself in a society that appears to be neutral but isn't. I can come off as self-assured, but it's always a force in me that says: "Be that way, you must, or you'll go under." Why can't I just be the way I want to be, simply, without any kind of battle stance?

May Opitz (age 25)

The Break

The day I was born, a lot of stories of my life came into the world. Each one carries its truth and wisdom. Those who were around me through my experiences would probably offer an entirely different story of my childhood than I would. I can only tell my story as it made its impression on me, and if the negative events remain clearer in my memory than the positive ones, no apology is necessary. That's just the way it is. I'm going to expose some of myself here. Without accusation or pardon, without claim to reality, in experiencing truth. And in the certainty that everyone who reads my story will understand it differently.

When I was born I was neither black nor white. "Half-breed child" was the first name I got. It is hard to surround a child with love when her mother's grandparents say that the child is out of place. It is hard if the child doesn't fit into the mother's plans and when there's no money. And it all becomes even harder when her white mother doesn't want her child to be taken away to a Black world. The laws don't even allow the African father to take his little German daughter to an African mother.

It's not easy to put a child into an orphanage. She stays there a year and six months.

On the radio a couple somewhere heard about children like me: about those who can't find parents because they are "GI children," because they are handicapped or not blond enough or were born in prison. I became the dream child of a white German family and forgot the months in the orphanage. From that period only my foster parents' stories remain: "You couldn't even stand up. Because of the unbalanced diet you had rickets. Your upper body was fat and overfed, your little legs so crooked that every doctor thought you would never halfway straighten up."

There aren't any "adorable" baby pictures from that period. I'm always mindful of my foster parents' repeated warning: "Be careful! If you were fat as a baby you'll be fat later on, too. Always take care not to eat too much!" From that period I had a constant fear of getting old and fat, later emphasized by the stereotype of the "fat black mammy," that was pointed out to me in many TV films as a frightful warning.

Childhood is when a child wonders a lot, and the words a child speaks aren't understood. Childhood is when a child wets the bed and the parents react with beatings. Childishness is a child doing everything wrong, misbehaving, not understanding anything, being too slow, and making the same mistake over and over.

Childhood is when a child continues to wet the bed and no one understands that the child doesn't do it to punish its parents. Childhood is living in fear of beatings and not being able to get over it. Childhood is getting bronchitis every year and being sent repeatedly to a sanitorium. Years later a doctor says in response to my surprise over the sudden disappearance of my chronic bronchitis after I was fifteen: Didn't you know that that, like bedwetting, is a psychosomatic illness?

Fear that constricts the air passage? There certainly was enough fear. Probably fear of the outside world. Or fear of bursting open. Fear of breaking to pieces from beatings and scoldings and of not being able to find yourself again. Don't protest, swallow instead. Until it can't go any further and seeps out: in the bed or as a brutal coughing pain that drives any person with normal hearing to sleepless nights and fits of rage. That's how it is with oppression. As soon as you start swallowing it, you can be sure that the cup will fill up. When the limit is reached, the bottom will crack or some will overflow. Your own form of "self-defense" is unfortunately completely misunderstood or not understood at all. I can hear my mother complaining: "That darn coughing. It's enough to drive a person crazy!"

Childhood is laughing, too! Playing in the sandbox, roller skat-

ing, scooter riding, and learning to ride a bike. Snagging thousands of pairs of tights and taking the maternal anger as the price for a wonderful day. And love!

Love is when Mama cooks something delicious and when the child gets to go along downtown. When the child gets a lollipop at the church bazaar, Christmastime when everything's enchanted, and the child gets to go to the movies. Love is getting up very quietly in the morning and setting the table for Mama and Papa and thinking up nice presents. Love is when everybody goes on vacation in a happy mood.

Longing is the need to sense someone saying: "Hey, little one, are you feeling all right? You mean so much to us. Whether you're Black or white, fat or skinny, dumb or smart, I love you! Come let me hold you." Longing is knowing what you want to hear and waiting in vain for it to be said. Sadness is when a child thinks she's too Black and too ugly. Horror, when Mama won't wash the child white. Why not? But everything would be much simpler. And the other children wouldn't shout "Negro" or "Negro Kiss." The child would no longer have to be ashamed or be especially proper or well-mannered. "Always behave nice and proper. What people think of you they think of all people of your color."

Life is too hard for me.

1. That damned fear of doing everything wrong. The crying all night if I lost something at school.

"Please, God, don't let Mama and Papa beat me when I tell them."

The constant trembling for fear of doing something wrong and then from such trembling breaking twice as many things as my other sisters and brothers. "No wonder nobody likes me."

2. The rotten grade school with the damn homework. Mama supervises everything with the kitchen spoon, especially the arithmetic homework. When the child doesn't figure fast enough she gets a smack on the head; when the problems aren't written neatly enough, the page gets ripped out. Except for recess and gym I don't especially like school. Why can't I ever invite or visit anyone? "Dear God, make Mama and Papa die and let us get other parents. Some that are only loving."

3. My parents say so often that I can't do anything, am nothing, and do everything too slowly. I secretly take one of my father's razor blades and hide it under my pillow. The fear and the longing for suicide—"The child plays with razor blades in bed! You must be out of your mind. Don't you know how dangerous that is? This child is driving me crazy!"

One time I decide to run away from home. I tell my little brother and say good-bye to him. I'm about nine and he is five. Recognizing the seriousness of the situation, he starts crying and tells my parents. They're a little nicer to me—"Dear God make me go to sleep and never wake up again."

4. Who destroyed my dream? The dream of "whiteness" ruined because of my parents' unwillingness and the weak cleaning power of soap. Even eating soap had no effect at all. The dream of "blackness" ruined because of the real-life appearance of my father. Before that, my secret: When I get big I'm going to Africa. There everybody looks like me. When Mama, Papa, and my white

sisters and brothers come to visit, people will point at them. I will console them and tell the people: "Don't do that!" And my parents will understand how it was for me in Germany.

Look! That's my father! He's really Black. "By comparison you're white."—"Does everybody in Africa look that black?"—"Well sure." You've all destroyed my dream.

One time when my father came to visit, all the kids ran away. But he had brought candy for all of us. Maybe we had played the game "Who's afraid of the Black man?" too often: "But what if he comes?"—"Then we run." Maybe the inoculations for black lies, black sins, and the black bogeyman had gone too deep. My brother and I would have liked to run away, but we knew we couldn't. Besides, there were nice presents.

My father was Uncle E. He was Uncle E because he was Uncle E for my white brother, and he was Uncle E because he was not my "father" to me. He remained Uncle E even in letters, when at some point I began writing, "Dear Father." My foster father wanted it like that. He thought that E would like that. Since I knew he was far away and would stay far away except for visits every few years, I did both of them the favor and wrote: "Dear Father." I wrote about my last vacation, my next vacation, my marks in school, and always about the weather. My foster father made sure that I did it right.

I never wondered whether I was supposed to be proud of him or hate him. From the few reports I got about him he seemed to be a positive, educated man, who for some reason had a child that he could not raise himself. I once asked for a story about the woman who brought me into the world. "A woman? She was a floozy." I never asked again.

In this feeling of exclusion I went around in circles. In particular, my foster parents' fear that I would end up on the "wrong track" kept me imprisoned. The fear that I would come home pregnant was the reason underlying every sanction against going out. Their worries and fears strangled me. Before I left home I spent one silent year in my family's home; that sealed the break.

In retrospect I know: my parents loved me. They took me into their care to sort of counteract the prejudice in this society. To give me the chance of a family life that I would never have had in the orphanage. Out of love, a sense of responsibility, and ignorance my parents reared me especially strictly, beat me, and imprisoned me. Cognizant of the prejudices that exist in white German society, they unintentionally adapted their rearing to those prejudices. I grew up with the feeling that they were committed to proving that a "half-breed," a "Negro," an "orphan child" is an equal person. Beside that, there was scarcely any time or space left to discover who I really was.

It took a long time until I became conscious of the fact that I have some value. When I reached the point where I could say "yes" to myself, without the secret wish to change, I was given the possibility to recognize the fissures in myself and my surroundings, to work through them and learn from them. I wasn't broken by my experiences; instead I gained strength and a certain kind of knowledge from them. The situation of not being able to be integrated forced me to the active struggle which I no longer regard as a burden, but rather as a special challenge for honesty. Always having to examine and explain my situation provided me with more clarity about myself and brought me to the recognition that I don't owe anyone an explanation. I hold no grudge against those people who subjected me to their power (and powerlessness) and who from time to time subordinated me or made me subordinate myself. Often I allowed others to make something out of me; now it's up to me to change that.

I've set out on the way.

calm of the storm

for my brother

sometimes
the beautiful moments shine until
today and
stroked wounds whisper
pain
in gentle dreams

best
I like to see us
playing in the sandbox
stirring earth and water to mudpies
the houses we built were beautiful and
fragile

the blows
to head and bones
bolts like lightning
when we laughed at THEM and cried
our nearness grew
i loved laughing with you!

sometimes the beautiful moments
shine until today
I stir mudpies
and draw our faces

fatherseeking

when i needed you
i held the picture on the wall
to be true
the most beautiful thing i had from you
the only thing

you were
as i wished you to be
serious and smart and tender. infinitely tender.

face to face
your glance caught me
serious and smart and cold. bitter cold.

without words
I hung the picture
that dreamed for me
a dream of father
bittersweet the parting

I go and wonder

almost not at all

i never knew you at all
and, after we
saw each other
for five minutes
years ago,
hardly at all

five minutes brown hair brown eyes nervous mouth
five minutes and back then nine months
forced child/motherhood
we never knew each other at all
and now, almost not at all

touching

i always sensed you there
even when rolling tears along branches
of loneliness
and especially then—
i sensed it
i know it

Katharina Oguntoye (age 27)

*What I've Always Wanted
to Tell You*

i dream of a common language. while my
heart beats in pulses thump. thump. thump.
and the fear prevents my breakaway.
1984

"Home Times Three"

Well, I might as well start at the beginning. I was born in January 1959, in the maternity hospital in Zwickau, the bells had barely begun to chime the noon hour. It was a beautiful day. (And to the best of my knowledge, a lot of people rejoiced at my arrival.)

Anyway, as far as I'm concerned, I felt perfectly content. So, Zwickau, where is it located? you'll ask. It is an industrial city in the foothills of the Erz Mountains and about an hour by train from Leipzig, where I moved three weeks later and would spend my next seven years.

Leipzig is the first stop for most African students who intend to study in the GDR. There they learn the German language before starting their respective majors at the various universities. For this reason there's quite a large African student community in Leipzig. My father and some of his relatives studied in Leipzig. At our house, there was often African food cooked, lots of people over to eat, and discussions late into the night. Thus, I and my brother who's two years younger than I grew up around white and Black people. Still I probably didn't perceive myself as Black, because one time looking out of the window of a rattling streetcar, I saw an African walking down the street and shouted, all excited: "Mommy, look! A Negro." This episode, which my mother often recounted, leads me to believe that I didn't connect my own color and my father's with the term "Negro."

Leipzig, which I now know to be one of the cultural centers of the GDR, is the place of my childhood, wrapped in memories and feelings. I regret that the images that for so long permeated my day- and night-dreams are now so hard to recapture. I remember Schreber Street, where we lived, and the way to the nursery school past the butcher shop, and the bakery opposite it. We played in the nearby municipal park with the big lake spanned by an old wooden bridge that I was scared to cross. Later I got up the nerve to peer through its wide slits into the shimmering water. Leipzig is a place where I experienced love and also learned to love. Mother worked hard, and yet she and Father were there for my brother and me. I felt safe.

With my brother and my mother, I went to Nigeria, my father's country. I was seven years old and my brother, five; for us the three-week trip on a freighter was a unique adventure which allowed us to gradually adjust to the move.

When we arrived in Lagos twenty years ago, before the civil war and the oil boom, life was very different from today—it was in no way as hectic. It pulsated with a colorful hustle and bustle and an ambience of well-being.

We lived in the luxurious faculty quarters of the university, which at that time was still under construction. There were plenty of children our age and of various nationalities to play with. A paradise of freedom for us city kids. We enjoyed prowling around in the dense woods behind our house or in the empty lot that had been cleared but not yet dug up for construction. Our games were called "preparing for an expedition" or "mud-hut-building" or the like.

Unlike the adults, the children had hardly any adjustment problems in our new living situation. We processed our many impressions by acting them out in our games. For example, it was a lot of fun harassing our mother by twisting ourselves in contortions, trailing behind her, imitating the beggar's call in a monotonous singsong: "Please Madam! Give me change! Please Madam! Give me change!"

Once I was supposed to recite a German poem at my new school. Having switched completely to the English language, I had to think hard. Then one came to me that I had learned in nursery school and liked a lot. It went like this:

> My cat is named Moor
> she's got a black ear
> and also black fur
> when there's something sweet to eat
> there she is right at your feet.

But when I had to translate it, I couldn't, and I got this painful feeling. Something was wrong about that little verse that I loved so much, even if, at age seven, I couldn't exactly figure out what it was.

Two years later I left Africa with my mother—that world that was getting to be more and more like home—to return to my first home. We lived in Heidelberg. But it wasn't my Germany that I went back to. It was *Germany*. And in the beginning I could hardly tell the difference, for this country resembled my native country as one egg resembles another. But an insidious communication problem in the same language made the difference unmistakable. Gradually I became aware that there was a way of being with people that I longed for and that was lost to me, just as it is impossible to stop or turn back time.

I'm happy about the varied nature of my early experiences, just as I have nothing against my life as an Afro-German. In collaborating on this book, a process began for me in which I'm learning to consciously use the possibilities that result from my background and my life.

toksi

i lived for three years in west germany separated from my brother. i was the only afro-german at the time. i remember well that when my brother finally came i loved his feet the most. i had missed him terribly the whole time. but now there was a totally new fascination. i was very surprised and had to look and look. i couldn't get enough. his fine young face, soft and sweet, his slim body and his hands, but all my love went to his feet. it was unbelievable. he had come from far away and had the same feet as me.

in the previous three years i had gradually figured out that every part of me looked different. now i knew what i had missed—having somebody around who looked similar to me. it felt so good that the form of his hands and feet looked so much like mine. i loved him for making me feel that i was not alone, not an accidental exception.

1984

Reflection

alone with my desperation. looking into your eyes, my brown, and oh so german sister. where is my peace? are *you* my reflection? is it the loneliness, the isolation that i see? the way to you is far and unknown. i go there unsure of my steps.

do you remember, my german, and oh so white sister, the feeling of desperation when you didn't yet know that there are other women who don't want to be just servants? women who nevertheless go their own way? when they became visible to you they gave you courage to find your own way? but how long did you have the feeling it wasn't possible to take a deep breath, in spite of the growing women's community, until you discovered you weren't the only one who loves women? that there were other lesbians who weren't willing to be played off against other women any longer?

now i'm telling you as your afro-german sister, that by choosing to see me as a woman without color and without her own heritage, or as a puzzling being, somehow exotic, somehow an object you are ready to leave me hanging in a similar desperation. and it is cynical when you say it's not *my* problem, only afro-german women have to deal with it.

1984

pain of separation

sometimes i'm tired. then i think the struggle is too hard and the pain is too much. but still while i'm thinking this i know that the effort is worth it. the joy of approaching my goal is wonderful. i've often been rewarded for my survival. and the warmth that i have from those experiences can't be taken away from me anymore. there's still the terror and mourning of separating, but these come precisely because something was there, something that came close to the dream.

i wouldn't want to give up because i want to feel it, this joy. i'd like to dive into the waves of the ocean. for it's a whole ocean of love that i know. perhaps the idea of wholeness in me, as it could be in you, is what i feel then.

leaving isn't going away for ever. to separate doesn't mean staying alone. not today. not for us. if hearts are connected, the miles can't hinder the flow of affection. and a psychic tie supports us along our different paths.

1984

being real

the way i perceive things, when I'm conscious of leaving, when i notice again. how i then begin to soak up everything around me. colors, forms, light. how everything fits together, how the rhythm keeps going. and i know i should always live this way. to enjoy and collect each thing, each gesture, for a later time when my reality has changed and i would remember that i once thought it would never be different from just that moment just because i was feeling it so strongly. but the images change. they don't stay real. it's only when they are completely gone that i notice what they had meant to me and whenever i want to i can return to my feelings for the smells, the trees or the river from that time while i was busy absorbing them. this is the way i experience every place. i learned this kind of being through my departures. it's harder when i simply want to be. sometimes it's such a perfect illusion that even i could believe in it myself.

1985

Relationships and Racism between Women
Our friendship or what i always wanted to tell you

up to that time racism wasn't a topic for me in my relationships with women. i accepted silently the taboo that existed between me and my women friends. sometimes i felt secure in the twilight zone of the unspoken. that way each could believe the best about the other. no embarrassing conversations would disturb the friendly woman-to-woman atmosphere or cause disharmony between friends. but sometimes i felt threatened by this silence which became more urgent as the years went by. i became aware that the not-knowing about the other's fears allows these fears to grow. then the fears become so strong for both that it's no longer possible to convey these feelings to each other. The longer and closer the relationship is, the more difficult it becomes because neither can escape from the confusion of her thoughts;

—she'll withdraw from me because . . .

—i can't tell her that . . .

—we're getting along so well, so why start talking about that . . .

—she's not interested or surely she'd have mentioned it . . .

—how shall i explain to her that i feel . . .

—i'll ruin everything if . . .

—she won't trust me anymore if . . .

—i don't want to hurt her feelings . . .

—she won't like me anymore . . .

—she won't answer frankly because she doesn't want to hurt me . . .

—i have/do i have racist thoughts . . .

—she despises me because i'm different

but these unspoken thoughts have an unsettling effect and can make it really hard for friendship between women. for me the worst was to sit by and watch as my friendships slowly dried up due to a lack of openness. that's like being in the middle of an oasis and dying of thirst because we think it's a mirage.

1984

"I never wanted to write,
I just couldn't help myself":

Conversation with
Raya Lubinetzki (age 23)
GDR

How did you come to write poetry?

When I was in school, about fourteen years old, I was in love with a woman who was my teacher. I've always read Afro-American literature, which I discovered in libraries. Richard Wright's *Native Son*, for example, and James Baldwin—that was the beginning of the "Black is beautiful" movement. Around that time I once wrote something about my feelings and thoughts, and it came out in the form of a poem. Then I wrote a bunch of poems and showed them to my German teacher. She said: "You have talent," and wanted to recommend me to the FDJ [Freie Deutsche Jugend (Free German Youth), a youth organization in the GDR] poets' seminar, but then she didn't do anything about it—I was terribly disappointed; I never found out why she didn't get back to me.

In tenth grade, for my senior essay I brought together all my ideas about the Afro-American literature I had read. Then I stuck the title of some book on it, and when I was asked where the book was, I said I couldn't find it. They gave me an A for the essay.

Did you consider yourself talented as a writer?

No, but writing was the only way I could express myself, because there was nobody I could talk to, because I felt nobody understood me. For example, one teacher said about a poem I had written about my mother: "Why such a serious piece?"

At that time I also read African literature. I always read a lot and my mother would often interrupt me to give me housework to do. Then I'd always get a guilty conscience. All my relatives were of the opinion that no one could make a living by writing.

The teachers wouldn't admit me to the diploma track because of my rebelliousness. So I left after tenth grade and started training to be a typesetter. Relatives had told me I could be more independent in that occupation, and I thought that in that way I'd be able to do everything myself, from writing to printing. Later I wanted to get my diploma but still wasn't accepted.

The training was disappointing; in the second year you were already locked into the production and exploited and didn't really learn anymore. So it took me three years, because I wasn't at all enthusiastic about it. Two years later I flunked the final exam. After that they gave me a three-month temporary contract, which stretched out to a year. Then they kicked me out. They took the others for retraining, since the typesetting machines we had learned on had become outdated by that time.

I moved from a little village to X into a boardinghouse. There they called me a "ring leader." I told the people who worked there: "I'm not your black sheep," because I felt their behavior was racist. Their reaction was: "We aren't racists." The subject of color was as much a taboo in the dormitory as at school and while I was in training. At the boardinghouse they just said: "We don't discriminate against you; if you talk about color, that's your problem."

At that time I continued writing, in whatever form it came out. Writing was a necessity for me. When I *have* to write something, it's like having to cut something out of myself.

Through Afro-American and African literature I could at least define myself. But my mother still always told me: "You can't do that. They've grown up somewhere entirely different and have different problems. They are really discriminated against."

In writing I've always just brought everything out of myself; no one ever critiqued my work.

While I was in training I had thought I wanted to become an actress. They told me I wouldn't be accepted because of my color.

There was one Black actress, she didn't get any parts except one in a film. She just collected her salary regularly and finally left for the United States.

At work I showed one editor my folder of poems. He liked them and published one. He recommended that I join a literary group. A writer there told me they weren't poems, I should write about being Black. We met once a week, and then he would read the pieces and tear them to shreds with his criticism. But it was a way for me to get away from my surroundings. We also took trips together, and I met other people. Then I fell in love again. She lived opposite me and I used to always stand at the window and gaze dreamily across the way. We took a few car trips together, but after I told her I was in love with her, she would continually explain to me that that was unnatural. It didn't work out with her, and that hurt, and in the beginning I thought that it had to do with my color.

I got out of the literary group, and it was all over with writing for a while. I applied to a school of sculpture, where I took evening courses. The school wasn't the best, and I couldn't take the regularity along with the work, which I hated.

I moved to Y, because a woman I was in love with had gone there and I also knew other women there. In X the subject "lesbian" was taboo. In Y, I had my first meeting with lesbian women in a women's group. I was so happy, here I was no longer alone, here there were several of us, I fell in love first with one and then the other.

The police picked me up from work for alleged "antisocial behavior." I spent a week in jail and started writing again. The matron said I could take my materials with me, but she took them away when I was released.

Then I got a job in a photo lab. I worked there for half a year and then quit. For a while I spent a lot of time with others who were also unemployed. In the search for a job I landed in a nursery. I desperately wanted to get the job and managed to persuade the woman to take me on. She looked at me and said "No" right away. At that point I started crying and then she took me on after all. On the job I had to run around all the time with a wheelbarrow, and it seemed like slave's works in the fields. She frequently criticized my life style with statements like: "You ought to go back to the bush." I always nodded. At some point I had had enough, so I left. After that I hung out for two months. Now I'm working as a house-keeper. The woman I work for has to listen to a lot of talk from friends like: "Well, how's your Negro doing?" Many of them are intellectuals. Recently we gave a reading, where I also read my things and there were some other Afro-Germans there. There were intellectuals who left the reading saying things like: "A damn nigger-reading, niggers and fags."

Can you say something about your childhood?

My mother wasn't married to my father. She left me in the hospital. Then my father tried to get citizenship from his country, Cam-eroon, for me, but it wasn't approved. He took me to a friend, who was really good to me. People didn't know I wasn't her child. Relatives and people in the village labeled her a nigger whore.

My foster mother always defended me fiercely. Even from chil-dren whose parents would put them up to it because of my color and because my mother was supposed to be a whore. People in the house went to the youth welfare bureau and said my mother couldn't raise me. Then they asked me whether I wouldn't rather go to an orphanage. I got into a lot of fights with other kids; once I got so beat up I had to have an operation. As a toddler, people used to constantly give me candy, saying: "What a sweet little thing." My mother told them not to do that. Later adults always avoided me. They smiled nicely in my face, but talked about me behind my back. The only one who was different was one teacher. She sup-ported me, encouraged me with rigor in class, and intervened to get me money from the youth welfare bureau. After school I'd often go home and paint for hours. Or I'd make myself leader of a group, so that everybody was afraid of me.

Money was a problem. Due to a heart ailment, my mother became an invalid. My father only paid for me after a court trial; my real mother never paid anything. My foster mother had not adopted me. Later, when the youth welfare bureau wanted to take me away, she was no longer able to adopt me, because they had cut off her money by then. She got 270 marks for herself and 90 for me.

When I was fourteen my foster mother told me she wasn't my real mother. My father, who was still living in Germany, felt I should meet my real mother. She lived in the vicinity, and I went to see her. She nearly fainted when she saw me. That was an awful experience. I stayed for two days. She tried to defend herself and pushed the blame on my father. She had two more girls by him after me. One she kept, the other she gave up for adoption. Now she's in the United States. My grandfather was really fascistic; he treated my sister badly. My mother didn't have the courage to keep me. My sister experienced a lot of discrimination. She dropped out of the university and got married.

My African uncles used to visit me sometimes. They got upset that my father neglected me like he did. I was ten or twelve when I saw him for the first time. He had a bad conscience. I didn't talk with him very much about my life. He knew there was discrimination here, but the only alternative was to go to Africa. He had children with his new wife. She wanted nothing to do with me and didn't like me. Then I would often go to Y to visit him. E would take me over to see relatives, where we would drink champagne. I'd always return to the provinces full of complexes.

Gray Tragedy

You say you feel, Mama, because you think.
Papa, you say you think because you feel.
Terrible torment of childhood,
single lucid eye.

Dissolving all desire, forgetting all pain.
Childhood: sunny wings flutter independent of the burning
the so hot burning of radiation.

Liqueur on the traveling train full of cowardice.
So they all suffer from their habits.
Hanging on. Feeling life.

And I in between, mommy's and daddy's outspoken
gestures, firm as walls, me feeling claustrophobic.

Oh my longing for the desert. The wide deserts without thinking,
without split feelings.
Just adapting without burning feet.
Aha, I understand. I understand without crying, without a smile,
without craving, or even more.
More was oceans more.

And I'm between all the fixed winds of
deserts. Depending on analyses of yesterday, day before, yesterdays,
before birth, after voiding.

Emptiness that is none.
Gray, my recognition. And the being forbidden to be here.
Without complaint.

Fragment

birth

mirrors break, habit skins crack
pigments overpainted in dismay
mediocre eyes lynching, hateful words tearing
stamp tested words trees, blood-swallowing grass tearing
mulatto is born
mulatto is here
frizzy curled hair breaking
euro-negro rhythms being ashamed
abandoned by notes songs remain silent
mulatto is born
mulatto is here

lamentation

something in me is so unreachable
even lips are still when crying
something in me i don't know
for i feel rejecting looks and kicks
in my soul and body too
something in me that i
can't love myself anymore

something in me that thirsts for love
but i am banned from it

call

young mulatto you i call
anointed with hope after the bath of pain
you, an exile among the exiled
my call joining your trembling your anxiety
no spot on earth you can call yours resting
but your ancestors' traditions far from each other
you who went the long way all alone
garbage-collector homeless complaining look
i the deserted call to unite with strength what
was thought incompatible contradicting what was and is
crazy-split between
feeling and thinking where has thinking
alone awakened the drums where has feeling
alone written a sentence
will you so scarcely understood you will
learn to understand yourself in your
thinking and feeling and conduct
the thousand-mighty chorus of your dreams

song

i am
thriller for european consciousness
return of the drums
whistle of the jaguar in the morning
in departure vomiting hunger
i am
widened hope of the confused
in rooms of locked smells
insecure pushing for more
and new
i am seeking in the old wresting from
the reservoir of future knowledge an echoing book
from the plant's thirsting roots in rushing winds
seeds falling to fruitful ground
birds' flight in spring
nests full of tender leaves

That i'm a Negro was pounded into me over and over.
Complete astonishment. Gray being. And maybe (not at all)
tears, catastrophic attack of tears, not restrained by
the seasons. The almighty. The love slouches
in four winds.

I won't catapult them out
of their coffee-fears from isolation.
Pardon? Pardon? I don't understand what i'm saying.
Since I've been looking for You, skins all around stomachs shrinking
everything's all right by me. Apart from working for money
in the over stuffed intestines of helpless
greed.
I'm sitting here birds singing outside.
And cry silently.
Excuse me.
More i can't do and it's "nobody's" fault.

Martyrs. Times have gone with
gray brain-twaddle.
Identifying . . .
Oh, quiet! Believe in myself. In spite of infamous
judgments. The whole world dares to judge. Only leaving
themselves out.
I kissed you when I was drunk. Courageous Being, when one
hardly dares to Be, without horrible finger-pointing fears.
I despise anarchy. Favorite color gray.
If it's not necessary, the anarchy.

Occupation: on the one hand—collecting myself in diversion.
And you?
do we want to go for love.
i'm at your mercy. Your Negro.
May i be your Negro . . .

Otherwise I feel free today. Being your Negro,
only yours, for everything else I've lost the feeling.
This awful mirror of antisentimentality.
Anarchy and motherlike touches alternate, come
and go, tear me apart. Let me collect myself.

Why am I lost from you? Writing, being alone,
without absurdity, unfinished twaddle of being lonely
or not.

I need the liveliness of the German mentality
machine scrubbing, worn out mouths, listening
to beliefs, raped ears without scruple.
Art and conceited know-it-alls can kiss
my ass. I'll bury myself in deserts or
fall over dancing ecstatically, mastering the skins, inner-scream.

german motherland
negroid features tearing
street smiles biting

cold eyes pointing
dance dreamy memory
outline senseless regret
moral training coming

who loved you more
was the inner rejected
my love knows
no measure no walls

senseless appetite of feet
winter-sweat pearls
dropping like soul
condemned bodiless

german motherland
asking for pardon not love

so wait mama
you kicked me
blind from your
body love into icy worlds

so wait mama
i hear your eyes
alone from the cold fields
staring like dying
condemned no
i don't want that

so wait mama
my hands hold you
without you i wouldn't be
without me you won't be left
alone pulled into the grave

but where am i supposed to die mother
in the dark of homes of chance
puzzled paths of the tam-tams
of derived sounds curious
yellow press shouting in
pavement babble of berlin

but where am i supposed to die mother
if berlin by chance paris nowhere
a tree indicates your hands joy
in dim summers pearls of sweat
curdling in houses that are not home

but where am i supposed to die mother
like judas i go astray and died
a thousand deaths in rainbow colored breezes
from the one river spitting love

and i was derided in my
powerlessness the mirror image
of its brothers and sisters
hidden tears in lonely nights

Recapitulation and Outlook

Stereotypes about people of African descent can be traced back to the Middle Ages, when the first Africans came to Germany with the so-called voyages of discovery. At that time they were marked by religious assumptions/prejudices. Because in the Western Christian tradition "black" embodied that which was undesirable and reprehensible, it is not surprising that the literature of the Middle Ages contains examples where through unacceptable behavior white people are "transformed" into "Moors." Not until the Enlightenment, however, were racial theories developed which claimed and judged cultural and social differences to be biologically based. Within Europe they served to ground and harmonize injustices that were based on certain class privileges and, outside Europe, to legitimize the subordination and annihilation of other peoples and cultures as the "natural right" and "cultural duty" of a higher "race." Social scientists and philosophers at that time very openly supported the values of a hierarchical society and its imperialistic interests. The discourse of race-theory was the expression of a polarization constructed of gender, class, and culture. Through their exploitation of military, economic, and political power, it was ultimately white European males who became the standard of the master race. Ranked beneath them were white women, then men of color and, finally, the women of these groups.

Hand-in-hand with the decline of feudalism and the waning influence of the Church as a normative authority went the decline of religious and aesthetic precepts as the basis for the devaluation of people of African origins. Replacing these was the new work ethic that accompanied the rise of industrial capitalism. Other peoples and cultures were assessed by ethnologists and anthropologists on the basis of their technological development in relation to white Europeans and were classified accordingly: as "people of nature," who in comparison to Europeans were "underdeveloped," "primitive," "uncivilized," or "backward." Also incorporated in this cultural devaluation was the emergence of sexist subjugation and disempowerment of women in Europe, whose increasing exclusion from public life was accompanied by a glorification of the traditional roles of housewife and mother. Men and women of other peoples were stereotyped with "female" characteristics, as they were embodied allegedly—from the white male viewpoint—in the modern middle-class woman: emotional, passive, orienting their own needs toward those of husband and family, unfit to stand on their own. To leading philosophers of the Enlightenment, white women signified the white man's "nature" and by analogy peoples of color were looked upon and treated as the natural resource of the white "race."

In the colonies it became evident that in actual confrontation with Africans, German women were often more brutal and intransigent than their men, who held positions of power. Their collusion in supporting and maintaining white men's power set them above any Black man and definitely above any Black woman. Only rarely was there actual solidarity with Black women, but in those cases where it did exist, it existed within specific boundaries. The myths about the particular brutality of Blacks and their sexuality bordering on perversion (myths that justified the enslavement and murder of Africans), the rape of Black women and the simultaneous protection of white women from Black men—all these continued uninterrupted, when, in the course of the occupation of the Rhineland, Black soldiers marched into Germany.

Racist colonial consciousness did not end with the forced relinquishing of the colonies. In the Weimar Republic the ideology of the existence of higher and lower races had its consequences in the defamation of Africans and in their deportation. This ideology found its most concrete realization in National Socialism. While a few Afro-Germans were given privileges for propaganda purposes, in order to protect the racist system against external attack, hundreds of others were persecuted, sterilized, or murdered.

After 1945, no substantive effort was made to come to grips with the German colonial history, and, furthermore, any settlements for National Socialist crimes were largely limited to financial "compensation" to persecuted Jews.

The emerging social sciences approached the new generation of Black Germans as the so-called children of the occupation. Researchers and sponsors of anthropological studies had no qualms about raising the question of hereditary peculiarities among the so-called half-breeds and addressing it with data that had been gathered during the Nazi regime, data that had earlier served to justify mandatory sterilization of Black Germans.

At the parliamentary level there was discussion in the mid-1950s of the possibility of transporting Black Germans abroad, using climatic considerations as the rationale. The possibility that it was the responsibility of the white German population to achieve an antiracist consciousness was not considered.

And so we see, for example, at the end of 1986 (half a year after this book's publication in German) a statement in a report about an interregional Afro-German conference on "Racism in the Federal Republic." "Being Black is not enough. Dark-skinned German citizens have a hard time in the search for identity" (*Frankfurter Rundschau* and *Die Zeit*).

It is high time that German society confronts the real issue and stops taking the victims of racism as the actual problem. The view of the German past is so clouded with guilt and fear that talking about it becomes taboo and engenders hatred and jealousy toward all those who even today number among its potential victims. In such a climate, no honest and constructive confrontation of Germany's own history, grief, fear, and anger can take place. What surfaces instead is, at best, revulsion and aggression toward anything that recalls the horrors of the German past and touches upon Germany's own responsibility for the present and the future.

Much remains to be done. Even today, racism is a basic component of children's, youth, and adult literature, textbooks, and mass media. Global interdependencies between poverty-ridden and wealthy countries lead to the exportation of this literature through "cultural exchange" and the colonization of people's consciousness around the world. In this way, the concept of "natural superiority and inferiority" of human beings of different heritages is supported and then given expression in a rejection of self by the supposed inferiors in their attempt to become like their oppressors. The use of skin lighteners, by women particularly, in Africa, the Americas, and Europe is one outward manifestation of this rejection of self. In complement to this there has developed among whites a kind of corrupted consciousness, expressing itself in well-intentioned paternalism and cultural arrogance toward people of non-European background. In this regard, the idealization of the "exotic" and "closeness to nature" is only the flip side of the same arrogance that leads to the distortion and blocking out of reality.

The cultural and social history of Afro-Germans is embedded within the context of society as a whole and of the world in general, in which racism, sexism, and class discrimination are interconnected on many levels. Thus it is not enough to direct a struggle against prejudice at specific individuals or to pull isolated racist books out of circulation. The structures of dependency must be brought into the open and dismantled at all levels.

To the degree that a society draws its cultural assumptions along strict lines of demarcation—foreigner/native, First World/Third World—it forces those who grow up with the knowledge that their heritage is rooted in other cultures to deal with their identity in a more intense manner. Even today Afro-Germans in West and East Germany often feel themselves to be in a kind of "limbo" between belonging and exclusion and are thus put to the test—far more often than white Germans—of attaining a form of self-consciousness that does not derive its strength from separatism. But white Germans, too, must work out an identity so that multicultural coexistence is not viewed as a one-sided process of accommodation and subordination, but as a rapprochement with mutual willingness for change.

Blues in Black-and-White

Over and over again
there are those who are
dismembered, sold off and distributed
those who are always are, were, and shall remain the "others"
over and over again
the actual others declare themselves
the only real ones
over and over again
the actual others declare on us
war

it's the blues in Black-and-white
1/3rd of the world
dances over
the other
2/3rds
they celebrate in white
we mourn in Black
it's the blues in Black-and-white
it's the blues

a reunited germany
celebrates itself in 1990
without its immigrants, refugees, jewish and black people
it celebrates in its intimate circle
it celebrates in white

but it's the blues in *Black*-and-white
it's the blues
united germany united europe united states
celebrates 1992
500 years since columbus
500 years—of slavery, exploitation, and genocide in the americas
asia
and africa

1/3rd of the world unites
against the other 2/3rds
in the rhythm of racism, sexism, and antisemitism
they want to isolate us; irradicate our history
or mystify it to the point of

irrecognition
it's the blues in Black-and-white
it's the blues

but we're sure of it—we're sure
1/3rd of humanity celebrates in white
2/3rds of humanity doesn't join the party

MAY OPITZ
October 1990
(translated by Tina Campt)

Translator's Afterword

ANNE V. ADAMS

Surprisingly, the term "Afro-German" is not immediately compre-
hended by most people who hear it. Virtually no Americans and
indeed few Germans have ever heard the term at all. But for those
who are now hearing it, an explication is usually necessary. Ob-
viously, the difficulty in comprehending the meaning of "Afro-
German" is not lexical but semantic. The two components of the
term are immediately recognizable to anyone with the least familiarity with names of European nations and with contemporary
"third world" discourse. But inasmuch as hyphenated or otherwise
qualified nationality designations are historical or geopolitical
products, it takes an understanding of the origins of the group so
designated in order to make something out of the name. Would the
term "Black German" be more transparent, like "Black French-
man" or "Black Briton," to mention other Black populations of
Europe? Does "Afro-German" correspond to "Afro-American"*
for Germans of African descent? (Or perhaps it's just a mocking
invention analogous to "Afro-Saxon")** Of the numerous designations that reflect the dynamics of the African diaspora, this one,

---

*For many Americans of African descent the designation "Afro-American" is
now being replaced by "African American" as a way of according full recognition to
our African ancestry, as is the case with *all* other ethnicities in the U.S. population,
for whom the full name, rather than a truncated adjective form, of their national or
cultural ancestry is used, e.g., Italian American, Chinese American, Jewish American. Thus, out of this preference "African American" is used in this translator's
afterword.

**Label coined by Kenyan writer Ngugi wa Thiong'o in criticism of some of his
fellow African ex-British colonials for being "more British than the British."

"Afro-German," is new. While Afro-Germans indeed share important historical, social, cultural, and political experience with Black French women and men, Black Britons, and African Americans, the German situation has its own unique definition, adding another dimension to the dynamics of the African diaspora.

While the shared history among Blacks in Europe derives, of course, from the European colonization of Africa, a discussion of which is not the intention here, the politics of naming are different in the specific cases. "Black French women or men" is the name that was accorded to Africans, specifically Senegalese inhabitants of the municipalities of Dakar and Saint Louis, on whom French citizenship was conferred early in this century, as a part of the French colonial program of cultural assimilation. Considered at the time to be a measure of status for those Senegalese, the designation "Black French woman or man" consequently served to impose a class distinction among Senegalese beyond the traditional determinants of group identity in Senegambian society. Through selected migration to the French metropole for education and professional opportunity throughout the colonial period, which furthered the assimilation process, and through the presence of African veterans of the French military from both world wars, Black people from all areas of French-colonized Africa as well as the Caribbean Antilles have settled in France for several generations, thus expanding the definition of "Black French woman or man" beyond the nineteenth-century Senegalese referent. "Black Britons," by contrast, is strictly a post–World War II appellation for British colonials, mostly from the West Indies, who, in the face of Britain's labor shortages in service industries following the war, were encouraged to immigrate to the metropole. A generation later, however, was to see a hue and cry among the British citizenry to halt such immigration, an attitude that continues to the present time. The name "Black Britons," therefore, designates the two generations of Black people born and raised in Britain as the product of this moment of economic history.

Unlike the names "Black French women or men" and "Black Britons," and even "African Americans," all of which designate overseas citizenship (in the case of the Senegalese) or transplanted populations and their descendants, the name "Afro-Germans" designates a population *native to* Germany, raised and enculturated as Germans, with little or no actual contact with their African cultural heritage. The ironic paradox of being viewed and therefore treated as foreigners but having, in most cases, no personal Black reference—conscious or unconscious, individual or collective—within their lives as Germans creates a limbo-life with no analog among Black populations in ex-colonial Europe or in North America.

Black people live all over the Germanys, at least in the major metropolitan areas and the university towns. But they are, for the most part, foreigners who are residents in Germany for a delimited period. The largest number are U.S. military and support personnel and their dependents. Before them, as this book documents, there were French African military troops. The other significant group of Blacks sojourning in Germany are students, mostly Africans, attending universities or other educational institutions. Beyond these there are other, smaller numbers of Black foreigners, some in the entertainment business, and a few migrants from Britain working as taxi drivers, and the like. Among the Black foreigners living in Germany, men outnumber women by a large proportion.

The Black foreigner sojourning in Germany experiences many of the same racially based encounters as does the Afro-German whose whole life has been spent in Germany. For the Black foreigner who has come from and/or can return to his/her own place of cultural reference, the day-to-day, "no-harm-intended" racial comments and questions have an ultimately less traumatic effect by virtue of two types of sociocultural "antibodies" practically imbibed with the mother's milk: (1) a psychological geocultural rootedness, or identity, historically vindicated; and (2) a historically toughened skin formed from generations of existence as a minority or a colonial under institutionalized oppression. The Afro-German, who is born and raised in Germany and whose place of cultural reference is Germany, but to whom a foreigner's identity is imputed, is not equipped with those same sociocultural "antibodies." As a Black foreigner living and moving in the German community off and on for a total of five years over a twenty-year span, mostly as a teacher or university lecturer, I had the means to handle the day-to-day encounters of racial insensitivity or ignorance through the reflexive deployment of those natural "antibodies" built up over my lifetime, sometimes mocking the incredible, provincial ignorance of the utterer of the comment or question and at other times correcting the ignorance.

It was, however, only through reading *Farbe Bekennen* and remarking upon the surprising similarities of my own experiences as a Black person, and particularly as a Black woman living in Germany, with those described by these writers, that I came to realize the *dissimilarities* in effect and reaction between myself and these writers. Reading this book revealed to me the perpetual psychological trauma that such day-to-day incidents generate for Afro-Germans, unequipped with the protective "antibodies" that have allowed some of those encounters to roll off my back or be otherwise handled with little lasting damage. So that, when faced with the patronizing You-speak-German-so-well-young-lady-do-you-come-from-Africa? line, with its subtexts of an implication of incompatibility between speaking German well and being from Africa and of the assumption that the Black woman being addressed is a "young lady," i.e., a student or in some similar status of "underdevelopment"—my own response is likely to address (patronizingly, sometimes) those subtexts (choosing to take up or dismiss the detail of being an African American rather than a continental African). The Afro-German, on the other hand, faced with that same line, is impelled to address the fact of her German origin and mother tongue in spite of obvious African blood.

Ironically, translating *Farbe Bekennen* led me to appreciate that whatever feelings of marginality or "otherness" might inform my existence as a Black person in the "recognized margin" that is the African diaspora community of the United States, Canada, Britain, or France, it is in fact a duly established, viable community, which has socialized me for the struggle with that marginality. Or, that whatever "foreigner encounters" might beset my life as a Black person sojourning in Germany, my sense of identity is a source of psychological sustenance. The Afro-German, until very recently, lacking such a source of sustenance, has been living a life of "otherness" on a margin that is not even recognized.

Literature and Addresses

Literature

Fremgen, Gisela. . . . *und wenn du dazu noch schwarz bist: Berichte schwarzer Frauen in der Bundesrepublik*. Bremen, 1984.

Lester, Rosemarie. *Trivialneger - Das Bild des Schwarzen im westdeutschen Illustriertenroman*. Stuttgart, 1982.

Mergner, Gottfried, and Ansgar Häfner. *Der Afrikaner im deutschen Kinder- und Jugendbuch bis 1945*. Oldenburg, 1985.

Pommerin, Rainer. *Sterilisierung der Rheinlandbastarde: Das Schicksal einer farbigen deutschen Minderheit, 1918–1937*. Düsseldorf, 1979.

Addresses

Contacts for groups in other cities are available at these addresses)

ISD Berlin (and the journal *Afro-Look*)
c/o BAZ
Oranienstr. 159
1000 Berlin 61

ISD Bremen
(Adefra Bremen and the journal *Afrekete*)
c/o Hagazussa e.V.
Friesenstr. 12
2800 Bremen 1

ISD Freiburg
c/o RDC

Egonstr. 54
7800 Freiburg

Black Unity Committee
Postfach 210212
1000 Berlin 21